TORMENTING

THOUGHTS

AND

SECRET

RITUALS

THE HIDDEN EPIDEMIC OF

OBSESSIVE-COMPULSIVE

DISORDER

IAN OSBORN, M.D.

TORMENTING
THOUGHTS
AND
SECRET
RITUALS

PANTHEON BOOKS / NEW YORK

Grateful acknowledgment is made to the following for permission to reprint previously published material:
American Psychiatric Association: Excerpts from the *Diagnostic and Statistical Manual of Mental Disorders, Fourth Edition.* Copyright © 1994 by the American Psychiatric Association. Reprinted by permission of the American Psychiatric Association. • Archives of General Psychiatry: "The Yale-Brown Obsessive-Compulsive Scale" by Goodman, Rasmussen, et al. *Archives of General Psychiatry,* vol. 46, 1989, pp. 1006–1011. Copyright © 1989 by the American Medical Association. Reprinted by permission of Archives of General Psychiatry. • Elsevier Science Ltd.: "The Padua Inventory" by Ezio Sanario. *Behavior Research and Therapy,* vol. 26, no. 2, 1988, pp. 169–77. Reprinted by permission of Elsevier Science Ltd., Oxford, England.

Library of Congress Cataloging-in-Publication Data

Osborn, Ian.
Tormenting thoughts and secret rituals :
the hidden epidemic of obsessive-compulsive disorder / Ian Osborn.
p.   cm.
Includes bibliographical references (p.) and index.
ISBN 0-679-44222-7
1. Obsessive-compulsive disorder—Popular works.   I. Title.
RC533.083   1998
616.85'227 — DC21   97-31226
CIP

Random House Web Address: http://www.randomhouse.com

Book design by Jo Anne Metsch

Printed in the United States of America
First Edition
2   4   6   8   9   7   5   3   1

*To my OCD patients at Penn State and
at the Clearfield-Jefferson Community Mental Health Center*

These things may seem ridiculous to others,
even as ridiculous as they were in themselves,
but to me they were the most tormenting cogitations.

JOHN BUNYAN,
Grace Abounding to the Chief of Sinners

CONTENTS

TORMENTING

THOUGHTS

AND

SECRET

RITUALS

PROLOGUE:
A PERSONAL PERSPECTIVE

I SUFFERED OBSESSIVE-compulsive disorder myself while in medical training. Terrifying, tormenting thoughts often popped unbidden into my mind, causing surges of panic and piercing discomforts. The thoughts usually took the form of vibrant, violent images, for instance, of a knife being thrust into my flesh, or of my nose being scraped right off in a car accident. A particularly frequent one was that of my hand being punctured by a phlebotomy needle. I would have the sudden, intrusive image of me standing at a patient's bedside ready to draw a sample of blood: I unsheath a large-bore phlebotomy needle, menacing, daggerlike in its appearance, and then inexplicably, instead of inserting the needle into my patient's vein, I thrust it to the hilt into the thenar eminence of my hand. Upon the occurrence of this frightful fantasy, my hand would ache in a manner that seemed indistinguishable from genuine pain. I would shake it to make it feel better.

It was fortunate that these troublesome intruders into my consciousness rarely struck when I was engaged in important activities and that therefore they did not upset my medical career because they were impossible to fend off. The more I resisted them, the worse they became. I often used counter-ideas, or restorative images, to neutralize them. To counteract the phlebotomy-needle thought, I would imagine an impenetrable cream covering my hand. The needle would strike and promptly burst into pieces. The image would fade. Yet the tormenting fantasy would always return at another time.

What I suffered, I learned later, was a typical form of obsessive-compulsive disorder. My tormenting thoughts were obsessions, and my counteractive ideas were compulsions. I know now that by fearing them and fighting them, I only made them worse. But back then I didn't know any better.

What did I do for help? Since I later went on to study psychiatry, you'd think that I might have gotten therapy: probed into my unconscious, teased apart my ego defenses, scrutinized my childhood—at the very least, come to some sort of an understanding of my problem. Nothing of the sort. When my obsessions were not bothering me, I didn't want to think about them. I kept my tormenting thoughts a secret, as most OCDers do. Given the treatments that were available back then, it was probably just as well.

In the early 1970s, mental health professionals knew next to nothing about obsessive-compulsive disorder. The field had come no further than had the great psychoanalyst Sigmund Freud, who candidly admitted that OCD baffled him. His own theories on the subject, Freud once said, were no more than "doubtful assumptions and unconfirmed suppositions."

When I was in training, the psychiatrists, psychologists, social workers, nurses, and counselors who treated OCD sufferers had trouble just identifying obsessions when they saw them. The self-tormenting thoughts were considered rare, and as a result they were rarely recognized. Severe cases were routinely misdiagnosed as hallucinations; mild ones were written off as examples of obscure unconscious conflicts.

On those occasions when OCD was correctly diagnosed, treatment was next to worthless. They tried years of psychoanalysis, counseling, and group therapy; they prescribed antidepressant medications, antipsychotic medications, even shock therapy; but therapists themselves believed that OCD was a dark and mysterious illness, essentially incurable. That's what I was taught in medical school. If a patient had severe OCD, my professors would just shake their heads, intimating, "We'll do our best, but don't expect much." One clinician of that era wrote, "Most of us are agreed that the treatment of obsessional states is one of the most difficult tasks confronting the psychiatrist, and many of us consider it hopeless."

The good news is that times have changed.

The study of OCD has undergone a truly remarkable shift in emphasis, as researchers have turned away from unproven theories and jumped with both feet into the research lab. As a result of this dramatic change, our understanding of OCD has leaped forward. At a recent meeting of the American Psychiatric Association, more special reports were presented on OCD than on any other topic. OCD has been referred to as the "hot topic" of the 1990s, and professional journals are overflowing with updates on the chemistry, genetics, psychology, and treatment of obsessions and compulsions. The great news for OCD sufferers is that obsessive-compulsive disorder is now recognized as a common, physical disease for which effective treatment is available.

OCD: THE HIDDEN EPIDEMIC

WHEN I WAS in training, psychiatrists estimated the incidence of a given mental disorder in the general population by extrapolating from the number of people known to be in treatment. Since back then only a tiny number of patients were diagnosed as having obsessive-compulsive disorder, OCD was thought to be very rare. The figure most commonly quoted for its overall incidence was a minuscule .05 percent.

What was not appreciated back then, however, was how adept OCDs are at keeping their disorder hidden. The effort they expend in scheming and lying often rivals that spent on the disorder. Afraid people will think they are crazy, OCD sufferers don't tell anyone about their illness—not their families or their friends, and certainly not their therapists. As Freud, who did not get much else right about OCD, astutely noted: "Sufferers [from OCD] are able to keep their affliction a private matter. Concealment is made easier from the fact that they are quite well able to fulfill their social duties during a part of the day, once they have devoted a number of hours to their secret doings, hidden from view."

The true incidence of obsessive-compulsive disorder was not uncovered until 1983, when the National Institutes of Health announced the findings of the first large-scale study on the rate of occurrence of mental health disorders in the general population of the United States. Researchers went from door to door in five different areas of the country, carefully interviewing 18,500 randomly selected people. The results took mental health professionals completely by surprise: OCD was found to occur in 1.9–3.3 percent of the population! Although some researchers have questioned the reliability of the NIMH study on the grounds that its diagnostic criteria were not sufficiently stringent, there is general agreement that OCD's incidence is at least in the range of 1–2 percent.

The experts had misjudged OCD's incidence by a factor of more than twenty. Instead of 150,000 people having the disorder, millions have it. OCD turns out to be one of the most common of all mental illnesses, with large numbers of people suffering the disease in silence. Harvard's Michael Jenike, a leader in OCD research, has referred to it as mental health's "hidden epidemic."

OCD AS A BIOLOGICAL DISORDER

WHEN I WAS in medical school, the leading theory on the cause of obsessive-compulsive disorder was Freud's: Obsessions and compulsions arise from unconscious conflicts between instincts, particularly the sex drive, and attempts at self-control. Once widely accepted, this theory no longer holds sway. Extensive research in biochemistry, pharmacology, radiology, and genetics has now demonstrated beyond a doubt that OCD results directly from an abnormality in the brain's chemistry, a malfunction that leads to faulty firing of the brain's neurons. As succinctly put by Yale Medical School Professor Richard Peschel, "Recent neuroscience research proves that obsessive-compulsive disorder is a physical, neurobiological disease of the brain."

That a physical, not a psychological, abnormality accounts for

OCD seems, at first, surprising, but the same discovery has been made in a number of other mental disorders. Neurosyphilis, a severe form of the venereal disease that causes heightened emotions and changes in behavior, and pellagra, a vitamin deficiency that leads to fatigue and anxiety, were once thought to be due to psychological conflicts. Early in the twentieth century, however, it became clear that both were entirely curable, biological diseases. More recently, bipolar disorder and schizophrenia, two of the most severe psychiatric problems, have been demonstrated to be physical illnesses. As England's Richard Hunter, past president of the Royal Society of Medicine, has pointed out, "Progress in psychiatry is inevitably and inexorably from the psychological to the physical—never the other way around."

In the case of OCD it is crucial that this shift in perspective, from psychological to neurobiological, be fully accepted as quickly as possible. For one thing, many people are convinced that if a disorder is called "psychiatric," it is not real. Insurance companies, ever eager to find ways of denying payment, routinely assert this fallacy. What a terrible burden it is for disabled OCD sufferers to be viewed as people who are too weak to deal with life's stresses, or worse, as impostors trying to get out work.

Furthermore, OCD patients themselves readily embrace the new neurobiological view. In the past when I explained to my patients that they had a disorder caused by childhood conflicts, they often promptly disappeared from treatment. In the rural area where I practice, at least, people do not want to hear that they have deep-seated problems resulting from the way they were brought up. Now when I explain to patients that they have a medical disorder—an illness like diabetes or heart disease—they nod in agreement. For those who suffer the disorder, the physical explanation of OCD has the ring of truth.

Most importantly, the unlocking of the neurobiological underpinnings of OCD has led to new and potent treatments for the disorder.

EFFECTIVE TREATMENT FOR OCD

BACK IN THE early 1970s, there were no effective treatments for OCD. Now there are not just one but two that work: behavior therapy and a new group of "serotonergic" medications. These two new therapies represent truly spectacular advances in the treatment of mental disorder. Certainly, if these therapies had been available twenty years ago, and I had known then what I know now, I would have unhesitatingly used them to treat my own OCD. As I will mention later, I do currently use an anti-OCD medication.

Behavior therapy came on the scene first, in the late 1970s. Bearing no resemblance to psychoanalysis's hunt for hidden conflicts, behavior therapy's goal is simply to transform troublesome behaviors. In behavior therapy for OCD, obsessions and compulsions are first clearly identified, then rated in order of severity, and finally targeted for special homework assignments. Behavior therapy has turned out to be a remarkably successful treatment for OCD. A dozen good studies in the last fifteen years have reported significant improvement in 60–70 percent of patients. A 1994 study using an intensive program developed by Edna Foa of Medical College of Pennsylvania showed a marked reduction in obsessions and compulsions in more than 75 percent of the patients.

Only a few years after the introduction of behavior therapy, a group of medications affecting the brain chemical serotonin appeared as a second effective treatment for OCD. It is truly amazing that two totally different, potent therapies for OCD emerged in such a short span of time. Five members of the serotonergic group of medications are now available in the United States: fluoxetine (Prozac), paroxetine (Paxil), sertraline (Zoloft), fluvoxamine (Luvox), and clomipramine (Anafranil). All work to lessen obsessions and compulsions. Clomipramine has been the most studied of the group. A 1989 study of a large number of OCD patients from twenty-one different university centers in the United States showed that 60 percent of the patients treated with clomipramine were much improved, while the number much improved with placebo was less than 10 percent.

Like most OCD specialists, I routinely treat OCD with a combination of behavior therapy and serotonergic medications. Happily, the two cause no problems when used together. On the contrary, each seems to enhance the effect of the other. According to John Greist, M.D., OCD specialist from University of Wisconsin, "Medications and behavior therapy now are able to help 90 percent of people with OCD." This in a disorder recently thought to be hopeless.

MY FIELD OF psychiatry—the branch of medicine that once brought you lobotomies and penis envy—has been getting things right lately. Tremendous progress has been made in the understanding and treatment of a number of syndromes, including schizophrenia, bipolar disorder, major depression, panic disorder, and attention deficit disorder. The advances in obsessive-compulsive disorder are the most impressive of all.

A good case can be made, in fact, that no other disorder in the history of medicine has ever experienced such an explosive growth in scientific understanding that has led to such a revolution in how it has been viewed: from regarded as rare to recognized as common; from presumed psychological to proven neurobiological; from written off as hopeless to accepted as one of the most responsive of all mental disorders to therapeutic interventions. All this has happened to OCD in about twenty years.

FILTH, HARM, LUST,

AND BLASPHEMY

OBSESSIVE-COMPULSIVE DISORDER can now be understood on a neurobiological level, yet its symptoms still seem altogether mysterious. How *could* I, in one of the best times of my whole life, suffer bloody images of stabbing myself? Sir Aubrey Lewis, the greatest English psychiatrist of the twentieth century, was struck by OCD's apparent contradictions "between kindness and cruelty, logicality and unreason, fear and desire," and by its overwhelming "variety of problems and the difficulty of stating them."

People who have never suffered the ravages of obsessions and compulsions can best get a sense of their puzzling power by examining clinical cases. This chapter presents four case histories, typical of severe OCD, that illustrate how the battle in the mind can come to rule peoples' lives. Commenting on the extreme variety of obsessions, Lewis concluded in 1935 that most could be grouped under four general categories: filth, harm, lust, and blasphemy.

OBSESSIONS OF FILTH: RAYMOND

ON A HOT summer day in June 1993, I shook hands with Raymond and escorted him into my office. He was a short, broad-shouldered man dressed in rugged work clothes and a baseball cap; his heavily lined face and shabby gray hair making him look ten years older than his forty-two years. Despite a somewhat rough demeanor, however, he spoke in a soft, gentle manner, with an exaggerated politeness.

"Doc," he began, "I've dealt with awful fears for over twenty years."

He proceeded to describe in enthralling detail—he was, I soon discovered, an accomplished storyteller—his twenty-five-year struggle with obsessions and compulsions. Fears that his hands were infected had caused him to wash and scrub them until they bled. Doubts that he might have committed the "unpardonable sin" had led him to innumerable consultations with ministers and friends regarding the use of birth control. Bloody images of people lying injured by the side of the road had almost made him give up driving. "Have you ever driven to Harrisburg a hundred yards at a time?" he asked. One evening, after finishing the two-hour trip home from our state capital, he became so distraught by the idea that he might have hit someone along the way that he spent the rest of the night completely retracing his journey, stopping every hundred yards to check whether someone lay critically hurt by the roadside.

Yet Raymond had conquered these and many other irrational fears by summoning all of his will power and standing up to them. He had forced himself to live with dirty hands. He had purposefully scheduled long drives every weekend.

Now, however, Raymond was beat. "My mind is handing me a crushing vision that I can't get rid of," he said. "I'm physically worn out from fighting it."

This new vision had started, Raymond explained, when he had taken his family to visit Disneyworld during Christmas vacation. On the second day, while walking through the vast, darkened Met-Life pavilion, he suddenly had the thought, "What if a disaster were to strike here at Disneyworld?" With an immediate heightened, focused acuity he heard Hispanics speaking in front of him and Germans behind him—over a million people visited each year from all parts of the globe, he had been told. Surely it would be a worldwide catastrophe. At that exact moment, having just caught a glimpse down a long, crowded corridor, a dreadful vision "jumped," as he put it, into his mind. In the middle of the corridor, a bucket, a jar—some sort of a container—was turning over and spilling contaminated material. Feces, germs, vile diseased substances, poisons that could cause devastation, were gushing along the floor.

Raymond knew rationally that this vision was a figment of his imagination. It was his mind presenting him with another "killer fantasy." The others had never come true, he tried to tell himself, and this one wouldn't either. Yet the strength, intensity, and persistence of this particular image overwhelmed him. It was, as Raymond put it, an "enormous heart-burden" that took his breath away. If a spill had occurred, and if he was the only one who knew about it, then the lives of thousands of people depended on his locating it. This electrifying realization prodded him, propelled him into taking immediate action.

Telling his family to wait by an exit, Raymond turned back to the corridor. He walked up and down, inspecting the carpet closely to make sure there were no telltale signs of dampness to indicate a poisonous spill. He wanted to get down on his hands and knees and go over it inch by inch, but he settled for kneeling down and touching the carpet a couple of times, rubbing it here and there, to make certain it was perfectly dry. Once satisfied, he returned to his family. A minute later, though, there was another long corridor, another vivid, fearful image, another reason to go back and check. The images kept coming, one dreadful spill after another.

That night, as he lay in his hotel bed, the rest of the family asleep, tears flooded Raymond's face. How could he slip away to check all these places? How could he live with himself if he didn't? Disneyworld, he reflected, had turned into a den of horrors. He tried to calm down by telling himself that things would be better when he got home. Then he would be able to look back and see that all these fears had been imagined.

But in the following days, gut-wrenching spill visions were continuously on his mind; when one began to fade, another took its place. Raymond fought to keep himself from checking. He was embarrassed by his excuses ("I need to get a drink," or "I want to go back and see that last exhibit again"), especially when his wife fixed him with what he called the "oh-no-not-again look." Yet the tormenting images drove him to glance furtively down every corridor, to walk back to scout for menacing spots frequently, to slyly brush floors with his hand, to nonchalantly, but firmly, rub carpets back and forth with his feet (this last ritual, Raymond realized, made no sense at all since he could not detect wetness through his shoes, but it somehow helped his mind to "click" and be assured that there had been no spill).

Still, arriving home in Pennsylvania after the vacation, Raymond was optimistic. He prided himself on his mental strength. Hadn't he kept his fears pretty much a secret for twenty years? Even his family was unaware of their true severity. Indeed, Raymond was known for his coolness under pressure in his job as railroad mechanic and as "Mr. Reliable" in his hometown of Altoona, Pennsylvania, where he was at once Sunday school superintendent, president of a fishing club, and leader of both an Explorer post and a Cub Scout den.

Yet in the six months since his return from Disneyworld, spill visions had been relentless, and the rituals Raymond was driven to perform had become increasingly complex and time-consuming. By the time he came to see me, Raymond said, checking compulsions were taking two to three hours a day.

A typical day would begin with clear and powerful spill fantasies charging into his consciousness at the ring of his alarm at 6 A.M. Someone had entered the house and urinated on the floor, or had poured out some poisonous substance. A rush of adrenaline would tense his muscles and speed his breathing. He had to check. If he didn't, the intensity of these images would increase until he was shaking uncontrollably, hyperventilating with anxiety.

First, Raymond would carefully inspect the outside doors, bolting and unbolting them several times until, as he put it, his mind "got to some high ground" from where he realized that it was very unlikely that somebody had entered the house during the night. The relief was only momentary. Attacked again by a vision, he would rush to his son's room, painstakingly examine the bed, carpet, chair, dresser, touching, patting, rubbing to make sure there had been no spill. Before leaving the room, he would say to himself, softly, slowly, deliberately, to make himself stay *convinced:* "Okay, I've thought that one out flat. There's no spill in the boy's room." Then he would walk quickly to the other bedrooms, the bathrooms, the basement, the living room, and take a glance in the kitchen.

With the completion of these rituals, a "safe, warm feeling" would remain with Raymond for a while, allowing him to shave, dress for work, and eat breakfast in relative comfort. But once ready to leave his house, he would again be assailed by fears. Over by the toaster, was there anything there? No. Just the toaster. What was on the breakfast table? Any dampness? If the table top was clear, Raymond ran his hands across its surface systematically, covering every spot. (It was easier for Raymond if the table was crowded with objects because then he could focus on them. "Okay, Cheerios and yesterday's mail," he could tell himself and be satisfied. But if the table was empty, it was agonizing.) Finally, halfway out the door to work: "Did I check the corner of the living room? Did I look closely enough at the stove burners?" Most mornings, Raymond was out the door and back at least six times before finally being able to leave for good.

The drive to work was filled with devastating spill fantasies, triggered by trucks "whooshing by" and kicking up dust. Suddenly, a menacing scrub bucket, a container of disease, was sitting in a hallway at his child's school. Raymond would be jolted by an urge, an overwhelming responsibility, to check the school. He would fight the urge with all his strength, remembering that if he gave in he would be late to work. But then a conflicting agony would assault him, just as bad: "If I don't check, how am I going to live with the pain of this fear all day?"

At first Raymond had been able to deal with these particular fantasies by simply telling himself strongly that they were not real. When that strategy started to fail, Raymond found that if he shook his head, or whistled, he could distract himself from his scrub bucket fears long enough to turn his thoughts to pleasurable subjects, like hunting or car racing. When that, too, began to fail, Raymond found that if he promised himself to check the school later in the day he could keep from needing to check at the moment. When postponement stopped being effective, however, Raymond discovered that the only way to lessen the force of the visions, the only way that he could keep himself from running to the school, was to perform a complicated part-mental and part-physical ritual that he was initially too embarrassed even to mention to me.

In this ritual, Raymond first confined the spill by focusing his imagination on a tiny, very specific place in the hallway of the school. He "tied it down," as he put it, by repeating to himself slowly, "The whole spill's right there on that spot." Then he pictured as clearly and vividly as he could a huge vacuum cleaner hovering in the air over the spill and sucking it up in one huge gulp. To add emphasis to this counterimage, he made loud "whooshing" noises as he breathed rapidly in and out; and he flailed his elbows up and down as he held on to the steering wheel. That a passerby might observe him in the midst of this ritual terrified him. The cleansing tornado worked 90 percent of the time, but when it didn't, Raymond had to turn his car around and go check.

When he finally arrived at work, Raymond would be much relieved. The familiar routine at the railroad works and the small talk with his coworkers drew his mind away from his fears. He still took frequent glances down hallways, and on a bad day he might have to call his wife, risking her annoyance, to ask her to feel the bed in his son's room, but these were relatively minor problems.

Returning home after work, however, brought back crushing obsessions. "As soon as I walk in the door," Raymond said, "I have the overwhelming sensation that the food in the refrigerator has been tampered with. I know it's extremely unlikely that anyone could have entered the house, but I have to check anyway." He would check the milk, the Kool-Aid, a half-full bottle of Coke, by carefully pouring a small amount into the sink to make sure there was nothing floating at the top. Then he checked for spills in every room in the house. If his wife was at home when he arrived the process was more difficult because he had to try to disguise and make excuses for the many rituals. Dinnertime meant sudden, piercing visions of disease organisms hidden at the bottoms of drinking glasses. Evenings brought more spill fantasies, worst of all when he had to leave his house for Scout meetings or church events, situations ripe for countless catastrophes. Raymond dreaded going out after dinner.

He welcomed any excuse to stay home. Rainy days were good. Thunderstorms were great.

Evenings finally brought on a new, excruciatingly embarrassing compulsion, the "last straw," which led to Raymond's coming to see me. The vision would strike of one of his children drinking something that had been poisoned or was "filled with disease." Sitting on his daughter's bed, he would ask, "What did you have in here to drink, Kristy?" "Nothing, Dad," his daughter would reply. But Raymond would persist, "You're sure there wasn't anything sitting here on the bureau?" "I'm sure, Dad." Relieved, Raymond would walk out, but no sooner did he get out the door than he would turn around and ask her again. "Come on, Dad!" his frustrated daughter would yell. Raymond badgered his children until they shamed him into leaving them alone, but later on, when the embarrassment had faded and the fearful image came back strong, he would hang his head and ask them again.

"Raymond," his wife told him at last, "you're driving the kids crazy. You've got to get help."

OBSESSIONS OF HARM: SHERRY

SHERRY SQUEEZED IN her appointment with me between Catholic Mass, where she was a lector, and the Art Alliance meeting, where she was the secretary. Every minute of her day was filled with activity, and that's the way she liked it—always helping others, the busier the better. Yet her overscheduled life was crumbling. She could no longer shove aside the horrors that were occurring in her own mind.

Petite and blond, hippie-looking but stylish, in jeans and a shawl, she rushed into my office, yanked her chair up close, leaned in, and took a deep breath. "I'm so scared," she confided. "I have terrible thoughts. I think of killing people. I think of stabbing my husband and my four year old, Megan. Driving over here I saw a little girl walking home from school, and I had the urge to swerve and hit her. Last night we drove by our old house, and my husband remembered that we still had the key to it. I started thinking: 'Oh good, we could sneak in at night and stab everybody.' I'm totally sick.

"Some days I can't think about anything else," she said, speaking more rapidly. "No thought is too awful for me. Sometimes I get the idea of gouging my daughter's eyes out. I used to think about throwing her in the microwave, but she's too big for that now, thank God. This morning I was shaving my legs in the shower, and I felt like cutting myself, slashing my neck open with a razor. I saw the blood pouring from my neck."

She leaned back and gave me a glassy look. "God, this sounds so crazy. I don't want to do these things I think about. At my worst moments, all I hold on to are God and Jesus. When will this hell I'm in end?" She sat quietly, wiping away tears.

I asked gently when these upsetting thoughts had started. Sherry related that she had been tormented by obsessions since age eleven, when, while baby-sitting, she had her first dreadful obsession. She was sitting on the kitchen floor, serenely watching her six-month-old niece rock back and forth in a swing set. Then, by chance, her eyes came to rest on a carving knife lying unsheathed on the kitchen counter. Suddenly, in her imagination, she grabbed it and slashed at the baby. Blood was everywhere. She froze in anguish and guilt. Her life was never the same.

Each night for a week afterward she dreamed that an evil witch had cast a spell on her mind. Finally confiding in her parents, she was taken to a therapist. A year of psychotherapy aimed at uncovering conflicts helped her feel better about herself but did not stop the tormenting images. "Why me?" she thought.

Knife fantasies continued to trouble her throughout junior and senior high school, and new obsessions cropped up as well. She learned to keep herself as busy as possible. As long as she was involved in an activity, the self-tormenting thoughts would usually leave her alone. If, however, she put herself under too much stress, then frightening thoughts would hit hard, like when she tried out for cheerleader and suffered terrifying urges to scream out obscenities at the top of her lungs. She made the team by keeping her teeth clamped together like steel traps; her jaw muscles ached for days afterwards.

In college she majored in art after discovering that her obsessions disappeared when she was fully involved in a creative task such as painting. Yet most hours of the day tormenting, violent thoughts were her secret companions. Thoughts to commit suicide were often on her mind as well. Strangely, these were usually consoling in their effect. "If my awful thoughts get too strong," she would think, "I can always kill myself before I murder someone else."

Her worst period ever followed the birth of her daughter. Overwhelmed by almost every awful harm obsession imaginable, including knifing, dropping, scalding, microwaving, and sexually molesting her infant, she developed a state of nervous exhaustion. She couldn't eat or sleep and finally just stayed in bed, leaving caring for her daughter to others.

A psychiatrist was consulted, and he recommended hospitalization because of the severity of her depression. She refused. "Please God, I'll make a deal," she prayed. "I'll go to the hospital if it gets really bad, but give me the strength to fight the thoughts." She began to see the doctor for psychotherapy and, with the help of antidepressant medication and the support of her husband, regained the ability to cope.

But four years later, after her husband landed a new job and the family moved to Pennsylvania, her equilibrium was shattered. She was again overwhelmed by OCD.

OBSESSIONS OF LUST: JEFF

JEFF, A THIRTY-YEAR-OLD high school science teacher, slightly built with delicate features and dressed neatly in a coat and tie, lumbered solemnly into my office. Speaking so softly that I could hardly hear him, he politely introduced himself, then sat down with a pained expression.

"There is a voice in my head that keeps saying . . . really awful things," Jeff said, stammering and pausing frequently. "It's hell. . . . It's just terrible. . . . I can't relax."

In an attempt to ease his discomfort, I began right away to ask questions. "Can you describe what the voice is like?" I said.

"It says various things . . . like that I'm homosexual," he said, adding quickly, "It's not that I have anything against gays. Anyone who wants to be gay, that's fine with me. But I have never been and I don't want to be gay."

"What else can you tell me about the voice?" I asked.

"It's loud. It's nonstop," Jeff said. "My mind has two levels. On the surface, I can think normally. I can still go to work every day and do an okay job. But in the back of my mind there is a voice that keeps repeating things over and over. It's like an endless loop cassette that's always there."

"What does it say?"

"Things like . . . 'Are you gay?' Or, 'Are you a pervert?' " Jeff looked anxiously around the room.

"Does the voice sound real?" I said. "Do you think other people can overhear it?"

"No, no," Jeff said. "It's just in my mind."

"Well," I said, "does it come from you or does it come from someone else?"

"That's what's confusing," Jeff said. "It seems as if I am the one who's saying these things, but these are not things that I would ever think. Believe me, they are not. Anyone would tell you that. . . . So that's why I guess I must be hearing voices."

"Okay, Jeff. I think I understand," I said. "You've got these thoughts, sort of like voices, that keep coming into your mind when you don't want them to, questioning whether you are gay. Is that the main problem?"

"Not exactly. There are pictures. . . . Explicit and very gross homosexual pictures. I can't even look at my male friends in the face any more because I will start to have these homosexual pictures. . . . I can't imagine what's happening to me."

"It would be very helpful," I said, "if you could pick one especially bad time you've had in the last day or two and describe it in some detail. You needn't go into all of the gory details. Just give me a sense of what goes on."

Jeff stared at the floor and I occupied myself taking notes. Then he shook his head with a sense of resignation. "I was doing my exercises before breakfast. I was working out on my rowing machine in my basement. My dog was there in the corner. And I started having thoughts and pictures come into my mind of going over and having sex with my dog."

I asked, "When these awful thoughts start coming into your mind, do you do anything to try to get rid of them?"

"I fight them with all my might," Jeff said, "but I can't stop them. The only thing that helps at all is to keep on answering them back. The pictures start coming, and I'm saying, 'That's not me, that's not me, that's not me." Or the voice says, 'You're a pervert,' and I'm answering back, 'No, I'm not, no, I'm not, no, I'm not.' My life is a mind battle. The thoughts control me."

It was now completely clear that Jeff suffered from obsessive-compulsive disorder. Nobody but those who share Jeff's peculiar combination of an extremely timorous conscience and an uncommonly deadly imagination can appreciate the gut-wrenching shame and profound guilt that can accompany sexual obsessions.

I leaned forward and attempted to reassure him. "You're not hearing voices. You're not a pervert. What is happening to you is that you are getting hit with obsessions—thoughts that come into your mind out of the blue, usually the worst thoughts that you could ever think. They do not in any way represent who you are.

"Sometimes," I continued, "terrifying urges go along with the awful thoughts. I see a loving young mother who gets hit with the obsession to kill her baby. Sometimes when the terrible thought hits, she has what seems like an urge to carry it out. But the urge is completely counterfeit. It is just another obsession. Following it is the last thing she would ever do."

"Yes," Jeff said. "I have urges, too."

"The truth is, Jeff, that most people get unwanted, terrible thoughts. The only difference between you and them is that they say, 'What a stupid thought!' and turn their minds to something else. You, on the other hand, become horrified by these thoughts and try to fight them, and by doing so, you make them worse."

After this Jeff perked up somewhat and talked more readily. His life had been going fairly well until he became romantically involved with Beth, another teacher at his school, about six months before he came to see me. Jeff, having had only one previous serious relationship, and that having ended painfully, felt insecure. Did he perform well enough sexually? Would he fail in this relationship as he had in the last? Did he have a good enough job to suit her? Yet although these worries were very stressful, Jeff still recognized them as normal.

Then his anxieties took a profound turn for the worse one day when he was carpooling to a conference with several other teachers. He had slept poorly the night before, and constipation was causing a discomfort in his lower rectum. Adding to his discomfort was being cramped in the backseat of the car, so that his shoulder and hip were unavoidably touching the man next to him. As Jeff shifted uneasily, he worried that his friends would notice his nervousness. He began to sweat profusely and swallow frequently. Suddenly, an exceptionally strong and vivid image flashed into his mind of his engaging in homosexual intercourse with the friend who sat beside him. Jeff was crushed. It literally took his breath away. He sat paralyzed in fear and disbelief. Shouting out in his mind was the question: "Am I gay?" To which he answered back, over and over, "No, I'm not. No, I'm not. No, I'm not."

Intense, homosexual fantasies proceeded to invade Jeff's consciousness over the subsequent weeks and months, sometimes continuing unabated for hours at time, particularly when he was alone and unoccupied. Jeff walked the streets near where he lived, crying, wondering whether he was going crazy, or becoming, against his will, homosexual. He tried shouting back at the thoughts. He tried substituting in heterosexual fantasies. He tried praying repeatedly, like a mantra, "God give me the strength to deal with this." Sometimes these countermeasures, compulsions, worked for a while to chase away the thoughts, but the unwanted ideas, images, and urges always came back.

It seemed to Jeff that his mind searched out those thoughts that were most base. When he was with Beth, thoughts of painful and perverted sexual acts prevented him from being able to enjoy their sexual relationship. When in the company of Beth's four-year-old daughter, ideas jumped into his mind of seducing her and fondling her. Much in the news at that time was Jeff Dahmer, the sexual psychopath who sliced out body parts and kept them in his refrigerator.

When Jeff heard these stories, thoughts rushed into his mind of his doing the same. Sometimes he was haunted by the "crazy idea" that since Dahmer shared his first name, Dahmer's spirit might be invading him and would force him to perform similar bloody rituals. Even though Jeff was able to realize that these ideas were absurd, he still became terrified and overwhelmed. Usually at those times he thought that he was going crazy.

As I explored Jeff's history, I learned that he had suffered OCD symptoms as a child. He checked the placement of every single object in his room before he went to bed, a ritual that took about twenty minutes. Then he often had to get out of bed and recheck items. He "went nuts" in the morning if he found something out of place. In fact, Jeff later learned that his older sister, well aware of his compulsions, sometimes played the trick on him of sneaking into his room late at night and ever so slightly changing the placement of one single item. (What OCDers have to put up with!) Jeff also always demonstrated the over-responsibility and guilt that typifies the OCD personality. He held himself to the strictest ethical standards and tended to blame himself for every failure that had ever occurred in his life. He did few things for fun. For instance, reading novels was impossible because he felt too guilty: All reading should be work-related.

Toward the end of our interview, I spelled out for Jeff a nuts-and-bolts understanding of obsessive-compulsive disorder. By then he was sitting up and animated. For the first time in six months he had reason to be optimistic.

OBSESSIONS OF BLASPHEMY: MELISSA

AN EIGHTEEN-YEAR-OLD freshman at Penn State presented to our University Counseling Service late in her first semester in 1992. She was accompanied by her parents, who had called earlier in the day saying that she needed to be seen immediately, that she had gone overboard in her religion and was behaving strangely.

I introduced myself to Melissa—tall, dignified, aloof, dressed neatly in a white shirt and plaid skirt—and walked with her into my office. Ignoring my inquiry about what brought her to the clinic, she sat perfectly still for a full minute, neither talking nor making eye contact, but simply staring straight ahead. Then she suddenly looked at me and said, in a halting voice, "If I'm going to talk to someone, it should be someone from my church."

I agreed that would be a good idea but suggested that she fill me in as well. There followed another minute or two of immersion in her own thoughts—I couldn't tell whether she had heard what I said or not—before she glanced at me and said softly: "The problem is questions. They keep coming into my mind, and I can't stop them." Melissa proceeded to share her story, all the while shifting abruptly back and forth between two very different mental states. For a few minutes she would speak normally in a composed manner, carefully choosing her words, at times becoming animated or humorous; then she would lapse back into her mute, staring state, as if something very important had come up in her mind that had to be dealt with right away.

Melissa explained that she was being bombarded by questions, all dealing with what was right or wrong for her to do. The questions were incessant and overpowering, causing her mind to, as she put it, "constantly spin." Is it right to listen to popular music? What is the greatest commandment? If someone commits suicide, do they always go to hell? Is it okay to use the telephone on the Sabbath? Should I wear a dress? The questions stopped only when she was asleep. No answers would satisfy them; every seeming solution was challenged by a new consideration. Should she decide that she could wear a dress, she would immediately have to grapple with whether it could be a colored dress. If she decided her dress should be black, she would next have to consider how long it should be. Soon she would be back to doubting whether she should even wear a dress at all.

When she needed to study for her classes, she would attempt to block out the questions, but to no avail. "I try to stop thinking them," Melissa said, "but I cannot get them out of my mind. It's like I'm involved in a battle with Satan, like he's forcing these thoughts in my mind."

I asked Melissa whether she ever performed certain actions over and over, or thought certain thoughts repeatedly, in order to get rid of the questions. "Yes," Melissa said, "there are things I do to make them go away. I'll say verses from the Bible. I say them continuously, over and over. It's the only way to stop the anxiety, the only way I can get through a day. 'Be ye perfect'—that's the one I've been saying as we've been talking. I'm saying it right now."

"Do you think that repeating verses like that is a good thing to do?" I asked.

"Well, actually," Melissa said softly, "the Bible prohibits vain repetition, and that is just what I'm doing. These aren't real prayers; I wish I didn't have to say them. It's stupid. I just say the verses to get rid of the anxiety."

I was soon fairly certain that Melissa was suffering from obsessive-compulsive disorder and had no other major psychiatric or medical problem. I asked Melissa whether I could speak with her parents for a few minutes. Her mother, a petite, energetic homemaker, and her father, a reserved elementary school teacher, informed me that Melissa had never before had mental health problems. The youngest of three children, she was always the quietest and the most anxious to please. She socialized only with a few friends and never dated. They were surprised when she joined a charismatic Christian church in junior high school since they seldom attended church themselves; but they considered it a good thing since the church provided a social outlet for their stay-at-home daughter. Melissa graduated as one of the top students in her high school class, with a particular aptitude in math and science, and came to Penn State to study engineering.

I ended that interview by explaining to Melissa and her parents that the problem appeared to be obsessive-compulsive disorder. I told Melissa that if she wished to look at her illness as being due to Satan, then Satan was causing a chemical disorder in her brain that rendered her incapable of ridding herself of fearful thoughts. I recommended that Melissa take a medical withdrawal from school, and Melissa was quite happy to move home immediately. Since she came from a nearby town, it would be possible for her to see me regularly for treatment. Melissa agreed to see me again in two days.

In subsequent interviews, Melissa was able in a composed manner to share further details on how her disorder had started. Shortly after coming to college, she had begun to feel vaguely unsafe. It was, she explained, as if she were missing something important and something bad were going to happen. Then as the weeks passed, this fear began to focus on the idea that she was in some way living wrong. Since junior high school, she had lived according to biblical convictions. She prayed regularly, attended Bible studies and prayer groups, and memorized Bible verses that she carried in her purse on index cards. Now a feeling of dread assailed her in this most important area of her life. She would be in class, in her dorm room, or just walking down the street, when suddenly, insistently, she would experience what she came to call "the first and the greatest question": Am I doing what's right in God's eyes?

She asked her pastors for advice. She cornered them in church or called them on the phone, and they patiently attempted to reassure her, suggesting Bible verses that might be consoling. "It's spiritual warfare," one campus minister stressed. "You can overcome it if you fight it with scripture and faith." She took to searching for the one verse that would give her a feeling of peacefulness, a sense that she was right with God. "I can do all things through Christ who strengthens me"; "Trust the lord with all your heart and lean not on your own understanding"; "We know that all things work together for the good for those who love God." Each verse would work for a day or two, quelling her fears, but then the first and greatest question would return.

She began to stay up late into the night sitting at the small desk in her dorm room, a study light illuminating the bulletin board, arranging and rearranging index cards of Bible verses. She would tack them up and take them down, shift their order back and forth, looking for the verse that would show her how to live perfectly for God. Many times she thought she had found it. She would grow excited, elated, after hours and hours of concentrated, intense searching. She would go to bed, some nights as the first rays of dawn were breaking, thinking that she had finally found the way she could be certain that she was always doing what was right in God's eyes.

On one occasion, Melissa found her answer in the verse, "Abide in faith, hope, love, these three, but the greatest of these is love." This,

Melissa thought, would cover everything. For a week she made a solid, determined effort to love everybody every minute of the day. What if her roommate left dirty clothes on her side of the room? No reason to be mad. What if people talked behind her back? She would love them, anyway. But after a week she was in shambles. "It seemed like by the end of each day I just realized how much I hate some people," Melissa explained. "I was just exhausted. It was too hard. I gave up."

Next she thought she found the answer in "Love is patient, love is kind." Accordingly, she undertook a full-scale effort to answer criticisms with kind words and selfish acts with acts of charity. Soon, of course, she was overwhelmed. "I worried and worried about what I said to people. Maybe I was short with them. I would have to go back to them and apologize. I was asking people's forgiveness all the time. It was very draining. I slept a lot. I couldn't take it."

Still another time Melissa settled on this verse: "Let no one seek his own good, but that of his neighbor." She resolved simply not to think of herself, living only for others. Why hadn't she seen this before?! But this yoke, too, proved impossible to sustain. She could not, to her satisfaction, eliminate self-seeking. Nor, although she attempted to follow yet another verse and fill herself always with joy, could she prevent herself from snapping back when someone made her angry. "I blew it! I blew it!" she would lament. Her thoughts became a frantic collage of questions and verses compelling her to love everybody, pray continually, spread the Gospel, fight the good fight, and be always gentle, kind, patient, loving, and joyous. "It never stopped," she told me, "and I felt guilty when it did."

By now the original question—Am I doing what's right in God's eyes?—had split into a number of more specific questions. Was it right to wear makeup? How about jewelry? As a woman, what was her greatest duty? Should she talk to non-Christians? How long should her hair be? Should it be worn up or down? Were curls all right? "I felt like digging at my skin," Melissa explained. "I felt sick in my stomach. I felt as though everything would crumble, as though the ceiling would fall in."

The Bible verses began to lose their meaning for her, turning into mere incantations. Melissa noted this change: "It got to be silly stuff. I no longer went for what the verses meant. I just said them to block out the questions, to fill the anxiety." Her choice of the words "to fill the anxiety" was interesting, I thought. It was as if doubt occupied her mind as an ominous void and rituals were the only thing that could give it substance.

Choosing the right verse now depended more on rhythm and rhyme. Short verses were best. "Love one another" and "Be ye perfect" could be said to a good beat. Sometimes Melissa would consult different translations of the Bible to find the wording that worked best. "Fight the good fight" was better than "I have fought the good fight" because it had a better sound to it.

After picking a verse she would repeat it over and over until she felt, as she put it, "sort of numb." She would attempt to say it every second of the day. "People would try to talk to me," Melissa explained, "but I was a zombie. I'd be trying to finish my verse." Often in her dorm room she would pace back and forth repeating the verse; at night, she would rock herself to sleep with it.

Not surprisingly, since the verses no longer held meaning, Melissa eventually began dispensing with them altogether and chanting other things. In the week prior to seeing me, she had started on numbers. She would secretly go to her room: "One and two and three and four and five," she would chant, getting a good rhythm, sometimes rocking back and forth, sometimes walking in a circle, sometimes saying it faster and faster until she was saying it as fast as she could. At times this was the only way she could escape the anxiety.

Also severe by the time she came to see me was another type of mental compulsion: the point-by-point, minutely detailed, over-analysis of conversations. Such prolonged trains of unproductive thoughts, done to chase away obsessions, are called compulsive ruminations. Melissa had always been sensitive to other people's feelings and had for years had the habit of apologizing to people in an overly scrupulous manner for things she feared had come out wrong. By the time she came to me, however, she herself realized that her concerns were out of control. Melissa was picking apart every encounter to see whether she may have been boastful, arrogant, insolent, a gossiper, or a slanderer. She would completely relive the words she had used, her tone and delivery, the other person's response, the order of speaking, and every other conceivable aspect of the conversation. It was a microscopic analysis that could easily go on for an hour.

As her disastrous first semester drew to a close, Melissa accelerated her phone calls to ministers, friends, and family. Some days she would make twenty or more calls—not to socialize by now, or even to ask for help in dealing with her problems, but simply for reassurance. Had she fallen away from God? Was she being a good Christian? Had she committed slander? She needed reassurance so that her anxiety could be "filled" for a while. Her calling had become a compulsion, just like the repetition of verses, the counting, and the over-analysis.

I admired Melissa for the way she had tenaciously struggled to find answers to her never-ending questions. I also respected a certain depth and potential richness in her religious quest. Indeed, it occurred to me that in the early part of her struggles, when, prodded by a vague uneasiness, she had turned to her Bible and prayer, Melissa could have been on a path to rich spiritual growth. Perhaps it is stretching the point too far, but Melissa's struggles did bring to my mind Saint Augustine's comment: "Our hearts are restless until they rest in Thee." But whatever potential there was, it was devoured by obsessive-compulsive disorder. Her questions became foolish obsessions, and her answers were reduced to meaningless compulsions.

THE READER NOT familiar with obsessive-compulsive disorder may find the cases of Raymond, Sherry, Jeff, and Melissa extraordinary, or even incredible. They are, however, quite typical of the severe cases of OCD that are routinely seen in clinical practice.

All four of these patients responded well to OCD treatments. The particulars involved in their behavior therapy, group therapy, and medication treatment will be discussed in subsequent chapters. First, however, it is important to understand exactly what mental health professionals mean when they say that someone suffers from obsessive-compulsive disorder.

DIAGNOSING OCD

OBSESSIVE-COMPULSIVE DISORDER is the simplest of all psychiatric disorders to diagnose. Unlike major depression, which requires the evaluation of nine symptoms (including depressed mood, diminished interests, weight loss, insomnia, and low energy), or panic disorder, involving the assessment of more than a dozen complaints (such as anxious mood, rapid heartbeat, and shortness of breath), obsessive-compulsive disorder requires the recognition of only two problems: obsessions and compulsions.

Traditionally, OCD has been diagnosed when a person suffers either significant obsessions or significant compulsions. The most recent research demonstrates, however, that virtually all OCDers actually have both symptoms. A practical, concise, and up-to-date definition of OCD, then, is the following: OCD is diagnosed when obsessions and compulsions interfere significantly in a person's life.

WHAT IS AN OBSESSION?

ONE MAJOR SOURCE of confusion must be cleared up right away: The term "obsession" has a totally different meaning for mental health professionals than it does for the general public. In magazines and on television, "obsession" has come to mean just about anything people want it to—as long as it has to do with thinking and carries a negative connotation. Most often, the word is used either for what is more accurately termed a preoccupation, like a coach's "obsession" with winning, or for an addiction, as in a gambler's "obsession" with horse racing.

But these "obsessions," clearly, have little in common with Raymond's tormenting spill fantasies, Sherry's heart-stopping knife thoughts, Jeff's torturing sexual urges, Melissa's mind-numbing religious interrogations, and my own thoughts to stab myself. What we suffered were *clinical* obsessions. This particular meaning of the word stays close to its Latin root, *obsidere,* meaning "to besiege," as an army would attack a city for the purpose of forcing surrender. What *clinical* obsessions represent is, truly, a battle in the mind.

The first good definition of clinical obsessions was provided in 1877 by the German psychiatrist Karl Westphal: "Obsessions are thoughts which come to the foreground of consciousness in spite of and contrary to the will of the patient, and which he is unable to suppress although he recognizes them as abnormal and not characteristic of himself."

A similar, precise definition is found in the official manual of American psychiatry (DSM-IV, see Appendix B): Obsessions are "recurrent and persistent thoughts that are experienced as intrusive and inappropriate and that cause marked anxiety or distress."

These definitions highlight the four main qualities of clinical obsessions. *Intrusive, recurrent, unwanted,* and *inappropriate.* Occasionally, not all of these characteristics are present, especially in children, chronic OCD sufferers, and OCDers with other psychiatric disorders in addition to OCD. In the great majority of cases, however, including those of Raymond, Sherry, Jeff, Melissa, and myself, all four are clearly recognizable. It is worth looking at each characteristic in some detail in order to become clear about just what an obsession is and what it is not.

AN OBSESSION IS AN INTRUSIVE THOUGHT

"INTRUSIVE" DESCRIBES THE way a thought may pop into the mind, interrupting the normal flow. A person will be thinking along, one idea leading to another, when all of a sudden—What's this!—a new thought butts in unexpectedly, involuntarily.

Intrusive thoughts are normal. Indeed, thoughts that show up suddenly and unannounced are often intensely creative. The French mathematician Henri Poincaré, perhaps the greatest scientist of his day, once described how he solved a particularly difficult problem just as he boarded a bus: "At the moment when I put my foot on the step, the idea came to me, without anything in my former thoughts seeming to have paved the way for it."

This quality of intrusiveness is acutely prominent in obsessions. Raymond, for instance, talked of crushing visions "jumping" into his mind and of his mind "handing" him terrible heart burdens. Since his obsessional thoughts bore no relationship to previous thoughts, there was no warning of their coming. Since they did not follow the normal flow of consciousness, there was the feeling that they somehow intruded on him from outside.

Similarly, a psychology graduate student described her obsessions in this way: "I can't stand to ride the bus any more, because awful sexual thoughts keep *jumping* into my mind—violent fantasies about men who sit next to me. I don't want to have the thoughts, but they keep *popping* into my imagination, *coming from out of nowhere.* I can't control them."

When I suffered from troublesome obsessions in medical school, I also had a disturbing sense of loss of control. Had my thoughts been leading logically from one to another, I could have intervened and halted the progression. But my obsessions—because they intruded suddenly and without warning into consciousness—seemed unstoppable.

An obsession is not a sensation. The buzz of a refrigerator late at night can feel like an obsession: intrusive, persistent, and bothersome. But a sensory experience comes from outside your mind, whereas an obsession is a thought within it.

AN OBSESSION IS RECURRENT

AN OBSESSION KEEPS coming back again and again. This can continue all day long. Melissa described the recurrent nature of her obsessions as a "constant spinning that never stopped." Sometimes an obsession repeats itself as a kind of undercurrent. Jeff, for instance, noted that his mind operated on two different levels at once. He could successfully teach a class while at the same time be continually tormented by unwanted sexual images.

A student who had been attending my university health services group for some time introduced herself to a new group member this way:

> My name is Stephanie and I'm a grad student in mathematics. I've been having weird obsessions off and on for years. Sometimes I get strangulation visions and images of gory things happening to my body. I will imagine a belt going around my neck, or I will see a knife being thrust into my back, or I'll see my ribs being cut open. These thoughts *keep coming into my mind, over and over, sometimes all day long.* Nothing stops them. Sometimes they really interfere with my work, which is bad, because I'm supposed to be getting my Ph.D. thesis done. This morning, thoughts were *running through my head nonstop.*

An obsession is not a phobia. Phobias are very similar to obsessions, both being recurrent, irrational fears. The difference is this: A phobia is a fear of a particular situation, such as riding on an elevator, entering a shopping mall, or speaking in public; and avoidance keeps a phobia at bay. A person with a public-speaking phobia will be fine as long as he or she is away from the lectern. With an obsession, in contrast, the focus is on a certain thought, such as knifing your daughter, crashing your car, or spreading germs. Avoidance doesn't work with thoughts. My fearful fantasy of pricking myself with a needle was most intense not when I was actually drawing blood but rather when I was alone and needle-free in my apartment.

AN OBSESSION IS UNWANTED

AN OBSESSION IS a gate crasher, an intruder in the night. The person afflicted with an obsession struggles mightily to resist it. This resistance can take up prodigious amounts of time and energy. Melissa said: "I try to stop thinking these thoughts but I can't. . . . It's like I'm involved in a battle with Satan, like he's forcing them into my mind." Jeff, sharing the OCD sufferer's most typical refrain, said: "I fight them with all my might, but I can't stop them."

Recently I saw a young mother who, like Sherry from Chapter 1, was having thoughts about harming her baby. Could there be any obsessions that are *more* unwanted? Hospitalized for exhaustion, thinking she had "gone crazy" and might actually harm her child, she told me:

> I was doing great until I got home from the hospital with my baby. All of a sudden, while I was feeding her, the thought came into my mind that I could choke her to death. I saw myself killing my baby. God bless her. I haven't been free of that thought since. I don't want my husband to leave me alone because I'm afraid of what I might do. I don't let myself go to sleep because I might let my guard down. *I try to stop these thoughts every second of the day with all my strength, but they don't let up.*

The terrible irony is that, indeed, the more strongly you resist an obsession, the more strongly it comes back. The mind does not work like a computer screen, where an unwanted thought is simply deleted. Rather, as a student patient of mine once observed, an obsession is like Freddie, the character in the *Nightmare on Elm Street* movies. Every time people thought they were finally rid of Freddie, he came *baaaaack* even stronger.

The strong resistance engendered by obsessions is probably their most defining characteristic. When I was in training at the University of Iowa, my chief of psychiatry, the noted researcher Dr. George Winokur, emphasized this point: "Look for how much the patient resists the thought—how much he or she fights it," Winokur used to say. "That will tell you whether you're dealing with an obsession or something else."

Again, to distinguish: *An obsession is not a depressive preoccupation.* A sixty-two-year-old man with intrusive, recurrent, and severely troubling thoughts was referred to me for "treatment-resistant OCD." The usual anti-OCD medications and behavior therapy had been tried. Nothing worked. He presented as a worn-out, agitated gentleman who spoke of nothing else but his fears of going into bankruptcy and losing his farm—concerns that were, in reality, totally groundless. He did not, however, resist these thoughts or consider them unwanted. On the contrary, to him these were realistic worries that needed to be dealt with immediately. What tormented him were recurrent, depressive thoughts, not obsessions. The patient responded to a standard antidepressant medication, imipramine (Tofranil).

An obsession is not an addiction. Degree of resistance also serves to differentiate obsessions from addictions. Obsessions are always unwanted—and not just 80 or 90 percent unwanted, but 100 percent. No part of a person wants an obsession. With an addiction, the unwanted urge carries a certain thrill. The gambling addict, for instance, gets a kick out of the action. A part of him looks forward to gambling, even while another part of him knows that he shouldn't do it. With an obsession, there is no enjoyment at all.

AN OBSESSION IS INAPPROPRIATE

GIVEN A CHANCE to sit back and reflect for a minute, the afflicted person just can't figure out why the tormenting thought would ever have occurred in the first place. There seems to be no earthly reason for it.

Mental health professionals use the term "ego-dystonic" to describe this characteristic. The term means "against a person's very nature," a mismatch to a person's sense of self. When I had my needle obsession, I knew it was irrational for me to be thinking such thoughts. They didn't match with who I was. They didn't fit in with my goals, my desires, or my fears. When an OCDer must check the light switch for the hundredth time, the reaction is: "Why am I thinking this crazy thought? This isn't me."

Raymond knew very well that his spill visions were only "killer fantasies." It was because he did that he went to such great lengths to hide his checking compulsions. A new student in our OCD group described her obsessions this way:

> *I will fully admit right now that my worries are unrealistic and completely stupid.* Like before I go to bed, I will keep having the thought that the door isn't locked. I lock it and unlock it, lock it and unlock it, a dozen times. But the thought still comes back: *What if I didn't lock it right?* I will get up and go over and check the door again. *It's so crazy that I'm reduced to tears.*

An obsession is not a psychosis. Sometimes the recognition of the ego-dystonic quality of an obsession—realizing that a thought is violating who you are—causes people to think that they are "going crazy." This is a common reaction to severe obsessions: "I should be locked up!" Jeff felt this way because he thought he was "hearing voices." Even though he recognized that these "voices" came from his own mind and did not sound like real voices, still, because his tormenting thoughts were so inappropriate and senseless, so unlike himself, he mistook his obsessions for psychotic hallucinations.

Melissa also feared that she was losing her sanity. At first, I myself wasn't sure on this point. Her inner preoccupations and abrupt lapses in conversation gave her the appearance of a person who might be actively hallucinating; furthermore, her intense concern about Satan raised the question as to whether she might be suffering delusions. When I questioned Melissa, however, as to whether she was in fact hearing voices, she said no. And when I asked her about common delusions—such as the idea that other people could overhear her thoughts, or the idea that messages were being sent to her over the television or radio—she denied these as well. Her beliefs about Satan turned out to be shared by other members of her church and therefore were not signs of mental illness. It was soon clear that Melissa had OCD, not a psychosis.

OCDers often feel like they're going crazy because they experience a loss of control over their thoughts. Yet obsessions never—repeat, *never*—lead to a true loss of contact with reality, to a psychosis. People who are psychotic lack the ability to discern what is sensible. OCDers, on the contrary, are intensely aware that their thoughts don't make sense. OCDers probably have *less* of a chance of going crazy than anybody else.

THE FOUR QUALITIES of *intrusiveness, recurrence, unwantedness,* and *inappropriateness* are what set clinical obsessions apart from the preoccupations, temptations, and worries of everyday life.

An adolescent male, starry-eyed over a new girlfriend, is not really "obsessed." He's merely preoccupied. Likewise, the lady who has to grit her teeth and punch down on the gas pedal to get past the liquor store is not "obsessed with alcohol," not clinically, at least. She is tempted, perhaps addicted. And consider what happened to me not long ago. I was fretting aloud about my ten-year-old daughter going away to college. Crime, cut-throat competition, men trying to take advantage of her. . . . My wife chided me, "Stop your obsessing!" But these were not unwanted thoughts that I resisted, nor were they completely inappropriate. It makes sense to be a bit fearful about your daughter's future. These were not obsessions; they were simply worries.

With ordinary temptations, addictions, and worries, there are ways to fight back—willpower, for instance, or thinking more rationally. But for obsessions there seems to be no defense at all. They are like body snatchers from outer space. A person will do anything to find relief. And that's where compulsions enter in.

THE NATURE OF COMPULSIONS

THE TERM "COMPULSION," like "obsession," has taken on a broad, which is to say vague, meaning. Popularly, it is used to indicate anything done to excess: compulsively eating Ben and Jerry's ice cream, for instance, or compulsively planning one's day. But again, the clinical meaning is much more specific.

A clinical compulsion is sometimes defined simply as "a repetitive act that is performed according to rules that must be applied rigidly." A better definition, however, is one that stresses the close relationship between compulsions and obsessions: A compulsion is a repetitive act that is clearly excessive and is performed in order to lessen the discomfort of an obsession.

An obsession strikes, anxiety mounts, and repetitive acts provide a way out. Why compulsions are effective in the short run to alleviate anxiety is not completely understood. As will be discussed in Chapter 8, animals are known to perform many stereotyped rituals when under stress (monkeys in the zoo strumming the mesh of their cage, or rocking back and forth continuously). Many OCD experts believe that compulsions are related to these and involve genetically programmed tendencies.

Compulsions can take an infinite number of different forms. Most often they are reasonable responses gone haywire, such as checking a gas stove a hundred times in a row for fear of a leak. They can also be acts that are completely foreign to reason, however, like jumping up and down eight times because of the thought that an accident will occur. But all compulsions have this property: Although they provide short-term respite from obsessions, in the long run they only make obsessions worse. Obsessions, in turn, make compulsions worse. It's a vicious cycle.

THE REMARKABLE CASE OF HOWARD HUGHES

THE BEST EXAMPLE of the depths of despair and disability to which this vicious cycle can carry a person is found, amazingly, in the case of a man who was once the richest person in America. Howard Hughes was a brilliant businessman, a pilot who set aviation records, a movie producer who courted beautiful starlets. Yet for the last twenty years of his life he lived as a complete recluse, spending his days in the darkened bedrooms of fancy penthouses with a small army of guards to insure his privacy. Newspapers portrayed him as an eccentric genius, but after his death in 1976 it was revealed that his strange behaviors were entirely due to compulsions run amok.

As a young man Hughes was, indeed, eccentric. Perfectionistic and domineering, he wrote pages of memos on inconsequential items. Friends knew that he had irrational contamination fears; they were not allowed to even touch his private refrigerator. Nevertheless, despite such peculiarities, Hughes was enormously productive and successful. All this changed in midlife after he was severely injured in the crash of an air force reconnaissance plane of his own design and subsequently became addicted to the narcotics that were prescribed for the pain of his injuries.

Thereafter, Hughes' life was dominated by compulsions. Afraid to eat, drink, be touched, wear clothes, or leave his room, he made his staff follow senseless, intricate checking and washing rituals that took hours and hours to perform. A typical memo to his staff, instructions for the "preparation of canned fruit," entailed no less than nine painstaking steps. Step 3, "washing of can," for example, read:

> The man in charge turns the valve in the bathtub on, using his bare hands to do so. He also adjusts the water temperature so that it is not too hot or too cold. He then takes one of the brushes, and, using one of the bars of soap, creates a good lather, and then scrubs the can from a point two inches below the top of the can. He should first soak and remove the label, and then brush the cylindrical part of the can over and over until all particles of dust, pieces of the label, and, in general, all sources of contamination have been removed. Holding the can in the center at all times, he then processes the bottom of the can in the same manner, being very sure that the bristles of the brush have thoroughly cleaned all the small indentations on the perimeter. He then rinses the soap. Taking the second brush, and still holding the can in the center, he again creates a good lather and scrubs the top of the can, the perimeter along the top, and the cylindrical sides to a point two inches below the top. He should continue this scrubbing until he literally removes the tin protection from the can itself.

Every other step is comparably detailed. From step 5: "While transferring the fruit from the can to the sterile plate, be sure that no part of the body, including the hands, be directly over the can or the plate at any time. If possible, keep the head, upper part of the body, arms, etc. at least one foot away." The memo finishes: "This operation must be carried out in every infinitesimal detail, and I would deeply appreciate it if the man would follow each phase very slowly and thoughtfully, giving his full attention to the importance of the work at hand."

Hughes' germ obsessions, paradoxically, drove him to hoarding whatever might cause contamination. His urine and feces was stored in large jars. He lived out his years in a tortured, solitary manner, his OCD relieved only by fixes of narcotic drugs.

The case of Howard Hughes is, indeed, very strange. Not only were his compulsions extraordinary, but it is almost unheard of for a person to develop such a severe case after age fifty. The objective observer must wonder whether Hughes' caretakers were purposefully keeping him disabled in order to take advantage of his wealth. His ability to cope with obsessions was certainly compromised when they helped him become addicted to narcotics. His OCD, it would appear, was also markedly worsened when they carried out what was in essence an "anti-behavior therapy" program, fully assisting in all of his wild rituals. Most tellingly, these assistants never tried to get Hughes any treatment. A physician remarked after his death: "He would have gotten better care if he were a penniless wino who collapsed on skid row. At least some passer-by would have called the paramedics."

TYPES OF COMPULSIONS

THE COMPULSIONS THAT crippled Howard Hughes, as well as those affecting his fellow OCD sufferers, can be divided into two groups: behavioral (observable acts) and mental (thought rituals).

Behavioral compulsions include all the classic and well-recognized OCD rituals. Hughes was troubled primarily by washing and checking, the two most common types of severe compulsions. Another widespread behavioral compulsion is asking for reassurance. Other common examples include hoarding, repeating, tapping, and ordering.

Washing
MANY EXPERTS THINK that washing is the single most prevalent type of behavioral compulsion. Judith Rapoport, M.D., of the National Institutes of Health, a top OCD researcher and author of

the acclaimed book, *The Boy Who Couldn't Stop Washing,* reports that more than 80 percent of the people who come to her clinic for treatment of OCD have been bothered at some time by washing rituals.

At the root of washing compulsions, not surprisingly, is an obsession that a part of the body is unclean. Washing eases the feeling temporarily, but once the scrubbing is done, the thought returns. More scrubbing follows. Dermatologists are often the first to diagnose this disorder, as people frequently seek treatment for the skin damage caused by this excess.

Handwashing compulsions are OCD's most recognized symptom. They are, indeed, the hallmark of the disorder. A typical example is provided by a math teacher:

> I get to thinking that my hands are unclean in some way. It's not that they look dirty. And it's not that I imagine germs on them, either. It's just that I have this feeling they're unclean. So I'll lather them up good, wash them for a couple minutes, and dry them carefully. But pretty soon I'll touch something and then I'll get the feeling again. Some evenings after work I wash my hands every five minutes. They're in bad shape. I have to put medication on them and wear gloves when I sleep.

The most famous description of excessive handwashing is found in Shakespeare's *Macbeth* (Act 5, scene 1):

> DOCTOR: Look how she rubs her hands.
> GENTLEWOMAN: It is an accustomed action. . . . I have known her to continue in this a quarter of an hour.
> LADY MACBETH: Yet here's a spot. . . . Out, damned spot! Out, I say! . . . will these hands never be clean? . . . Here's the smell of blood still: All the perfumes of Arabia will not sweeten this little hand.

Although this would seem to be a good description of compulsive washing, in the context of Shakespeare's play it probably does not represent true OCD. Lady Macbeth's handwashing occurs during sleepwalking, and her ritual is driven not by clinical obsessions but rather by depressive delusions or preoccuptations fueled by her guilt over Duncan's murder.

Checking

CHECKING COMPULSIONS IS also very common. A recent study of 250 consecutive patients from Harvard's outpatient OCD clinic found that 63 percent complained of checking rituals.

With this type of compulsion, a person must examine a situation over and over to make sure that no harm will come of it. Obsessions such as, "Is the gas shut off?" and "Are the doors locked?" drive the checking. A young wife described the torment and disruption that these rituals can cause:

> I stand there and turn the light switch off and on, off and on, off and on, off and on. I can't make myself stop. It's crazy. What happens is that I have the thought that maybe I didn't completely turn it all the way off. Maybe the switch is somewhere inbetween the off and on position and a fire will start because of a short circuit. I know that this does not make sense. Still, I have to keep on switching back and forth until I get it just right. I might stay there for ten or fifteen minutes. One time the light switch started smoking. Now my husband swears at me and yells, "Leave the light switch alone or you really will start a fire!"

Requesting Reassurance

THIS TYPE OF compulsion tests the patience of family members more than any other. Here, a sufferer becomes obsessed that something terrible has happened and is compelled to coax a pledge from another person that everything is okay. "I didn't hit anybody with the car, did I?" "That lump doesn't mean I have AIDS, does it?" The OCDer asks over and over, unable to stop, knowing the answer she'll get, but needing to ask again anyway. Reassurance must be endlessly provided. A newlywed explained how her marriage was almost on the rocks due to her reassurance compulsions:

> I love my husband more than anything. But I get the crazy thought that I might be interested in other men. I'll be walking in the mall and I'll notice a handsome guy, and afterward I'll get to wondering if

I looked at him too long, if maybe that means I'm interested in him. I'll worry all day; I can't stop myself from thinking that I might have had thoughts of unfaithfulness. Then, because I feel so guilty, I'm driven to tell my husband. I know it makes him feel bad, but I have to. He says that it's okay, that he knows I'm not interested in anyone else. Then I feel better. But I've been doing this every day, and it's driving him nuts.

Hoarding

HERE, THE NATURAL tendency to save things is stretched to a pathological degree. A young man whose apartment was more than half filled, floor to ceiling, with magazines and newspapers explained that he was afraid to throw an article away because he might later remember that there was something critically important in it. Then, if he couldn't find it, he might get so upset that he would have a nervous breakdown.

Repeating

WHEN A ROUTINE action is repeated compulsively, and when—unlike in washing, checking, reassurance, and hoarding rituals—it bears no logical relationship to the obsession preceding it, this is called a repeating compulsion. One student, when struck by a harm obsession, compulsively repeated the action he was engaged in; this could be combing his hair, crossing his legs, or writing his name. Several quick repetitions usually sufficed to chase away the obsession. Repeating compulsions often must be performed a certain specific number of times. A young woman, in response to "a feeling of dread," scratched her head, brushed her teeth, or chewed on Lifesavers four times, no more no less.

Rubbing, Touching, and Tapping

THESE COMMON COMPULSIONS also defy logical analysis. A student with harm obsessions needed to tap her fingers ten times to prevent her tormenting thought from coming true.

Ordering

HERE, ITEMS MUST be arranged so that they are "just so." These rituals differ a bit from all others: They occur frequently in young boys, and their corresponding obsessions are often hard to identify.

It has been hypothesized that ordering compulsions bear some resemblance to another kind of abnormal, repetitive action, the jerky movements referred to as "tics." Ordering compulsions may represent a hybrid symptom between OCD and the related neurological disorder of tics, Tourette's syndrome.

MENTAL COMPULSIONS

IN CHAPTER 1, I mentioned that when I was in medical school I suffered the obsession of a phlebotomy needle suddenly plunging into my skin. It was a startling image that shook me to my bones, like fingernails raking across a blackboard. To lessen its effect I developed the habit of immediately bringing to mind a certain protective image: my skin being covered by a soothing, impenetrable cream.

That was a mental compulsion, an attempt to escape an obsession by employing a special, counteractive idea. With mental compulsions, as with behavioral compulsions, something is done repeatedly, mechanically, for no purpose other than to lessen the discomfort of an obsession. As one person may repeatedly check the stove, another may habitually conjure up a corrective fantasy.

Ten years ago, mental compulsions were not even known to most mental health professionals. The last edition of the official manual of American Psychiatry, the DSM-III-R, published in 1987, defined compulsions as "intentional *behaviors* that are performed in response to an obsession." It is now recognized, however, that compulsions occurring in the form of thoughts are extremely common, probably even more common than behavioral compulsions. How far our knowledge of OCD has come in just a decade!

Counter-image

PERHAPS THE MOST prevalent type of mental compulsion is the type I developed in med school, the counter-image. In my OCD group, a student described her counter-images in this way:

> I get pictures in my mind of knives being stabbed into my grandmother. These thoughts cause me so much anxiety that I have to re-

think them whenever they occur. I have to get a good image of my grandmother in my mind, one where she doesn't have the knife sticking in her. So I see the knife going in, and then I have to pull it out. But as soon as I pull the knife out, it's there again. So this goes on and on. I think a bad thought, then I have to think a good one.

Repeating of Prayers

ANOTHER COMMON TYPE of mental compulsion is the rote repetition of a prayer. The words no longer have real meaning, they have been reduced to ritualistic incantations performed exclusively to drive away an obsession. A Catholic woman in her fifties described her ritual:

> I say to myself "Holy Mary mother of God have grace on us sinners" over and over. It's because an awful thought keeps coming into my mind. A thought to stab Jesus. God knows why it happens. The prayer used to work to make it go away; but now I say it over and over, for hours, and the terrible thought keeps on coming back anyway.

Counting

THIS COMPULSION INCLUDES numbering objects as well as repetitively counting to a certain number. The key is that the compulsion is in the process of counting itself. A thirty-five-year-old man, totally disabled by OCD, needed to count anything in sight. In my waiting room, he counted the tiles in the ceiling. In my office, he counted the books on the bookshelf. He said he just had "an urge to do it."

Ruminations

ALTHOUGH THERE IS little written about this type of compulsion, it seems to be fairly common, especially in students. A rumination has been defined as "a train of thought, unproductive and prolonged, on a particular topic or theme." Sometimes, ruminations clearly represent mental compulsions. An engineering student described his unwanted musings:

> I constantly over-think things. I'll be out with my girlfriend, and suddenly I say to myself, "Oh no, here come the thoughts!" I know

then that I'm going to get carried away with thinking things over. The thought comes that I'm not real. I'll have to answer endless questions regarding whether my girlfriend and I are actually here or not. The metaphysical analysis goes on and on and on. I get an isolated, alone feeling. Then I may start questioning why I'm thinking these crazy thoughts in the first place. My whole evening will be ruined.

Mental compulsions, like behavioral compulsions, in the long run only worsen obsessions. A particularly devastating outcome is when the obsession itself starts to be triggered by the very images used to counteract it. A gentle, civic-minded man described how this happened to him:

> I'd kill myself before I'd harm a kid. I have kids myself. I'm a Scout leader, for God's sake. Yet I will be walking along and I'll see a little boy across the street, and then the thought will come into my mind to run over and strangle him. Nothing will get rid of the awful idea. I used to play a trick to try to get rid it. When the terrible idea would hit, I'd immediately imagine myself teaching the child how to play baseball. This worked for a while; but now things are even worse, because now whenever I see a baseball game on TV, it brings the terrible thoughts right into my mind.

The compulsions mentioned above—washing, checking, reassurance, hoarding, repeating, ordering, and various mental rituals—do not exhaust all possibilities, but they are the types most commonly seen. All of them share one feature: They are defensive, done solely to lessen the torment of obsessions. Yet, from the extreme checking rituals developed by Howard Hughes, to my own more modest protective fantasies, compulsions in the long run only guarantee that the self-tormenting thought that caused them will return again and again.

THE DIAGNOSIS OF obsessive-compulsive disorder presented no major difficulties in the cases of Raymond, Sherry, Jeff, and Melissa. All four had typical obsessions and common compulsions. Usually OCD is like that, very easy to diagnose. Anyone who has obsessions and compulsions that are interfering in their lives has obsessive-compulsive disorder, unless proven otherwise. Occasionally, however, there are times when it is not completely clear whether a person suffers from OCD or from another somewhat similar psychiatric disorder, such as hypochondriasis or body dysmorphic disorder, or from a related neurological disorder, such as Tourette's syndrome. Phobias can also overlap with OCD. These more complicated situations will be discussed in chapters 9 and 10.

To put the whole process of psychiatric diagnosis in broader context, it has been observed that medicine has three levels of diagnostic sophistication. The first stands on the recognition of specific symptoms ("pneumonia is a cough with a fever"). The second level founds diagnosis on measurable biochemical changes in the body ("pneumonia is congestion in the lungs"). The third, the highest level of diagnostic refinement, fixes diagnosis firmly on the ultimate cause of a disorder ("pneumonia is a bacterial infection of the lungs"). Psychiatry, for the most part, is still in the first stage, whereas the other branches of medicine have advanced to levels two and three.

Later in the book it will become clear that psychiatry, in the case of OCD, is on the threshold of moving up one or two levels in diagnostic sophistication. For now, though, OCD continues to be diagnosed completely on the basis of the recognition of its symptoms, obsessions and compulsions.

SELF-ADMINISTERED QUESTIONNAIRES FOR DIAGNOSING OCD

THERE ARE SEVERAL pencil-and-paper tests that can provide a fairly good idea of whether a person suffers from OCD. Taking these tests requires only sitting down and answering a number of multiple choice questions to determine whether common obsessions and compulsions are present. Although these tests do not take the place of diagnosis by a competent psychiatrist or psychologist, they can be effective screening devices.

Below is the questionnaire that I find the most useful, the Padua

Inventory, which was developed in Italy in 1987 and has been standardized on thousands of people here and abroad. I suggest you take this test. Apart from diagnostic considerations, reflecting on the questions contained in the Padua Inventory will increase your understanding of OCD, as these represent a fairly comprehensive list of the most common obsessions and compulsions. In them you will recognize the problems of Raymond, Sherry, Jeff, and Melissa. The test requires only about ten minutes of your time.

THE PADUA INVENTORY

Instructions: Reply to each question with a rating of 0 to 4: 0 = not at all; 1 = a little; 2 = some; 3 = a lot; 4 = very much.

1. I feel my hands are dirty when I touch money.
2. I think even slight contact with bodily secretions (perspiration, saliva, urine, etc.) may contaminate my clothes or somehow harm me.
3. I find it difficult to touch an object when I know it has been touched by strangers or by certain people.
4. I find it difficult to touch garbage or dirty things.
5. I avoid using public toilets because I am afraid of disease and contamination.
6. I avoid using public telephones because I am afraid of contagion and disease.
7. I wash my hands more often and longer than necessary.
8. I sometimes have to wash or clean myself simply because I think I may be dirty or "contaminated."
9. If I touch something I think is "contaminated," I immediately have to wash or clean myself.
10. If an animal touches me, I feel dirty and immediately have to wash myself or change my clothing.
11. When doubts and worries come to my mind, I cannot rest until I have talked them over with a reassuring person.
12. When I talk I tend to repeat the same things and the same sentences several times.
13. I tend to ask people to repeat the same things to me several

times consecutively, even though I did understand what they said the first time.

14. I feel obliged to follow a particular order in dressing, undressing, and washing myself.

15. Before going to sleep I have to do certain things in a certain order.

16. Before going to bed I have to hang up or fold my clothes in a special way.

17. I feel I have to repeat certain numbers for no reason.

18. I have to do things several times before I think they are properly done.

19. I tend to keep on checking things more often than necessary.

20. I check and recheck gas and water taps and light switches after turning them off.

21. I return home to check doors, windows, drawers, etc., to make sure they are properly shut.

22. I keep on checking forms, documents, checks, etc., in detail, to make sure I have filled them in correctly,.

23. I keep on going back to see that matches, cigarettes, etc., are properly extinguished.

24. When I handle money I count and recount it several times.

25. I check letters carefully many times before posting them.

26. I find it difficult to make decisions, even about unimportant matters.

27. Sometimes I am not sure I have done things that in fact I know I have done.

28. I have the impression that I will never be able to explain things clearly, especially when talking about important matters that involve me.

29. After doing something carefully, I still have the impression I have either done it badly or not finished it.

30. I am sometimes late because I keep on doing certain things more often than necessary.

31. I invent doubts and problems about most of the things I do.

32. When I start thinking of certain things, I become obsessed with them.

33. Unpleasant thoughts come into my mind against my will and I cannot get rid of them.
34. Obscene or dirty words come into my mind and I cannot get rid of them.
35. My brain constantly goes its own way, and I find it difficult to attend to what is happening around me.
36. I imagine catastrophic consequences as a result of absent-mindedness or minor errors that I make.
37. I think or worry at length about having hurt someone without knowing it.
38. When I hear about a disaster, I think it is somehow my fault.
39. I sometimes worry at length for no reason that I have hurt myself or have some disease.
40. I sometimes start counting objects for no reason.
41. I feel I have to remember completely unimportant numbers.
42. When I read I have the impression I have missed something important and must go back and reread the passage at least two or three times.
43. I worry about remembering completely unimportant things and make an effort not to forget them.
44. When a thought or doubt comes into my mind, I have to examine it from all points of view and cannot stop until I have done so.
45. In certain situations I am afraid of losing my self-control and doing embarrassing things.
46. When I look down from a bridge or a very high window, I feel an impulse to throw myself into space.
47. When I see a train approaching I sometimes think I could throw myself under its wheels.
48. At certain moments I am tempted to tear off my clothes in public.
49. While driving I sometimes feel an impulse to drive the car into someone or something.
50. Seeing weapons excites me and makes me think violent thoughts.
51. I get upset and worried at the sight of knives, daggers, and other pointed objects.

52. I sometimes feel something inside me which makes me do things that are really senseless and that I do not want to do.
53. I sometimes feel the need to break or damage things for no reason.
54. I sometimes have an impulse to steal other people's belongings, even if they are of no use to me.
55. I am sometimes almost irresistibly tempted to steal something from the supermarket.
56. I sometimes have an impulse to hurt defenseless children or animals.
57. I feel I have to make special gestures or walk in a certain way.
58. In certain situations I feel an impulse to eat too much, even if I am then ill.
59. When I hear about a suicide or a crime, I am upset for a long time and find it difficult to stop thinking about it.
60. I invent useless worries about germs and diseases.

To score the Padua Inventory, add up your ratings (o to 4) for the sixty questions.

The average result for unscreened groups of people (usually hospital employees and university students) is about 40. The average result for people in treatment for OCD is about 80. I took this test remembering back to when I suffered OCD in medical training and got a 72. Taking it now, I get about a 50.

There are several other questionnaires worth mentioning. The Maudsley Obsessive-Compulsive Inventory, developed in 1977 in England, has been used more than any other test. Unfortunately, in light of our current knowledge of OCD, it is clear that the present version concentrates excessively on checking and washing compulsions. (A new, improved version of the Maudsley Inventory will be released soon.) The Leyton Obsessional Inventory and the Compulsive Activity Checklist are also excellent screening tests but are, perhaps, not quite as comprehensive as the Padua Inventory.

The Yale-Brown Obsessive-Compulsive Scale (Y-BOCS), developed in 1989 by Yale and Brown universities, asks ten questions that assess the strength of a person's obsessions and compulsions. It is a very useful and widely used test, but it was designed mainly to follow people's progress in treatment, not to diagnose OCD. It is included in Appendix A.

If you think that you might possibly have obsessive-compulsive disorder, please do take the Padua Inventory. OCD sufferers tend to walk through life in a sort of numb confusion, approaching their obsessions and compulsions like bad weather—to be lived through and then forgotten as soon as possible. They never come to grips with the fact that they have a real psychiatric disorder. This is a major mistake.

Anyone who scores well above average on the Padua Inventory should consider that they may have obsessive-compulsive disorder. If you have it, you should treat it. There is no shame to having OCD. In fact, I am rather proud to be included in the company of the people discussed in the next chapter.

3

WHO GETS OCD?

"THEY ARE MOSTLY good people, for bad men rarely know any-thing of these types of thoughts." That comment was made by En-glish Bishop John Moore in 1692. Many similar observations have been made over the centuries by people, usually clergymen, called on to provide help to OCD sufferers.

Contemporary helpers have largely agreed with these observa-tions. Psychologist Stanley Rachman of the University of British Columbia, perhaps the leading expert on OCD over the last two decades, summed up the opinions of specialists in the area of obses-sive-compulsive disorder in 1979: "Our clinical impression is that people with OCD are correct, upright, moral citizens who aspire to high standards of personal conduct."

In the 1980s, researchers began to study personality and OCD scientifically, confirming that people with OCD do share certain personality traits, specific life-long tendencies to think and act in particular ways. One research group suggests that OCD sufferers may be summed up as fearful, introspective, and depressive. An-other group of investigators has found that there are three other qualities that are common to OCD sufferers: a tendency to avoid harm at all cost, a lack of interest in novelty, and a great need for ap-proval from others. A third group of investigators finds that the core of OCD sufferers' personalities is a tendency to take excessive personal responsibility for others. Indeed, it seems that people with OCD do make upright citizens.

This chapter begins with a review of historical figures who have had symptoms of OCD. Then, taking these cases as examples, it will explore research into the unique personality traits of OCD sufferers.

JOHN BUNYAN

AUTHOR OF THE Puritan allegory, *Pilgrim's Progress,* John Bunyan (1628–1688) has been called, next to Shakespeare, England's most influential author. Coleridge referred to *Pilgrim's Progress* as "the model of beautiful, pure, and harmonious English." Rudyard Kipling labeled Bunyan "the father of the novel."

Bunyan had clear-cut, moderate to severe OCD; his case is our best historical example of the illness. As William James stated in *The Varieties of Religious Experience,* Bunyan had "a sensitive conscience to a diseased degree, beset by doubts, fears, and insistent ideas."

In his powerful autobiography, *Grace Abounding to the Chief of Sinners,* Bunyan vividly describes attacks of intrusive, tormenting thoughts. Most were obsessions of blasphemy. Nothing would stop the onslaught. "A very great storm came down upon me . . . whole floods of blasphemies, both against God, Christ, and the Scriptures, were poured upon my spirit, to my great confusion and astonishment. . . . I felt as if there were nothing else but these from morning to night." Bunyan agonized over obsessional impulses to scream out profanities in public, urges that drove him to physically restraining himself: "The tempter would provoke me to desire to sin . . . if it were to be committed by speaking of such a word, then in so strong a measure was this temptation upon me, that often I have been ready to clap my hand under my chin, to hold my mouth from opening." Bunyan endured other obsessions as well, perhaps murderous or sexual obsessions, which he considered too vile to discuss: "Many others at this time I may not, nor dare not, utter, neither by word nor pen."

Bunyan developed extensive compulsions, such as endlessly repeating certain phrases while rocking back and forth: "For whole
hours together . . . my very body would be put into action by way of
pushing or thrusting with my hands or elbows; still answering 'I
will not, I will not, I will not, I will not, no not for thousands, thousands, thousands of worlds."

In describing an obsession that a church bell would fall on him,
Bunyan illustrates the torturing doubt that assails the obsessional:

> I began to think, what if one of the bells should fall? I chose to stand
> under a main beam . . . thinking there I might stand safely. But then
> I thought again, what if the bell fell with a swing, it might first hit
> the wall, and then rebounding upon me, might kill me, despite the
> beam. This made me stand in the steeple-door; and now, thought I, I
> am safe enough. But then it came into my head, What if the steeple
> itself should fall? And this thought did continually so shake my
> mind, that I dared not stand at the steeple-door any longer, but was
> forced to flee, for fear the steeple should fall upon my head.

Through it all, Bunyan showed the insight of a true obsessional.
He knew his worries were irrational; he just couldn't stop thinking
them. "These things may seem ridiculous to others," Bunyan notes,
"even as ridiculous as they were in themselves, but to me they were
the most tormenting cogitations."

SAMUEL JOHNSON

POET, PLAYWRIGHT, BIOGRAPHER, and scholar, the greatest
literary figure of his age, Samuel Johnson (1709–1784) once wrote,
"Disorders of the intellect happen much more often than superficial
observers will easily believe. Perhaps if we speak with rigorous ex-
actness, no human mind is in its right state." His interest in the
subject was due to concern for his own sanity. In *Young Sam Johnson,*
James Clifford writes that Johnson "would become oppressed, again
and again, by the morbid obsession that he was losing his mind."
Johnson was a great admirer of John Bunyan. Historian W. Hale

White notes that Johnson was "haunted by Bunyan's specters." That is not surprising, as Johnson, like Bunyan, clearly had obsessive-compulsive disorder.

James Boswell, Johnson's famous biographer, notes that his subject had "queer habits which amazed all beholders," habits we now recognize as touching and repeating compulsions. Johnson "sometimes seemed to be obeying some hidden impulse, which commanded him to touch every post in a street or tread on the center of every paving-stone. He would return if his task had not been accurately performed."

Johnson also performed compulsive rituals before entering houses: "I have upon innumerable occasions," writes Boswell, "observed him suddenly stop, and then seem to count his steps with a deep earnestness; and when he had neglected or gone wrong in this sort of magical movement, I have seen him go back again, put himself in a proper position to begin the ceremony, and, having gone through it, break from his abstraction, walk briskly on, and join his companion." Similar compulsions are described by another Johnson biographer, Miss Frances Reynolds, who writes that upon entering a house Johnson "whirled and twisted about to perform his gesticulations; and as soon as he had finished, he would give a sudden spring and make such an extensive stride over the threshold, as if he were trying for a wager how far he could stride."

Johnson frequently suffered a nervous tic disorder, not uncommon with OCD sufferers. Sometimes, his compulsions and tics were the object of ridicule. Boswell writes: "Once Johnson collected a laughing mob by his antics; his hands imitating the motions of a jockey riding at full speed and his feet twisting in and out to make the heels and toes touch alternately."

THERESE OF LISIEUX

PATRON SAINT OF France, author of a still popular spiritual autobiography, *Story of a Soul,* Therese of Lisieux (1873–1897) appears to have endured disabling obsessive-compulsive disorder that started at age twelve. Interestingly, her OCD improved when she entered a Carmelite convent at age fifteen. Therese tells in *Story of a Soul* of that early period in her life:

> It was during the retreat for my second communion that I was assailed by the terrible sickness of scruples. One would have to pass through this martyrdom to understand it well, and for me to express what I suffered for a year and a half would be impossible. All my most simple thoughts and actions became the cause of trouble for me, and I had relief only when I told them to Marie. This cost me dearly, for I believed I was obliged to tell her the absurd thoughts I had even about her. As soon as I laid down my burden, I experienced peace for an instant; but it passed away like a lightning flash.

While in the midst of an obsessional crisis Therese writes: "If you only knew what frightful thoughts obsess me! . . . I would like to be able to express what I feel, but alas! I believe this is impossible. . . . Must one have thoughts like this when one loves God so much? . . . I undergo them under duress, but while undergoing them I never cease making acts of faith."

The obsessions that tormented Therese were primarily excessive fears of committing sins, or "scruples." That her scruples represented what we now call clinical obsessions is indicated by her strenuous resistance to them, as well as by her full insight into their "absurd" nature. Her compulsions included constant reassurance seeking, as well as, perhaps, "ceaseless acts of faith." Note that Therese herself tellingly refers to her problem as a "sickness."

WINSTON CHURCHILL

AT THE FUNERAL of Winston Churchill, the novelist Rebecca West summed up the feelings of those acquainted with the great British statesman: "Really, the world will not come to peace with itself except as it acknowledges that some men are simply superior." Yet Churchill himself suffered from classic harm obsessions: intrusive impulses to suicide. They did not interfere into his life in a major way, and it is not at all certain that Churchill had diagnosable OCD, but his obsessions were anxiety provoking and a nuisance.

Churchill once confided to his personal physician, Charles Moran: "I don't like standing near the edge of a platform when the express train is passing through. A second's action would end everything. I like to stand right back, and if possible to get a pillar between me and the train." Because of similar obsessional impulses to jump to his death, Churchill didn't like to travel by boat. "I don't like to look down into the water," he once told Moran. "A second's action would end everything. A few drops of desperation." For the same reason, Churchill didn't like to sleep in rooms with access to a balcony.

Yet Churchill was not suicidal. As is always the case with obsessionals, to follow through on his tormenting thoughts was the last thing he wanted. He explained to Moran, "I don't want to go out of the world at all in such moments. I've no desire to quit this world, but thoughts, desperate thoughts, come into my head."

MARTIN LUTHER AND IGNATIUS OF LOYOLA

LASTLY, WE MAY consider two great historical figures who, even though they were bitter enemies, had much in common. Both marked turning points in 1521: Luther was condemned by the Catholic Church as a heretic; and Ignatius of Loyola experienced religious conversion. Both men started great movements: Luther, the Reformation; and Ignatius, the Jesuits. Both men, too, suffered obsessions.

Martin Luther underwent severe mental turmoil with obsessions and depression. In *Young Man Luther,* the psychiatrist Erik Erikson notes that during his first years in the monastery, Luther's mental state was so disrupted that "it seems entirely probable that young Luther's life at times approached what today we might call a borderline psychotic state." Ignatius endured similar, if not quite so severe, afflictions. W. W. Meisner, M.D., writes in his biography *Ignatius of Loyola* that Ignatius's early life was "filled with inner torment" due to "intense, destructive obsessions."

Luther and Ignatius both endured tormenting obsessional doubts and, to a lesser degree, other types of obsessions as well. Religious doubts, a form of scruples, were indeed a common problem in past centuries; they qualify as obsessions when they are persistent, tormenting, and recognized as inappropriate. Luther writes in his *Commentary on Galatians:*

> When I was a monk I thought that I was utterly cast away. If at any time I felt fleshly lust, wrath, hatred, or envy against any brother, I assayed many ways to quiet my conscience, but it would not be; for the lust did always return, so that I could not rest, but was continually vexed with these thoughts: This or that sin thou hast committed: thou art infected with envy, with impatiency, and such other sins.

Because of these excruciating scruples, Luther could not feel certain that he had confessed all his sins. He would confess for hours and hours, splitting his transgressions smaller and smaller. He would go back to childhood and endlessly enumerate possibly sinful acts. After finishing he would ask for special appointments to correct previous statements. His preceptors, confused by his obsessiveness, threatened to punish him for obstruction of confession. As quoted in *The Way of Interior Peace,* one of them told Luther: "You have no real sins with which to reproach yourself . . . give up your nonsensical and ludicrous notions."

Ignatius suffered similar battles with confessional scruples. He writes in his autobiography *St. Ignatius' Own Story:*

> Even though I had confessed . . . my scruples returned, each time becoming more minute, so that I became quite upset, and although I knew that these scruples were doing me much harm, and that it would be good to be rid of them, I could not shake them off. . . . I continued with my seven hours of prayer on my knees, rising faithfully every midnight, and performing all the other exercises. But nothing provided me with a cure for my scruples.

Luther and Ignatius also suffered violent and blasphemous obsessions. Luther once declared at the dinner table that the sight of a knife conjured up "painful pictures" before him. He writes: "For more than a week I have been thrown back and forth in death and

Hell; my whole body feels beaten, my limbs are still trembling. I almost lost Christ completely, driven about on the waves and storms of despair and blasphemy against God." Ignatius notes: "While these thoughts were tormenting me, I was frequently seized with the temptation to throw myself into an excavation close to my room. But, knowing that it was a sin, I cried again: 'Lord, I will do nothing to offend you,' and I frequently repeated these words."

Who knows how many other great historical figures suffered obsessions? Charles Darwin, arguably the single most influential scientist who ever lived, suffered frequent attacks of heart palpitations, shortness of breath, fainting, a buzzing noise in his head, stomach pains, and eczema. Most of his recent biographers agree that he had panic disorder. Darwin's letters and diaries suggest he may have also been plagued by obsessions. Darwin mentions having "much involuntary fear" and sudden "insane feelings of anger." He reports: "I awake in the night and feel so much afraid, though my reason laughs and tells me there is nothing to fear. . . . By habit the mind fixes on the same object." In the 1977 medical biography of Darwin, *To Be an Invalid,* Ralph Cope, Jr., M.D., concludes that Darwin was "tortured by obsessional thoughts."

EXCESSIVE PERSONAL RESPONSIBILITY

WHAT ARE THE similarities between the personalities of these "great obsessionals"? What are the deep-seated ways of looking at life that make a person vulnerable to OCD?

A good place to start in looking for an answer is a recent theory advanced by Oxford psychologist Paul Salkovskis. The critical factor in the development of obsessions, Salkovskis hypothesizes, is an inflated sense of personal responsibility—a deep-seated, automatic tendency to feel accountable for anything bad that might happen. This tendency can turn unwanted, intrusive thoughts into disabling obsessions. Since Salkovskis first demonstrated this idea in 1985, other investigators have confirmed his finding. A 1992 study, for instance, found that of five factors related to intrusive thoughts, only personal accountability significantly predicted compulsions.

According to Salkovskis's theory, a potentially upsetting thought causes no emotional reaction when it first comes into the mind. Indeed, if a person regards it as simply a piece of mental flotsam—as an idea of little or no importance—then the thought will just drift on by without a ripple. What happens with OCD sufferers is that they appraise the thought—a split-second evaluation that is not in full awareness—and conclude, as Salkovskis puts it, "that they might be responsible for harm to themselves or others unless they take action to prevent it." All of a sudden an alarm sounds: "I'd better pay attention to that thought!" Now the thought will not float by. It must be dealt with.

This exaggerated sense of personal responsibility is demonstrated most dramatically by people with checking compulsions. A patient of mine, an articulate, middle-aged mechanic with OCD, described it this way:

My compulsions are caused by fears of hurting someone through my negligence. It's always the same mental rigmarole. Making sure the doors are latched and the gas jets are off. Making sure I switch off the light with just the right amount of pressure, so I don't cause an electrical problem. Making sure I shift the car's gears cleanly, so I don't damage the machinery.

I went to a sale at Tru Value hardware Saturday and bought a Weed Eater marked down from $34.99 to $26.88. After I checked out, I got to wondering if it was really on sale. The sales slip said it was, but I still wondered if I had cheated the guy, if maybe his computer wasn't up to date. So I went back in and, pretending I was looking at something else, made sure the sale price was under the item I had bought. It was, but after leaving the store I was still afraid I got sale prices I didn't deserve. I wanted to go back in again, but since I'd already spent a long time in there, people would have noticed me. I stood in the parking lot trying to decide what to do. Finally I drove away, but I was troubled all day long.

I fantasize about finding an island in the South Pacific and living alone. That would take the pressure off; if I would harm anyone it would just be me. Yet even if I were alone, I'd still have my worries, because even insects can be a problem. Sometimes when I take the garbage out, I'm afraid that I've stepped on an ant. I stare down to see if there is an ant kicking and writhing in agony. I took a walk last week by a pond, but I couldn't enjoy it because I remembered it was spawning season, and I worried that I might be stepping on the eggs of bass or bluegill.

I realize that other people don't do these things. Mainly, it's that I don't want to go through the guilt of having hurt anything. It's selfish in that sense. I don't care about them as much as I do about not feeling the guilt.

When the exaggerated sense of personal responsibility is violated, the result is guilt—a major driving force in the lives of all obsessionals. In *Young Sam Johnson,* James Clifford writes: "Johnson was the kind of man who magnified his sins, and instead of forgetting them brooded over and stressed past offenses. . . . He had a deep-seated sense of guilt." Boswell tells the story of Samuel Johnson's visiting his hometown. Johnson remembered that, fifty years before, he had refused his father's request that he sell books at a stall. He went to that stall and stood in front of it for an hour in the rain, ignoring the sneers of passers-by. Johnson explained that he did this "to do away with my sin of this disobedience . . . and to propitiate Heaven for my only instance, I believe, of contumacy to my father."

Johnson himself observed the close tie between guilt and obsessions. "No disease of the imagination," Johnson wrote, "is so difficult to cure as that which is complicated with the dread of guilt: fancy and conscience then act interchangeably upon us, and so often shift their places, that the illusions of one are not distinguished from the dictates of the other."

Guilt and obsessions sometimes feed on each other, leading to a frenzied state in which an OCD sufferer may even confess to crimes he knows he didn't commit. I had a patient who, on the basis of violent obsessions, turned himself in as a murderer. Yet, in fact, the OCD sufferer who has thoughts to harm others is the least likely person of all to commit a violent act. The obsessional's personality is the antithesis to that of the hard-core criminal, or antisocial. Thomas Insel, M.D., specialist in OCD at the National Institutes of Mental Health, summarizes this contrariety: "Antisocials are severely aggressive and never feel any guilt, while obsessionals do nothing aggressive and feel guilty all the time."

Having an exaggerated sense of personal responsibility is not all bad, of course. It can be a spur to greatness. When the mental mechanisms work together fortuitously, it may find expression in a sense of lofty mission. Churchill felt he was chosen to lead Britain to its finest hour. "This cannot be accident; it must be design," the prime minister once noted. "I was kept for this job." Similar sentiments are echoed by Luther, Ignatius, and Bunyan.

Salkovskis's idea that a deep-seated, exaggerated sense of personal responsibility lies at the root of obsessions is particularly appealing because it accounts for many of the well-known character traits of OCD patients. As noted by Stanley Rachman, Ph.D., in his 1980 text *Obsessions and Compulsions,* foremost among those traits are fearfulness, introversion, and a tendency to depression.

FEARFUL, INTROVERTED, AND DEPRESSIVE

JEREMY TAYLOR, A seventeenth-century cleric who wrote a great deal on mental problems, said of OCD sufferers:

> They dare not eat for fear of gluttony; they don't sleep for fear of sleeping too much. If they are single, they fear their temptations. If they are married they fear doing their duty, then fear that the very fearing of it is a sin. They repent when they have not sinned, and accuse themselves without reason. Their virtues make them tremble, and in their innocence they are afraid.

People with OCD fear that they will act on impulses of violence, fear that they will be damned for ideas of blasphemy, fear that they will be contaminated by images of germs, and fear generally that they are going insane. Fearfulness is their most commonly described personality trait.

In fearing their thoughts, unfortunately, they only fuel them, however. Somehow, in the mind, fearing a thought exaggerates the importance of that thought, guaranteeing that it will return again and again. Fearing unacceptable thoughts turns them into obsessions.

The trait of introversion refers to a tendency to be absorbed in the inner world of the mind rather than in the world outside. This inclination to look inward throws a person repeatedly back into any ongoing battles with obsessions and by doing so escalates the problem.

It might be argued that since obsessionals are driven to spend hour upon hour analyzing, repeating, correcting, regretting, and fighting their thoughts, it is having obsessions that makes a person introverted, not the other way around. However, studies show that obsessions usually develop after age twenty, when the major personality traits, including introversion, are already in place. Introversion precedes obsessions and almost certainly increases the likelihood of getting OCD. Rachman observes that extroverted obsessionals are quite rare.

A tendency toward depression also goes hand in hand with severe obsessions. Anyone who works with OCD patients can't help noticing this relationship. Recent research confirms that depression is the most common complication of OCD and that approximately two-thirds of people with OCD suffer severe depression at some time during their lives.

Serious bouts of depressions were suffered by all the historical figures discussed above; most of them tended toward chronic melancholy as well. Biographers write that Ignatius had "an essentially depressive core to his personality." Luther was "a melancholic." Churchill had a "depressive temperament," and was subject to deep depressions, which he himself referred to as his "black dog." Johnson suffered "constitutional melancholy."

It is obvious that the long, demoralizing battles OCD sufferers wage with their thoughts could lead them to depression. It now also appears certain that depression leads vulnerable people to experience more and more obsessions. In 1986, researchers in Australia showed that intrusive thoughts in college students are closely related to mood and speculated that depressed people experience more intrusive thoughts because of an impaired ability to process and get rid of them. This is seen on a clinical level. As depression saps people's confidence and breaks down normal means of coping, the result is more difficulty dealing with potentially troublesome thoughts. Samuel Johnson recognized this clearly: "If the imagination presents images that are not moral, the mind drives them away. But if a person is melancholic . . . the images lay hold on the faculties without opposition."

PERSONALITY CLASSIFICATIONS AND OCD

THE DSM-IV DIAGNOSTIC manual used by mental health professionals in the United States contains a set of diagnoses called personality disorders that are applied to people with long-term maladaptive patterns of thinking and behaving. Many of the labels are well known: paranoid, hysterical, psychopathic, narcissistic, and, yes, obsessive-compulsive.

You probably recognize what obsessive-compulsive personality disorder is like. It represents the extreme of what in general parlance is referred to as obsessive-compulsive behavior. It describes the person who is perfectionistic, punctual, aloof, and inflexible, when severe obsessive-compulsive personality results in a sort of malignant fussiness. One patient of mine timed family members every time they showered, yelled when anyone put a fork in the dishwasher with the prongs facing down, and insisted on saving the carpet by having family members walk up and down the stairs on newspapers.

Until recently, the unquestioned assumption among mental health professionals has been that obsessive-compulsive personality leads directly to obsessive-compulsive disorder. That is why, of course, they were both referred to as obsessive-compulsive in the first place. The two disorders were thought simply to represent different levels of severity of the same basic problem; the rigidity and inflexibility of obsessive-compulsive personality was thought to cause by unconscious mechanisms the obsessions and compulsions of OCD. When I was in training there was no doubt about this link. Yet, although this theory is still cited in newspapers and magazines, the fact is that experts in the field no longer believe it.

First of all, researchers have found that obsessive-compulsive personality is not, after all, a necessary condition for the development of OCD. Recent studies suggest that obsessive-compulsive personality disorder is not even the most common personality disorder that is found among people who have OCD. A 1993 study by Russell Noyes and colleagues at the University of Iowa, for instance, found that although 80 percent of OCD patients suffer from personality disorders, it is dependent personality disorder—fear of decisions, under-assertiveness, excessive leaning on others—that is present in more than half of patients. This finding agrees with what is found in clinical practice. Instead of being detached and emotionally cool, as are people with obsessive-compulsive personality disorder, OCD patients are nervous and clinging.

Secondly, the idea that OCD is caused by any personality disorder has been called into question. In a 1992 study at Harvard, Michael Jenike and his colleagues looked at seventeen patients who were diagnosed as having both OCD and personality disorders. Ten of these patients responded well to medications and behavioral therapy for their obsessions, and when tested again after treatment, nine of the ten no longer had their personality disorders. What these findings suggest is that when people with OCD have personality disorders, it may well be the obsessions and compulsions that are causing the personality problems, not the other way around.

Studies such as these cause mental health professionals to question whether the diagnoses referred to as personality disorders are truly valid and reliable. Other approaches to personality may be better. One well-researched new scheme for describing personality is that introduced in 1987 by Dr. Robert Cloninger, chairman of the Department of Psychiatry at Washington University in St. Louis. I like Dr. Cloninger's approach and so do my patients. It's easy to understand, and it doesn't involve negative labels, such as "hysteric" or "paranoid."

THE TRIDIMENSIONAL PERSONALITY THEORY

IN ITS SIMPLEST form Dr. Cloninger's model suggests that most of the important differences between our personalities may be accounted for by three key qualities or dimensions: harm avoidance, novelty seeking, and reward dependence.

"Harm avoidance" refers to the urge to escape from unpleasant experiences. People low in harm avoidance tend to be carefree, confident, relaxed, optimistic, uninhibited, outgoing, and energetic. Those who are high in harm avoidance, on the other hand, tend to be timid, inhibited, apprehensive, tense, shy, easily fatigued, and pessimistic about the future.

"Novelty seeking" describes a capacity to be exhilarated by new experiences. Everyone likes excitement now and then, but people who score high in this dimension live for it. They are impulsive, fickle, quick-tempered, extravagant, and disorderly risk-takers. Daredevils fit here. Those who are low in novelty seeking are reflective, loyal, stoic, slow-tempered, and orderly. They're good scouts.

"Reward dependence" refers to the need to be reinforced by approval from others. Those on the low end of this personality dimension tend to be detached, emotionally cool, practical, and tough-minded. People high in reward dependence are sympathetic, eager to help, and sentimental. They're people-pleasers.

Consider some of the combinations. A person who is low in harm avoidance, high in novelty seeking, and low in reward dependence is fearless, impulsive, explorative, and doesn't care what people think. In the extreme this is the criminal personality type. Think Charles Manson. If reward dependence is changed from low to high while the other two factors stay the same, then a person is impulsive and explorative but also emotionally vulnerable. He or she craves activity and excitement but needs positive feedback. This is the attention-seeking, dramatic, gullible individual; perhaps an example would be Marilyn Monroe. Each of the combinations of Cloninger's traits corresponds to a recognizable character.

OCD sufferers, according to Dr. Cloninger's theory, are high in harm avoidance, low in novelty seeking, and high in reward dependence. Recent studies from the universities of Iowa and Toronto have confirmed the strong correlation of OCD to high harm avoidance and low novelty seeking. There is suggestive evidence tying OCD to high reward dependence. OCD sufferers are timid, sentimental, good scouts, people-pleasers. That description fits a surprisingly large number of my OCD patients.

The term harm avoidant fits me to a T. Novelty seeking? When I was a child, my family visited New York City. My brother wanted to see Broadway; I wanted to stay in the hotel room and play cards. My brother is now in the foreign service; I'm living in my hometown. And reward dependence? I can't remember even once making my parents mad at me. This is simply the typical personality pattern of the person who develops OCD.

Of considerable value in Cloninger's personality classification scheme is the fact that, for the first time, personality types have been connected to brain chemistry. Correlations are introduced between, for instance, harm avoidance and the level of the neurotransmitter serotonin; between novelty seeking and the neurotransmitter dopamine. This link allows patients to gain an appreciation of the interrelation between OCD's psychological roots and the biochemical causes of the disorder.

4

OCD'S BEST TREATMENT: BEHAVIOR THERAPY

TWO TREATMENTS HAVE been established effective in the majority of cases of obsessive-compulsive disorder: behavior therapy and medication. According to research studies, behavior therapy has the edge, markedly helping up to 80 percent of people who complete treatment, compared to medication's 50–70 percent. Behavior therapy is also less costly than medication, and it causes no side effects. Behavior therapy is thus the premier treatment for OCD, indicated for all who suffer the disorder.

From a theoretical point of view, behavior therapy is extremely simple. It requires no plumbing of the unconscious, exploring the distant past, or examining tangled motives. Instead, it stands on a basic, physiological property of the nervous system that is found in all animals from mollusks to man: habituation.

If a snail's head is lightly touched, it recoils quickly into its shell. If it is touched fifteen times in a row, however, it stops withdrawing. The snail, in effect, gets used to being touched. That's habituation. The same type of response occurs in the infinitely more complicated case of a human who is afraid of a certain situation. Like the snail, if a person is presented with a noxious stimulus repeatedly and neither escapes from it nor is harmed by it, then he or she will eventually get used to it.

Applying the law of habituation, behavior therapy has proven to be extremely effective in the treatment of simple phobias. Take, for example, a man who is afraid to ride in elevators. In order to get over his fear, he must first go into an elevator; this is called *exposure* to the anxiety-producing situation. Next, he must prevent himself from running off the elevator; this is called *response prevention.* Research shows that if the man places himself in elevators a sufficient number of times, and each time stays on the elevator long enough for his anxiety to diminish (as a rule, not longer than an hour), then eventually he will habituate to fear of elevators. He will overcome his phobia.

The same principles apply when behavior therapy is used to treat OCD. A woman has obsessions that her hands are dirty and washes her hands compulsively. What she must do is expose herself to the anxiety-producing thought of dirt (the equivalent of going into the elevator) while resisting the response of washing (preventing running off). If she can do this often enough—twenty to thirty total hours of exposure and response prevention is usually sufficient—the idea of having dirty hands will no longer make her severely anxious, and she will no longer be driven to wash. She will conquer her compulsions.

The gist of behavior therapy is found in an old adage that most people have heard all their lives, but too few OCDers have taken to heart: *Face up to your fears.* Behavior therapy simply takes this wise counsel and applies it systematically and scientifically.

A number of different procedures may be employed in implementing behavior therapy for OCD. Usually, patients begin by recording in a diary the severity and duration of all obsessions and compulsions as they occur throughout the day. Situations that are being avoided because of OCD are carefully noted as well. Obsessions and compulsions are then ranked according to the degree of discomfort and disruption they cause. Specific symptoms are chosen for exposure and response prevention tasks. Progress is recorded daily in a journal or log.

The meat of behavior therapy—the part of treatment where great gains are made—is in the tasks, or homework assignments, where patients must expose themselves to obsessional situations while preventing themselves from performing compulsions. Most commonly, the situations targeted for exposure and response prevention are the everyday triggers of OCD. A person with handwashing compulsions, for instance, may be asked to touch the toilet and refrain from washing her hands for two hours. An exaggerated measure of exposure may be encouraged: Touch the toilet then touch her clothes and furniture with her "contaminated" hands. Such exaggerated exposure, or "flooding," speeds up the process of habituation, as it keeps a fearful thought prominently and inescapably in the forefront of a person's mind. Sometimes, a therapist first models a task. For example, a patient might be asked to bring a "dirty" object into a session, and the therapist could rub it all over himself, demonstrating that it is not dangerous. Occasionally it is helpful for a therapist to accompany a client home and model an assignment in its natural setting.

Exposure and response prevention can also be carried out in the imagination. Here, a patient is asked to bring to mind a fearful obsessional scene and to keep it in vivid awareness until the anxiety it causes begins to fade. For people who possess a strong capability in visual imagery (OCDers, it seems, usually do), this technique can be just as effective as exposure in real life.

There are other techniques, as well, that help to implement exposure and response prevention. The popular form of psychological treatment known as cognitive therapy aims at changing people's attitudes and outlooks toward their problems. We incorporate this approach extensively in behavior therapy for OCD. Putting a new spin on an obsession, taking a different view of it, can allow exposure and response prevention to be accomplished much more easily. A simple example would be helping a person to view an obsession as being like an obscenity shouted by a harmless drunk.

Given the many different procedures that can be used in behavior therapy for OCD, one might think that this treatment is quite difficult, always requiring close professional supervision. Actually, however, twenty years of research into behavior therapy has led to a progressive diminution of the therapist's role in its use. In the 1970s, for instance, it was thought that a therapist should always model exposure tasks and do home visits as well. Now it is clear that neither is necessary. What studies demonstrate is that the only absolute requirement for effective behavior therapy is enough exposure and response prevention to allow habituation to take place, and that this can be accomplished by a patient without the help of any therapist at all.

In this regard, behavior therapy for OCD is much like physical rehabilitation for a shoulder or knee injury. Both can be accomplished without external help. More often than not, however, some assistance is essential. In the first place, just as it is not obvious that one should exercise a painful joint, it is not intuitively obvious that one should expose oneself to frightening thoughts. Secondly, exercising a knee, like preventing compulsions, is hard work. To extend the analogy further: If one has a minor shoulder injury, it may be fairly easy to devise and implement an exercise rehabilitation program. If the injury is severe, however, almost certainly a professional must be consulted in order to prevent exacerbating the injury with incorrect exercise. Thus, in milder cases of OCD, for the self-motivated person who has learned the principles of behavior therapy, no therapist may be necessary. Otherwise, however, it is wise to seek consultation (for information on how to find a behavior therapist, see Appendix D).

This chapter will first illustrate professionally directed behavior therapy for OCD by following treatment of the cases of filth, harm, lust, and blasphemy that were introduced in Chapter 1. Then we will look at the special problems that arise when behavior therapy is ineffective. The chapter will conclude with a bare-bones, informal program of behavior therapy that will be sufficient to allow some OCD sufferers to help themselves.

One more thing can honestly be said about behavior therapy in the treatment of OCD: Spectacular improvement is the rule. The cases of Raymond, Sherry, Jeff, and Melissa are not at all unusual. Most OCDers who follow behavior therapy programs through to completion will have therapeutic successes in the same range. They will not cure their OCD, but they will be able to live normal lives. And that qualifies as spectacular.

AN EXAMPLE OF BEHAVIOR THERAPY:
THE CASE OF RAYMOND

RAYMOND'S CASE, INTRODUCED in Chapter 1, is instructive because he responded well to a very simple behavior therapy program. All that was necessary for marked improvement was for Raymond to systematically expose himself to his everyday obsessions while doing his level best to prevent compulsions.

When Raymond first came to me, he was in the midst of a severe OCD crisis. He was unable to work. His days were filled with obsessions of poisonous spills, and he performed hours of checking rituals in order to prevent imagined catastrophes. Raymond thought that he had lost control of his mind, that his life was ruined. He fully expected to be hospitalized.

Instead what happened was that Raymond worked hard at behavior therapy for six months, seeing me every one to two weeks for consultation. By the end of that time, his symptoms were more under control than they had been since he was a teenager. Antiobsessional medications were also quite helpful in Raymond's treatment, especially in the beginning. Group therapy was very beneficial, too. But Raymond and I both believe that behavior therapy was the critical factor in his striking improvement.

Raymond's behavior therapy was divided into three stages. Our first four sessions together were educational. He learned the nature of OCD and how to clearly recognize his obsessions and compulsions. Sessions five through seven were concerned with assessment; here, we identified all of Raymond's symptoms and ranked them by severity. Our last nine sessions formed the active behavioral therapy phase, during which exposure and response was accomplished.

As is often the case, Raymond was greatly comforted right at the beginning of treatment when he learned that obsessions and compulsions are caused by a physical, chemical disorder. Like most OCD sufferers, he had never carefully considered the root of his symptoms but rather had blindly assumed that, somehow, he was to blame for them because of some mental weakness. Learning the truth about OCD began a revolution in the way he looked at himself. For twenty years, although he had been an excellent worker, citizen, and family man, he had thought himself mentally inadequate and half crazy. That he is neither of these things but instead the sufferer of a specific brain disorder continues to surprise him even now.

Identifying obsessions and compulsions—the critical step in the early part of therapy upon which all further progress depends—presented no special problems for Raymond. His intrusive thoughts of vile and dangerous spills were classic, easily recognizable obsessions. Carefully looking for spills, feeling carpets, checking hallways, and conjuring up visions of vacuum cleaners while making "whooshing" sounds were obvious compulsions. With Raymond as with all OCDers, however, identifying obsessions and compulsions was easier when he was sitting in the office calmly discussing his symptoms than when he was in the heat of an OCD attack.

In the assessment stage of therapy, the important work is to take a comprehensive inventory of obsessions and compulsions and then to rank them according to their severity. In order to accomplish this, I first asked Raymond to keep a daily diary of compulsions for three consecutive days. Here is a typical day of entries:

DAILY DAIRY OF COMPULSIONS—JULY 22, 1993

HOUR	COMPULSION (ritual)	MINUTES SPENT	SITUATION	OBSESSION
6 A.M.	Check whole house, look, touch	30	Getting up	Spills in house
	Turn car around in lane once and come back	5	Leaving home	
7 A.M.	Whooshing rituals in car	10	Trucks blasting	Spills in school, bank, church
8 A.M. 9 A.M. 10 A.M.	At work: now and then looking for spills	10 total	Walking around	Spills

11 A.M.	down halls, but not too bad			
	Check coffee cups	2	Getting coffee	Disease or poison
12 noon	Restaurant: turn around and look carefully, walk back to table once	2	Leaving restaurant	Spill on table or on floor
1 P.M. 2 P.M. 3 P.M.	Not too bad at work, again; occasional checks	5 total	Halls	Spills
4 P.M.	Leaving work: go back and check mail room	5	Just as I get to my car	Spill in mail room
	Driving home; stop in church and walk through classrooms	10	Passing church	Spill in church
	A few whooshing rituals	2	Trucks passing	Spills
	Arrive home: dump out liquids in refrigerator	5	Walk in kitchen	Poisons
	Check whole house	20	House empty all day	Spills
5 P.M.	Watch my wife pour drinks, check glasses and food	5	Kids eating dinner	Poisons
6 P.M.	Make excuses to check aisles at Sears	5	Shopping	Spill
7 P.M. 8 P.M.	All evening I am asking kids if	60 total	Watching TV, reading	I'm constantly

| 9 P.M. | they've eaten or anything I don't know about, each one, three or four times an hour | imagining disease or poison |

10 P.M.   Fall asleep quickly

Even though Raymond's symptoms were significantly improved by the fifth visit, his daily diary shows that compulsions were still taking up almost three hours a day. Obsessions, Raymond told me, were on his mind virtually every minute, except at work, when perhaps a half an hour would go by when he was completely free of them. The diary demonstrated that his obsessions were of two types: "spill fantasies," in which he vividly imagined a container full of a deadly liquid ready to tip over and cause a disaster; and "poison fantasies," in which he conjured up the image of a poison or diseased substance either accidentally present or deliberately planted in the food or drink of family members.

Using his daily diaries as a starting point, Raymond then constructed a list of all the various situations in which compulsions commonly arose and ranked these situations according to the degree of anxiety he experienced when the obsession struck. His anxiety ratings were purely subjective—estimates of his level of anxiety during certain situations relative to others. To rate the anxiety, he used an "anxiety thermometer," on which "o" represented no anxiety at all and "100" was the most anxious that it was possible for him to feel. We divided the OCD situations into those involving "spill" and those involving "poison" obsessions.

OCD SITUATIONS RANKED
ACCORDING TO ANXIETY LEVEL, AUGUST 2

SITUATIONS TRIGGERING SPILL OBSESSIONS	ANXIETY LEVEL
Getting up in the morning	100
In car driving to work and trucks blast by	100

Trying to leave a large store	100
Arrive at home after work	80
Leaving work (spill in mail room)	50
Driving back from work passing church	40
Watching TV in evening (spill at parents')	40
Walking down hallways at work	40
Leaving restaurant at lunch	30

SITUATIONS TRIGGERING POISON OBSESSIONS

Watching TV (kids drinking or eating something)	80
Arriving home (refrigerator)	50
At work getting coffee	30
Dinner time, wife serving drinks	20

With the critical data in hand, Raymond was ready to begin the action phase of behavior therapy. During this stage, I met with Raymond every other week to help him methodically implement exposure and response prevention.

It is best to start with a task that is not too difficult. I asked Raymond to pick an OCD situation that he thought he could confront without severe distress. He chose "leaving a restaurant at lunch," a compulsion that involved stopping somewhere between the checkout counter and the door of the restaurant and staring intently all around the restaurant for thirty seconds to a minute and sometimes pretending that he left something at his table in order to once more walk through the aisles of the restaurant, carefully checking for spills.

For his first behavior therapy assignment, Raymond agreed that he would go into the restaurant as usual (exposure) but would prevent himself from doing any checking (response prevention). He would perform this task at least three times a week. In addition to this primary behavior therapy homework, he would, as much as he felt up to it, limit or delay other compulsions throughout the day. In order to track his progress, Raymond would keep a daily journal, noting both how the day went in general and how he did on his specific homework assignment.

An excerpt from his journal after two weeks of active behavior therapy illustrates his progress.

> *August 20—Overwhelming sensations all day that something has just spilt in my house, at work, in the next room, or wherever. Checked a number of times, just walking around and looking. When I couldn't do that, used the whooshing ritual.*
>
> *For lunch I went to Bill's Sports Club. After I finish I usually go on a pivot, studying the carpet, the steps, everything. But today I psyched myself up, walked right over to the cash register, ignored my surroundings, and escaped to my car easily. I knew that if I turned around and looked it would be really bad, so I didn't let myself. Driving back to work I kept worrying that my mind would come up with a catastrophe that would make me go back and check, but it never happened.*

Carrying out his first assignment was fairly easy. Raymond never once had to return to a restaurant for extra checking. Since the goal in a behavioral assignment is a success rate of 80 percent or greater, we were ready to move on.

Over the next month, Raymond worked on two more exposure and response tasks: driving by his church on the way home from work and not checking it, which he had been doing at least every other day; and watching TV as usual, suffering the spill-at-his-parents'-house obsession, and not checking their house, which he had been doing almost every evening. During this time Raymond made excellent progress, not only in combatting these two compulsions, but also with a number of others, as is illustrated by this journal entry:

> *September 19—I'm proud of the things I've done today. On the way home from work I drove by the church and my mind reached out and created a terrible vision of a container of disease. I have a key, and it would have been the easiest thing in the world to go in and check. Instead, I drove right by. I kept looking back in my mirror and I wanted to stop so bad it hurt. I kept think-*

ing, "How am I going to live with this?" I was in dire straits, but I didn't go back. About an hour later it was not as real.

Then this evening I had a stabbing vision of a spill at my parents' house. I didn't know how I would cope with it. Usually I would have gone over and peered in the window, or if they weren't home I would have gone in and walked around. But I told myself it wasn't real and that I could go over later if I needed to. It was hard, hard work, but I waited it out.

I also have had many victories this week with the whooshing compulsion. I am not going through the mental gymnastics of a month ago when I would work myself up into a frenzy. I just keep telling myself that this ritual is absurd. My mind can't do magic.

The next behavior assignment was to deliberately enter large stores (exposure) and not check the aisles (response prevention). As indicated on the OCD situations list, these situations were associated with a considerably higher anxiety level. Raymond worked on this assignment for four weeks, and by the end of that time he was able to enter and leave stores without resorting to time-consuming rituals. Again, an excerpt from his journal demonstrates his progress.

October 14—Went to the Sears store and deliberately walked from one end to the other and out again. I only had to look back down an aisle with cans of paint a couple of times. It was very hard for me to leave because I was afraid that five minutes down the road uncertainty would jump into my mind and say, "Are you sure there wasn't a wet spot on the floor down that aisle?" After I left the store I could feel it coming: Terror rushed into me and my mind conjured up a very real image of a bucket about two feet high filled with some liquid that would make people sick. I knew that this was absolutely at the edge of reality, but I felt I had the responsibility to go back and check. I was really hurting. I forced myself not to, and about a half an hour later, I realized that what I was thinking about was probably not true. That was a terrific feeling: I won a big victory by not checking.

I am convinced that to lick this OCD the key is tons of exposure and response prevention. I am making every effort. No one understands this, but I am literally fighting for my life.

After this string of successes, Raymond chose to work on preventing the ritual of asking for reassurance from his kids that they had not eaten or drunk anything that he didn't know about. It had been the extreme embarrassment resulting from this ritual that had driven him to seek help in the first place:

November 12—I have gone for two whole days without asking my kids whether they've drunk or eaten anything. It is very painful, because this obsession is so strong. No one knows how much pain and embarrassment it causes. When the obsession hits, I am going into the next room and just letting myself soak in the anxiety, telling myself that it's not real. I also tell myself that if it gets too bad, I can go into my kids' rooms and ask. But my fear usually lightens up within an hour.

This afternoon was wonderful. I took my boy to the football field. As I was leaving, I was beside myself because my mind kept presenting me with visions of him sitting on the bench and drinking a can of something that had been sitting there for about a week and had AIDS in it. It hurt a ton, but I didn't check and I never asked him about it later.

At the end of six months, instead of living in almost continual torment, Raymond was living a normal life. He put it this way:

When I first came here, I was at a real squeeze point. I thought there was no way out. The fears wouldn't go away unless I checked, but when I checked one thing, it always led to another. Now I have reached a level of understanding where I am sure that my spill fears are based on false thoughts, and when they jump into my head, I don't react to them so much. And now I know that there is a way for me to deal with my obsessions. I have confidence that when a spill fantasy hits, it will go away. I just stick in there and sweat it out.

COMBATTING AVOIDANCE: THE CASE OF SHERRY

RAYMOND'S CASE ILLUSTRATES the basics of behavior therapy for OCD: exposure to obsessions accompanied by prevention of compulsions. But there is another aspect of treatment that can be of great importance: prevention of avoidance. Avoidance occurs when a person stops doing certain things or going certain places that bring on self-tormenting thoughts. Like compulsions, it is a way of trying to escape from obsessions.

Severe avoidance frequently accompanies obsessions of doing violent harm to others, perhaps because there is no obvious ritual to perform to escape from this type of tormenting thought. Obsessions of contaminated hands lead naturally to washing; obsessions of electrical fires lead directly to checking the light switch; obsessions of offending God lead to confessing; but nothing provides easy relief from an obsession to stab your daughter.

The case of Sherry demonstrates the treatment of harm obsessions accompanied by disabling problems with avoidance. In such cases, two behavior techniques are especially helpful: direct limitation of avoidance, and prolonged exposure to obsessions in the imagination.

Sherry, you may recall, presented in a panic because of violent fantasies of the worst types imaginable, including stabbing her daughter, slitting her own throat, and crashing her car. Each obsession was a split-second mini-series of images, urges, and ideas that jarred her like a knockout combination. Compulsions were not a significant problem; she was primarily disabled by the terror caused by her obsessions and her avoidance of the many different situations that brought them on. She often could not cook because of her fear of using knives. Sometimes she could not bring herself to drive the car. Occasionally, she would stay in her bed almost all day long out of fear that she might act on one of her violent urges.

After three sessions spent gathering history and educating Sherry on the nature of OCD, I asked Sherry to keep a diary of her symptoms as they occurred throughout the day. Her fear of her obsessions was so strong, however, that this proved too painful. "Please don't make me try that again," she begged. We compromised, and Sherry agreed to write a short note each evening. Here is a sample of her first week of journaling, her fourth week in treatment overall:

Tuesday—Woke up in the middle of night and again in the morning with the obsession of stabbing myself. Thought how I could walk down to the kitchen and get a knife and push it in my stomach. Saw blood everywhere. Bob wakes up and I'm dying, covered with blood.

Avoidance: Stayed away from knives all day. Did go in the kitchen, but used "alternative cooking."

Wednesday—Obsessions while driving were constant: Crash into this car, swerve over and hit that little boy. I'm praying, "God, get me through this."

I must really be sick to have these thoughts. Helped to remember that the doctor said that everyone has crazy thoughts. Didn't want to cook dinner, but I did and I forced myself to use knife (a dull one). Hurrah!

Thursday—Awful day. Started with obsessions of slitting my throat while shaving my legs in the shower. Thoughts of knives all day long. Read magazines to get away from them. Watched TV. Tried to go to sleep as fast as possible.

Avoidance: Spent a lot of time in bed today. Didn't cook with knives.

Friday—Better than yesterday. 99 percent of obsessions today were knife thoughts. Was vacuuming the floor and had the thought to grab a knife and slit my throat. Or to stab myself in the belly. Same ones over and over. At dinner time the thought of knifing Bob. I kept telling myself: "This is gross. Stop it!"

Saturday—Obsessions in and out of my mind all day long. Thought of stepping out in front of a truck. Then while I was driving I thought of running off the road. At Art Alliance, thought: "I could chop all their heads off." Gross. At dinner time, thought of grabbing a knife and slitting Bob's throat. The thoughts just pop in and out, but when they occur they're so powerful.

Avoidance: Some avoidance of knives and driving. Increased time in bed.

Based on her journal, Sherry and I constructed an OCD situations hierarchy.

OCD SITUATIONS RANKED ACCORDING TO ANXIETY LEVEL

SITUATIONS TRIGGERING KNIFE OBSESSIONS	ANXIETY LEVEL
In kitchen: slitting my throat or my wrists or stabbing myself in the stomach with the kitchen knife, or else stabbing Megan or Bob	100
In shower: slitting my throat or my wrists with a razor while shaving my legs	90
In bed: stabbing Bob in the stomach while he's sleeping	50
In bed: slicing up Bob while we're making love	30

Anywhere: slitting Megan's or Bob's throat
or stabbing them   20

Meetings, malls: stabbing people, cutting
their heads off, etc.   20

SITUATIONS CAUSING CAR CRASH OBSESSIONS	ANXIETY LEVEL
In car: seeing little kids and swerving my car to hit them	70
In car: truck or overpass coming and pulling the wheel and swerving into it	60
Anytime in car: crashing it	30

Our goal in behavior therapy was to expose Sherry to her obsessions and to continue her exposure long enough for habituation to take place. But before describing that treatment in detail, let me point out one other extremely important aspect of Sherry's therapy.

In no other type of OCD is it so important to address shame and self-reproach as in that characterized by obsessions of doing harm to others. Sherry felt wretchedly, inescapably guilty over her violent fantasies. Sometimes they piled up, each one more painful than the previous, cascades of calamitous thoughts climaxing with the ultimate guilt-inducing obsession: the idea (usually based on the misinterpretation of a slight body movement) that she was actually beginning to carry out an awful fantasy. Deep down inside, Sherry was afraid that, for reasons that were beyond her understanding, she was a sick, perverted murderer.

Her previous two therapists had done little to relieve her guilt. Tracing her self-tormenting thoughts back to a time when her "overly perfectionistic" parents had prevented her from expressing anger, these doctors had made the standard interpretation: Sherry's obsessions were due to bottled up hostility that leaked out of her unconscious and took the form of violent thoughts. Yes, Sherry was told that her murderous fantasies were not her fault, but she was not reassured. The theory that she had bottled-up hostility, in fact, had the perverse effect of validating her guilt by endorsing the idea that her murderous thoughts were nothing less than a very important part of her personality.

In cases of harm obsessions, the OCD sufferer must be taught, and reminded again and again, that obsessions are not a part of one's basic personality. They have no bearing on who a person "really is." Intrusive, violent thoughts are normal for the human race, and overly responsible, guilt-prone OCDers are the least likely people ever to act on them. The OCD sufferer must strive continually to keep a rational perspective and a therapeutic distance from these most gut-wrenching of obsessions.

In order to do that, Sherry kept in mind several different ways of looking at her obsessions. She often reminded herself that her obsessions were not a real part of herself but rather were due to a chemical disorder. She sometimes viewed her obsessions as a joke. When walking in the mall she would be hit by a thought "to grab strange men in the crotch." After a while, she could look on this obsession as being so funny that it just didn't bother her. To help herself think rationally, she used the "panhandler analogy." Suppose a person is walking down Broadway in New York City and is suddenly accosted by a street person aggressively asking for money. What to do? Not fight. Not run away. Just turn the eyes forward and walk, *ignoring* him. Sherry, having had few encounters with panhandlers but many experiences with "jerks making passes," sometimes changed the "panhandler" to the "unwanted suitor": Give him the right to exist but ignore him, don't let him bother you.

Sherry began the active phase of behavior therapy with homework assignments directed toward confronting her avoidance. For two weeks she worked on forcing herself to get out of bed every morning and not allowing herself to retreat to her room later in the day. After accomplishing these goals, she began taking long drives in her car. Later in treatment, she exposed herself to the more fearful task of using sharp knives while preparing dinner.

In confronting avoidance, it is important to go slowly. Exposing oneself too quickly can result in the opposite of habituation—sensitization—wherein the fear of the situation increases rather than diminishes. Sherry overdid it one day when she spotted a knife store while walking in the mall. As she told the story, she marched up to the counter, looked the salesman in the eye, and asked, "What's the biggest goddamn knife you have?" The salesman replied, "This pig knife right here," opening the showcase and putting a foot-long butcher's blade in her hand. Sherry froze, then panicked, dropped the knife, ran out into the mall, and vomited. Despite that setback, which she took with admirable humor, she progressed to using knives with every meal, driving when she needed to, and keeping out of bed.

The second emphasis in Sherry's behavior therapy was exposure to imagined scenes. Here, the assignment was to hold an obsession, in its complete awfulness, in her mind's eye for a sufficient length of time to allow anxiety to fade (usually twenty to sixty minutes) and habituation to take place. There are several ways to implement this technique. The most time-honored is for the therapist to talk a patient through an obsessional scene using the most vivid imagery possible. The patient can tape the session and play it back for homework. Another method is for the patient herself to produce a written rendition of an obsession and then to imagine it in great detail, bringing back the obsession every time it fades by rereading the script. Yet another method is for the patient to record an obsession on a loop cassette and play it over and over.

Patients must be thoroughly prepared before they begin exposure in the imagination because it can be startling and upsetting. They must clearly understand that the only purpose of the painful exercise is to make the mind get used to, habituate to, an awful image. Patients worry that picturing a terrible act could lead to doing it. As discussed previously, they must be reassured that OCDers never follow through on an obsession, that they are the last people who would ever harm anyone.

Sherry used exposure in the imagination to treat several of her obsessions. Toward the end of therapy she wrote a script of her number one worst fear.

Here goes! It's winter and it's ugly outside. I have been feeling down and have been unable to shake it. I've tried all day to concentrate on other things. It's 4:30 P.M. and I've been to the grocery store and am feeling nervous. Life is so painful; nothing will ever be right. I'm putting things away in the kitchen, and I spot the carving knife. Megan is sitting at the table. The urge hits to slash at her. I shake with anxiety. The urge takes over. I am unable to control it. I sneak up behind Megan, and I stab her in the back, over and over. I see the blood spurting out. I think that I am out of control; that it's really happening this time. Megan flops onto the floor, dead, into a pool of blood. I vomit hysterically. I've killed my daughter!

Sherry recorded this scene on a cassette loop tape, and played it back to herself every day for twenty to thirty minutes, long enough to allow her anxiety level to drop significantly. She needed occasionally to step back from the scene and remind herself, "This is my OCD, it's not me"; or, "This does not mean that I'm going to really do it, but I must learn to live with the idea of doing it if I want to overcome my OCD." Such psychological distancing is usually necessary, but I encouraged her to minimize it, because the fuller the immersion in the frightful fantasy, the faster therapy proceeds.

After twelve weeks of active behavior therapy, seventeen weeks total in treatment, Sherry had markedly improved. Her journal, in which she was now taking note of her attitudes as well as her obsessions, reflects her progress:

Monday—Very mild obsessions. Ideas of knifing myself. Passed easily.

Self-talk: "Oh, it's a knife. I could hurt myself with that if I wanted to. Well, it's dinner time. I could stab myself if I wanted to." I took out a knife and used it easily for cooking.

Tuesday—Rating: 8. Very mild obsessions. Was busy all day. Felt sad in the afternoon.

Self-talk: "What a nasty illness. Why did it have to happen to me? Why couldn't I have gotten help sooner?"

Wednesday—Had obsessions off and on all day. Don't know why. Got up in the morning and thought of knifing Bob in the stomach. Image first, then urge.

Self-talk: "Oh, not you again. Stop bugging me, jerk. You're bothering me, but you're just an obsession." Went away after a while.

Thursday—Stayed busy all day. Some thoughts about hurting myself.

Self-talk: "It's just OCD. These thoughts can't harm me."

Friday—Fleeting obsessions of knifing and running people over. Not bad.

Self-talk: "Obsessions, I'm not scared of you any more! If I bear the anxiety, I know you'll go away."

Saturday—Had two hours of a pretty bad obsession after an argument with Bob. Kept my anger in. Variety of thoughts. Knifing myself. Running car into overpass. Took a long time for them to go away. Crying. Why does this happen while I'm driving?

Self-talk: "Come on, Sherry, shape up!"

Sunday—Good day with family. Only a few obsessions all day. Very mild. Life can be good.

Sherry's most satisfying moment of all came a few months later. Not since age eleven had she carried a knife with the blade pointed outward when another person was in the kitchen. Instead, she always carried it pointed toward her belly, so that if she stabbed anyone, it would be herself. But one day while she was carving a roast, her daughter calmly munching snack food nearby, Sherry slowly and purposefully grasped the knife, held it pointed outward, and walked carefully, as if on slick ice, across the kitchen. At the finish of her journey, she put down the knife and gave her startled daughter a joyous, gasping hug. Sounds simple, but Sherry said it was like winning an Olympic gold medal.

The treatment of Raymond and Sherry demonstrates the nuts and bolts of behavior therapy for OCD. The same basic techniques of exposure and response prevention were used to help Jeff, whose lust obsessions were discussed in Chapter 1. Jeff purposefully exposed himself to situations where his sexual obsessions occurred strongly, such as sitting close to other men. At the same time, he worked hard to prevent his mental rituals, such as repeating, "I am not gay," over and over in his mind. Jeff's formal behavior therapy lasted for approximately four months, and by the end of that time he was, like Raymond and Sherry, markedly improved.

Melissa, whose religious obsessions were also presented earlier, was also treated with standard behavior therapy and responded well. Melissa systematically exposed herself to her nonstop obsessions of doubt ("Should I listen to non-Christian music?" "Should I wear dresses?" "Am I being a good enough witness?") while limiting her compulsions to chant prayers, ask reassurance, and overanalyze situations. A couple of points about Melissa's treatment deserve special comment.

A theory on the cause of OCD that is especially good for explaining obsessions in the form of questions has been advanced by psychiatrist William Hewlett of Vanderbilt University. Hewlett's theory holds that the basic problem in OCD is a broken "uncertainty system" in the brain. The uncertainty system, it says, is a mechanism that developed through evolution to help animals deal quickly and efficiently with danger. Suppose our prehistoric ancestor was walking through the forest and heard a twig snap. His uncertainty system would spring into action and cause the following: first, an uncomfortable feeling of doubt; second, fantasies of various possibilities to explain the twig snap; and third, an insistent demand to take some sort of action to resolve the situation. Such a chain of responses, it can be easily seen, could be very advantageous. But for a person with OCD, Hewlett suggests, the uncertainty system discharges for no reason at all. Spontaneous fits of doubt occur, similar, perhaps, to an epileptic's sudden grand mal seizures. The OCD sufferer is then repeatedly overwhelmed by agonizing questions, fantasies of catastrophe, and powerful urges.

When I explained this to Melissa, her eyes lit up. "If I were that caveman and heard a twig snap," she laughed, "I'd look for a Bible verse that said all twig snaps are dangerous animals, and I'd say it over and over. But then I'd have the question 'Does that mean a tiger or a bear?' and I'd have to look for another verse." This model helped Melissa to see that her tormenting questions were the result of a brain disorder and that her prayer rituals were simply acts she was driven to perform in order to turn off the questions.

Another important point to be made about Melissa's treatment is that her behavior therapy did not conflict at all with her religious beliefs. Many people, particularly Christian evangelicals, accuse psychiatrists of being opposed to religion. This criticism has some validity, unfortunately, since Sigmund Freud, the father of American psychiatry, did proclaim religion a "universal neurosis"; and many psychiatrists still do subtly, if not overtly, discourage people from their faiths. But it worked fine for Melissa to look on her obsessions as being caused by Satan; in fact, that view should be given a certain distinguished status because of the many great people who have held it, as discussed in the previous chapter. Furthermore, the fact that some of her prayers had turned into compulsions did not lessen the importance of true prayer for Melissa; her prayer life is now better than ever. And, finally, Melissa still attends the same evangelical church, where her pastor is now a believer in this form of psychiatric treatment.

WHEN BEHAVIOR THERAPY FAILS

BEHAVIOR THERAPY IS not effective in all cases of OCD. Studies show that up to 30 percent of patients either refuse to try behavior therapy or quit it early, and an equal number improve only minimally or not at all after a full course of treatment. My own experience is that at least one third of OCD patients will not be helped significantly by behavior therapy.

Some types of OCD symptoms, it has been demonstrated, respond much better than others to behavior therapy. Luckily, clearcut washing and checking rituals—the most common symptoms of severe OCD—respond especially well. Most other types of rituals, along with episodes of avoidance, are also fairly easily treated as long as they can be clearly identified and thus readily targeted for exposure and response prevention. However, if compulsions and avoidance are not obvious, then behavior therapy becomes difficult.

"Pure obsessionals," people who are tormented by obsessions yet have few other obvious symptoms, have been identified as one group of patients who do very poorly with behavior therapy. Fortunately, increased use of the technique of exposure in the imagination (as was used with Sherry) has improved their prognosis considerably.

OCD sufferers with "obsessional slowness" are another group known to do poorly with behavior therapy. Unfortunately, no new techniques have improved the outlook here. I see a middle-aged woman who spends two and a half hours dressing, bathing, eating, and getting out of the house every morning. Where does the time go? A few checking and washing rituals never take her more than ten minutes. Hours go by that simply cannot be accounted for. She is, it seems, just painstakingly slow. She will study every detail. She will move from one tiny task to the next only after thorough deliberation. To make anything happen, it is as if she must overcome a great inertia. Such slowness seems itself to be a form of compulsion—or more likely the result of hundreds of mini-compulsions. In any case, it is extremely difficult to target for exposure and response prevention.

Severe depression also makes behavior therapy extremely difficult. Low energy, inability to concentrate, decline in interests, loss of motivation, and drab pessimism all rob a person of the ability to accomplish what is necessary for successful behavior therapy: a great deal of effort directed to exposure and response prevention. Depression must be addressed first, and only after that OCD.

Another problem sabotaging the therapeutic effects of behavior therapy is a strong belief that obsessions are real. You will recall that an obsession is, as a rule, recognized in a moment of quiet reflection as senseless. When that insight is lost, behavior therapy becomes impossible. My clinical observation is that this apparent loss happens for two reasons. Some patients with schizophrenia-like disorders have obsessions that represent delusions, or fixed, false beliefs. In these cases, the main problem is not OCD but a brain disorder that interferes with the ability to know what is real and what is imagined.

Other patients, though, suffer no such serious disorder, yet still insist on the truth of their obsessions. A student I treated recently insisted that her roommate really could catch her germs and die, and that scrubbing out the bathroom every day really was the right thing to do. She knew that no one else took such precautions. She even admitted that the chance of her roommate's dying from her bathroom germs was less than the chance of her being struck by lightning. Yet she still defiantly claimed that it could happen and therefore that she should perform her cleaning rituals. There was no reasoning with her. It seemed to be a matter of her heart ruling her head, along with a good dose of bullheadedness. After many unproductive sessions, I strongly confronted her. She would never get better, I told her, unless she stopped being stubborn and started using her brain. I am hopeful that this helped but I don't know because she terminated her therapy after that visit.

Finally, perhaps the most common reason for behavior therapy failures is a lack of will to change. As pointed out at the beginning of this chapter, behavior therapy is the single best treatment for people who make the necessary *effort*. But some OCD sufferers, particularly those who have had the illness for many years, become accustomed to an impaired life; they call a truce with their rituals. I treat a middle-aged man, a chronic OCD sufferer, who works eight hours a day pumping gas and then returns to an empty house where he puts in two hours performing rituals. He understands the irrationality of his OCD; he was able to lay the groundwork for behavior therapy by keeping an accurate daily diary of his symptoms. But when it came to practicing exposure and response prevention, he could not get the job done. He would forget to do it, or there wouldn't be time, or the assignment would be too difficult. After many unsuccessful attempts to make therapy work, he himself discovered the reason for his lack of success. "Well," he said, "I guess I really don't have anything better to do than the rituals."

SIX STEPS TO CONQUERING OCD

IT IS A fact that minimal instruction in behavior therapy can be all that is necessary for dramatic improvement in OCD. This has been demonstrated by psychiatrist Isaac Marks of the University of London. Marks, widely regarded as the world's leading expert in behavior therapy, demonstrated in 1988 that OCD sufferers taught the basics of behavior therapy could do just as well as patients who made frequent and lengthy visits to behavior therapists. Marks observed that the key to improvement was patients engaging in exposure and response prevention by themselves. This agrees with a common clinical observation: Once patients learn how to do behavior therapy, they don't need to come in for regular visits any more. Raymond told me, "Once I got the hang of exposure and response prevention, I was able to handle things by myself."

This being true, I have no doubt that many cases of OCD do not require professional help. What is necessary is only to understand the principles of behavior therapy and to put them to use.

You may benefit from a self-help approach if you are a self-motivated person and if your symptoms are relatively mild. You should consult a therapist, on the other hand, if your obsessions, compulsions, or avoidance are causing major distress or disruption to your life, or if your OCD resembles the cases described above in which behavior therapy is especially difficult. It may well be helpful, if you are going to attempt to treat yourself, to pick up a book that deals with self-help in greater detail than I do here. I often recommend *When Once Is Not Enough* by Stektee and White, *Stop Obsessing* by Edna Foa, *Getting Control* by Lee Baer, or *Brainlock* by Jeffrey Schwartz (see Appendix C).

The following six steps cover the essential ingredients of effective behavior therapy for OCD. A note of caution: Isaac Marks comments that using self-treatment is far from a "glib exercise" in using willpower to face up to fears. Progress depends on mastering definitions and principles, then putting them to use in a systematic and disciplined way. That said, here is a bare-bones self-help program for OCD:

Step 1. Understand that your OCD is a brain disorder. What you are fighting is a chemical problem that makes certain fearful thoughts (obsessions) stick tenaciously. The discomfort caused by these thoughts forces you to perform silly, repetitive acts (compulsions) and to limit your life (avoidance).

Know these facts so well that you can explain them to others. Test yourself: What is OCD? What exactly are obsessions, compulsions, and avoidance?

Step 2. Fully grasp the principle of habituation, nature's way of getting rid of fearful thoughts. Your job is to put habituation to work through the use of exposure and response prevention.

You will know that you have the main idea when you are able to comprehend this concise statement: "The problem with compulsions is that they chase away obsessions before a person habituates to them."

Step 3. Make a list, at least mentally, of your obsessions, compulsions, and avoidance. Give them a general ranking according to how seriously they interfere with your life. (If clearly identifying obsessions and compulsions proves very difficult, which it is in some types of OCD, then you should see a professional.)

Step 4. Your goal is to learn to live with obsessions—even though you dislike them intensely—while combatting compulsions and avoidance. To accomplish this, *do an exposure and response prevention task at least three times a week.* Pick an instance of compulsion or avoidance that is relatively mild, set up an exposure situation, and tolerate the ensuing anxiety until it decreases by at least 50 percent, which may take up to one to two hours. As you "get the hang of it," move on to more difficult tasks. (If you find that your anxiety is getting worse rather than better, you may be sensitizing to your obsessions rather than habituating. See a therapist.)

Step 5. Get support. You may be a lone-ranger type, but it is extremely helpful to have contact with other OCD sufferers and to keep abreast of new developments in OCD research. An excellent way to do this is to join the OC Foundation (see Appendix D).

Step 6. Try out different strategies to assist in exposure and response prevention. My patients' ten favorites are discussed in Chapter 6.

5

USING MEDICATIONS

OCD SUFFERERS ARE immensely fortunate that in addition to
behavior therapy, a second treatment has recently been found to be
markedly effective for obsessions and compulsions: medications.
Medications can work when behavior therapy doesn't; moreover, the
combination of medications and behavior therapy usually works
better than either remedy alone. Most OCD clinics, including my
own practice, routinely employ a combination of these two proven
treatments.

The medications that are most useful for OCD are the serotonin
reuptake inhibitors (SRIs), including clomipramine (Anafranil),
fluoxetine (Prozac), fluvoxamine (Luvox), sertraline (Zoloft), and
paroxetine (Paxil). These drugs, which had previously been known
to have antidepressant effects, have now been discovered to possess
distinct, specific anti-OCD effects as well. Over a hundred well-
controlled research studies involving thousands of patients have
now conclusively proven that the SRIs are both safe and effective in
the treatment of OCD.

Unfortunately, the intense media coverage of these medications,
particularly Prozac, has left many people scared to take them. On
television, it seems, a few dramatic, personal testimonies that Prozac
has caused addiction or suicidal ideas speaks louder than the thera-

peutic experiences of millions of people. But among the leading psychiatrists in America there is *unanimous* agreement that these medications are both very helpful and very safe in the treatment of OCD.

The serotonin reuptake inhibitor medications take their name from a unique, biochemical action: their ability to influence a certain brain chemical that has been found to play a key role in the production of obsessions and compulsions. Serotonin is a neurotransmitter; it serves as a messenger between brain cells. Molecules of serotonin are released from one brain cell, carry impulses to a second, and then are reabsorbed back into the first, to be used again.

The SRIs specifically interfere with the reabsorption, or reuptake, of serotonin. Research into how they do so has yielded two outstanding findings. First, SRIs are extremely selective in their effect; they have little impact on other neurotransmitters in the brain, of which over a hundred have been identified to date. Second, in the treatment of OCD, the SRI medications have their major therapeutic activity in one small area of the brain. Brain-imaging techniques, able to show the brain at work, reveal that OCD is caused by a hyperactive circuit of nerve cells running from the basal ganglia to the orbital frontal area of the brain (see Chapter 9). SRI medications decrease the firing of nerve impulses in this circuit.

From a practical standpoint, what patients report is that the SRIs allow them to let go of obsessions more easily and to resist the urge to do compulsions more readily.

Five members of the SRI group are currently marketed in the United States, and all are now approved by the Federal Drug Administration for the treatment of OCD. They are classified under the general heading of "antidepressants" because even before their anti-OCD effect was discovered, all had been shown to reverse the severe states of depression characterized by loss of energy, interests, appetite, and sleep. The antidepressant effect, interestingly enough, appears to be unrelated to the anti-OCD effect.

GENERIC NAME	TRADE NAME	EFFECTIVE DOSE
Clomipramine	Anafranil	200–300 mgs
Fluoxetine	Prozac	20–80 mgs

Fluvoxamine	Luvox	200–300 mgs
Paroxetine	Paxil	40–60 mgs
Sertraline	Zoloft	50–200 mgs

Clomipramine (Anafranil), the oldest of these drugs, was first discovered to be useful in the treatment of OCD in Spain in 1967. Since 1980 there have been more than fifteen double-blind and placebo-controlled studies that have demonstrated its efficacy beyond a doubt. The largest study, the Clomipramine Collaborative Study Group, a model of modern pharmacological research, examined the effect of Anafranil versus placebo in 520 OCD patients over a twelve-week period. The results, published in the *Archives of General Psychiatry* in August 1991, showed that 60 percent of patients improved markedly with Anafranil, whereas placebo was effective in less than 5 percent of patients. Prozac—first introduced in the United States in 1987—and Luvox, Paxil, and Zoloft, which were introduced in the early 1990s, have also been demonstrated to be effective anti-OCD medications by large multi-center studies similar in design and outcome to the clomipramine study.

Does any of the SRIs work better than the others? Few "head to head" studies have been undertaken, but those that have been done failed to show any one drug superior. A statistical review of a large number of studies published in January 1995 suggested that Anafranil is slightly superior to the others. This result, however, has been questioned, since the Anafranil studies included a much higher percentage of patients who had never before been tried on medications and who were therefore more likely to respond. What is clear is that all of these medications significantly help 60–70 percent of patients with OCD—a figure remarkably similar to the percentage of people helped by behavior therapy.

When is it appropriate to use SRIs? The decision to initiate drug treatment should be made on an individual basis, balancing the true risks of side effects against the probability of therapeutic gain, and taking into consideration the severity of symptoms, the age of the patient, and the chronicity of the disorder.

In general, when OCD is moderate to severe—when the sufferer is experiencing significant distress and is substantially impaired by obsessions and compulsions—medication should be used right away. In these situations, anti-OCD medications not only provide relief of symptoms, they also help a person to get a good start on behavior therapy, which is sometimes difficult when obsessions and compulsions are at their absolute peak.

In some cases, even when OCD may be fairly severe, it may be better first to try behavior therapy alone. For children and adolescents, medication treatment should be avoided, if possible, because the effects of these drugs on the developing brain are not fully known. For children with severe OCD who do not respond to behavior therapy, however, the data are very encouraging that the SRIs are both effective and safe. Another situation in which medication should be a last resort is the treatment of pregnant women. Again, however, the data are encouraging that these medications can be safely used.

What about young adults and college-age OCDers? I like to try behavior therapy first in this age group, as they often respond especially well to psychological therapies. If OCD is affecting a student's performance in class, however, I do not hesitate to use medications right away.

In general, when OCD is mild—when the sufferer has troublesome symptoms but is getting along satisfactorily despite them—it is best to try behavior therapy alone before medications. Yet if behavior therapy is not effective, and particularly if the symptoms have been present for a year or more, medications should definitely be given a try. No one should have to put up with OCD—a medical, neurological disorder—when good treatments are available.

ONCE THE DECISION has been made to use SRI medications to treat obsessive-compulsive disorder, a number of general principles must be kept in mind.

Complete versus Partial Cure

SOME PATIENTS, AFTER hearing of the great advances in treatment of OCD, expect that their OCD can be completely cured by SRIs, just as penicillin eliminates pneumonia. Unfortunately, this rarely happens. A closer parallel for the manner in which SRIs work is the use of anticonvulsants for treating epilepsy, or insulin for treating diabetes: They bring symptoms under control but do not eliminate the underlying disorder.

Studies such as the Clomipramine Collaborative Study Group demonstrate that SRIs usually bring about a drop in OCD symptoms in the range of 30 percent—from a Yale-Brown Obsessive Compulsive Scale rating (see Appendix A) in the mid-twenties, for instance, to a level in the mid-teens. This might mean a change from performing rituals three hours a day to doing them for one hour. Typically, what SRIs do when they work is to free a person from being disabled by obsessions and compulsions, allowing a return to a relatively normal life. Although this is a great boon to the OCD sufferer, it is not a complete cure.

Trial and Error

WHEN TREATING EPILEPSY or diabetes, tests can indicate which drug will work best and what dose is likely to be effective, but prescribing for OCD is still more of an art than a science. Studies have shown that one SRI medication will work when another does not and that there is no clear way to predict effectiveness. Further, adding a second medication, an "augmenting agent," to an SRI can often "kick-start" a treatment that at first seemed ineffective. The OCD sufferer, therefore, must be prepared to view medication treatment as a process of trial and error. I find it helpful to say to patients: "Let's agree to give medication treatment a try, and we may need to use several different agents, or combinations of agents, before we find the right one."

Medication treatment should generally begin with one of the five SRIs used alone. Different teaching centers have differing opinions as to which to use first. Whichever one is chosen, it should be given sufficient time to work. Although OCD sufferers often report a beneficial effect from medication after only a week or two, studies indicate that it may take four to six weeks before an effect is obvious, and much longer, up to three months, before it is maximal. Therefore, a reasonable trial period for a given drug is often ten to twelve weeks.

If there is no improvement after the initial trial, then an augmenting agent should be added in an attempt to bolster the anti-OCD effect. If this, too, fails, then a second SRI should be tried, and after that a third, and perhaps even a fourth and fifth. Studies have demonstrated that a particular SRI can work where others have failed. A recent study, for instance, showed that 20 percent of patients who had not responded to either clomipramine (Anafranil) or fluoxetine (Prozac) did well on fluvoxamine (Luvox). When it is necessary to try several SRIs, one of them should always be clomipramine (Anafranil), which is the only one that can be accurately measured in the blood, allowing a test of whether a therapeutic amount of medication is getting into the body.

After trials on at least three SRIs, with augmenting agents, combinations of SRIs may be tried. Although there are few good studies to date on the combined use of SRIs, clinical experience shows that this can be an effective strategy. A number of my patients, for example, have benefited from the combination of Anafranil with another SRI.

An important consideration in prescribing for OCD is whether a second, distinct psychiatric disorder is present along with OCD. If so, then it is imperative that this second condition be treated as well. Severe depression, panic disorder, bipolar disorder, and tics all occur with an increased frequency among OCD sufferers. For reasons not well understood—psychological, biological, or a combination of the two—OCD often will not respond to treatment until after these accompanying disorders have been addressed.

Dose Variability

THERE ARE LARGE variations in the dose of medication required to treat OCD effectively. This is due to a number of factors, including how well a drug is absorbed into the body, how efficiently it is metabolized by the liver, how quickly it passes through the blood–brain barrier, and how strongly it affects serotonin. It is known that with standard antidepressants there are tenfold differences in effective doses between patients. The same probably holds true for SRIs.

Finding the optimal dose of medication must be approached with the same "whatever works best" strategy as finding the right type.

Studies suggest that higher doses of SRIs are needed to treat OCD than to treat depression. Quite commonly, OCD sufferers require 80 milligrams per day of fluoxetine (Prozac), and I have had patients on up to 150 milligrams. Many patients, on the other hand, respond well to the standard antidepressant dose of just 20 milligrams a day. A few people with OCD respond to ultra-low doses of medication. I have patients doing well on just 2 milligrams a day of Prozac. To take such a low dose, the liquid form of medication can be used; or the capsule can be taken apart and the contents mixed in juice and saved in the refrigerator.

Two different approaches are used to begin people on anti-OCD medications: Start low and increase slowly, or move quickly to the highest safe dose. The advantage of the latter, of course, is that it saves time. Trials on a number of different agents, if the dose is slowly increased, could easily last up to a year. The advantage of going slowly, on the other hand, is that no one suffers harsh side effects, and therefore medications that might work if given enough time will not be quickly abandoned. Both approaches have their place. Academic centers, perhaps because many of their patients have already been tried on several medications, tend to prefer the faster approach, whereas psychiatrists in primary care, such as myself, usually start slowly.

Maintenance Treatment

THE PERIOD OF time from when medications are started to when a good therapeutic effect occurs is referred to as the acute phase of treatment. The period after that, during which medications are continued in order to maintain therapeutic gains, is referred to as the maintenance phase. In OCD it is clearly wise to continue medications for some period of time after acute treatment, but there is disagreement as to how long.

A number of studies have shown that when SRIs are stopped, relapse is highly likely. In a 1991 investigation of moderate to severe OCD, for instance, 89 percent of patients who had responded to clomipramine (Anafranil) relapsed within seven weeks of stopping the drug; all patients subsequently responded again when Anafranil was reinstituted. As mentioned above, the SRI medications work like anticonvulsants or insulin: They bring symptoms under control but do not eliminate the underlying disorder. The effects of SRIs last only as long as the drug is being administered.

More recent studies, however, show that it is often possible to discontinue medications, even in cases of fairly severe OCD, if effective behavior therapy has been implemented. Studies from England, in particular, suggest that a majority of patients can stop medications if they practice behavior therapy faithfully. My clinical experience is that many OCD patients can, indeed, stop medications. Some work hard at behavior therapy; others, it seems, experience such a lessening of life stresses that drug therapy is no longer necessary. Still, I find that more than half of patients need long-term maintenance treatment.

In maintenance treatment, happily, the medication dose can usually be decreased without losing therapeutic effect. A study of the use of Anafranil in long-term treatment of OCD, for instance, demonstrated that the average dose of medication required during acute treatment was 270 mgs, whereas the average dose needed to maintain treatment was only 164 mgs. Such a decrease is often enough to eliminate any remaining side effects.

A reasonable approach to maintenance treatment is to stay on an SRI for at least six to twelve months after symptoms have been brought under good control. During this time, maximal effort should be invested in behavior therapy. The medication dose can then be slowly lowered. If there is no recurrence of symptoms, medication can be discontinued. Yet OCD sufferers should be ready to accept the possibility that long-term treatment with an SRI, with regular trials at obtaining the lowest effective dose, may be best.

SIDE EFFECTS

PERHAPS THE MAIN reason why SRIs are among the most widely prescribed drugs in the world is that they have relatively few side effects. A recent study involving more than six thousand patients showed that far fewer patients (13.9 percent) stopped SRIs because of side effects than stopped standard antidepressants. In my own clinical practice I have treated hundreds of patients with SRIs. The dose has usually needed to be adjusted, the type of SRI has often needed to be changed, and on occasion medication has needed to be stopped all together. But I have never had a patient who experienced either a nonreversible or a medically harmful side effect.

Unfortunately, misinformation abounds regarding the side effects of these drugs. Probably the most common unfounded belief about SRIs is that they cause addiction. The truth is that not a single study has shown them to be habit-forming. Furthermore, the personality of the OCDer, guilt-prone and overly responsible, tends to prevent addiction to anything. I have never treated, nor even heard of, a patient who became addicted to an SRI prescribed for OCD.

Another common but unfounded fear is that the SRIs can cause suicidal, or even homicidal, behaviors. This specter was raised by a 1990 article in the *American Journal of Psychiatry* which reported that 6 out of 172 hospitalized patients on Prozac had become preoccupied with suicidal thoughts. Subsequent studies on many thousands of patients, however, proved that suicidal and homicidal thoughts are no more common with Prozac than with other antidepressants. The number of people who have been prescribed Prozac to date—over 40 *million*—dictates that almost everything will have happened to someone while on the drug, simply by chance. Yet the mistaken idea that Prozac causes Jekyll-and-Hyde personality changes surfaced once again when defense lawyers tried to argue that David Wisbecker, who in 1989 killed eight of his coworkers in a plant in Kentucky with an assault rifle, did it because he was on Prozac. The issue, hopefully, was put to rest permanently in 1995, when the courts completely discredited the "Prozac defense" in the Wisbecker case. The Federal Drug Administration, whose mission it is to oversee the safety of medications prescribed in the United States, and which is often criticized for being too restrictive, subsequently rejected a petition that the Prozac label include even a warning about suicidal or violent behavior. The FDA has repeatedly reaffirmed the safety of Prozac and the other SRIs.

Some widely available books do a good job of realistically appraising the risks of side effects of SRIs and other psychiatric medications. I found three good ones in my local bookstore: *Complete Drug Reference* (Consumer's Reports Books, 1994); *Essential Guide to Psychiatric Drugs* by Jack Gorman (St. Martin's Press, 1995); and *Prozac: Questions and Answers* by Ronald Fieve, M.D. (Avon Books, 1994), the eminent psychiatrist at Columbia University who did much of the pioneering work on bipolar disorder. Unfortunately, the "product inserts" that accompany medications and the Physicians Desk Reference, a compilation of product inserts, do a poor job of appraising side effects. They are designed largely to prevent malpractice suits against pharmaceutical companies and simply list every side effect that has ever been reported.

The truly significant side effects of the SRIs—all affecting only a minority of patients—are nausea, nervousness, sexual problems, irritability, and nightmares.

Gastrointestinal Symptoms

NAUSEA, AND SOMETIMES vomiting or diarrhea, are among the most common side effects of SRIs: 20–30 percent of people experience them in the first one to two weeks of treatment. These side effects usually respond to either dose reduction or taking medications with food; often, however, they are the reason patients stop treatment with a given agent. These side effects are most troublesome with sertraline (Zoloft) and fluvoxamine (Luvox).

Nervousness, Headaches, and Insomnia

THESE SIDE EFFECTS, affecting 15–20 percent of people taking the SRIs, are all related to an activating effect of these medications that some patients describe as being like the "caffeine jitters." Such reactions are strongest with fluoxetine (Prozac) and are, indeed, the most common reason why people stop that medication. These side effects usually last only a few months, and then the body adjusts to them. After that, they are sometimes replaced by their opposites, apathy and sleeping too much. All respond immediately to lowering the dose of medication. All can also be effectively treated by the addition of an antianxiety medication such as clonazepam (Klonopin) or lorazepam (Ativan).

Interference with Sexual Functioning

THIS SIDE EFFECT—most often either an inability to attain or-
gasm or a loss of interest in sex—was underreported at first, but it is
now clear that it occurs in fully 30–40 percent of people taking
SRIs. This side effect, too, usually responds to dose reduction. A
number of my patients on short-acting SRIs, such as paroxetine
(Paxil), sertraline (Zoloft), and fluvoxamine (Luvox), have reported
that skipping medication for two days allows a return of full sexual
function without a loss of antiobsessional effect. Two recent studies
have supported this observation. Adding medications of various
types to an SRI can also reverse sexual side effects, and yohimbine
(Yocon), buspirone (Buspar), buproprion (Wellbutrin), trazodone
(Desyrel), and cyproheptadine (Periactin) have all been tried in this
regard. In my practice, however, these counteractive drugs have
proved disappointing. Only Yocon and Desyrel have worked at all,
and those in only a few patients.

Irritability and Nightmares

SINCE THE DATA are strong that the neurotransmitter serotonin
plays a role in regulating anger (for instance, violent criminals have
low levels of serotonin metabolites in the spinal fluid), it is not surprising that SRIs have an effect on irritability. Fortunately, this is
usually a positive effect. Typical is the story of an eighteen-year-old
woman who had been kicked off sports teams, run away from home,
and been punished by her parents since age six for her short fuse and
overly aggressive behaviors. After three months on an SRI she told
me, "I'm much calmer now. I think before I act. For the first time
ever, I sat down and talked to my sister for a full hour." A study at
Harvard in 1991 looking at outbursts of anger among people on
SRIs found that outbursts went down in 71 percent of patients and
up in 6 percent.

The increased irritability that does occur in a small number of
people can, it must be admitted, be a problem. I have had several
patients, all with prior histories of hostile behaviors, who had to
stop SRIs because of marked increases in anger. One patient, for
instance, who had served time for assault and battery, had to stop
his SRI because, as he put it, "It made me feel like when I was on

steroids: say hello and I snap out." I should add, however, that I have never had a patient who acted harmfully because of the effects of these medications.

A larger problem with the SRIs is the occurrence of nightmares, often of physical harm. Rather than the 0–5 percent reported in clinical trials, perhaps 10–15 percent of my patients are bothered by vivid, troublesome dreams. These patients respond to decreasing the dose of medication, or changing to a different SRI.

Other Side Effects

TREMOR AND SLEEPING excessively can occasionally become problems after many months of treatment with an SRI. Patients so affected usually respond to a lowered dosage. Allergic reactions, primarily rash, occur in about 3 percent of people taking SRIs. Because teratogenic effects (adverse consequences of drugs on the developing fetus) have not been well studied, SRIs should be stopped, if possible, during pregnancy. Large numbers of pregnant women have taken SRIs, however, and so far there have been very few problems reported.

Dry mouth, constipation, drowsiness, and memory loss occur as a group and are referred to as anticholinergic effects. They are by far the most frequently seen with clomipramine (Anafranil) and occur to a lesser extent with paroxetine (Paxil). Anticholinergic side effects always respond to dose reduction. Chewing sugarless gum or sucking on lemon drops (which stimulates salivation) can also be helpful for dry mouth. Other potential problems specific to clomipramine (Anafranil) are heart conduction abnormalities (patients who are over forty should have an electrocardiogram before starting Anafranil) and a lowering of the seizure threshold.

Medication Interactions

THE SRIS — IN this case clomipramine (Anafranil) much less than the others—have a strong effect on the liver's metabolism of certain medications. As a result, the SRIs have the potential to dangerously increase the blood levels of many drugs, including antidepressants, anticonvulsants, blood sugar medications, heart medications, pain medications, and allergy medications. Although I have never had a patient who ran into a major problem in this regard, these drug interactions are potentially serious. For the older person on a number of medications, these drug interactions represent the major drawback to the use of an SRI.

Alcohol

CAN A PATIENT drink while on medications? Psychiatrists tend to take the conservative position that it is better not to consume any alcohol while on any psychiatric medication. It should be pointed out, however, that many patients drink socially while on SRI medications without a problem. There is, in fact, no direct, harmful interaction between alcohol and the SRI drugs. The case is somewhat different with benzodiazepine medications, such as lorazepam (Ativan), clonazepam (Klonopin), and alprazolam (Xanax). Here there is an interaction, and alcohol should be avoided.

OTHER MEDICATIONS HELPFUL
IN THE TREATMENT OF OCD

Benzodiazepines (BZDs)

THIS GROUP OF anti-anxiety agents, which includes chlordiazepoxide (Librium), diazepam (Valium), alprazolam (Xanax), lorazapam (Ativan), and clonazepam (Klonopin), is taken by approximately 15 percent of American adults, making them among the most widely prescribed of all medications. Next to the SRIs, these are also the most useful medications in the treatment of OCD. In my practice, approximately one third of my OCD patients take a benzodiazepine, almost always in conjunction with an SRI. The more severe the OCD, the more likely a BZD will be helpful.

The benzodiazepines are remarkably free of side effects. Oversedation, and in some cases short-term memory loss, are the main problems, and they are seldom severe. The primary concern with the BZDs is that, unlike SRIs, they can be addicting. Even here, however, the danger of addiction must be put in perspective. I remind my patients that addiction is, in essence, a loss of personal freedom. The addict's choices lessen as she is controlled by the desire to obtain and ingest a substance. Yet the OCD sufferer, too, is enslaved— to obsessions and compulsions—and medications help reverse those. In this sense, BZDs are the opposite of addicting; they help open life up, they are freeing. Of course, these drugs must be properly prescribed. The dose should be kept in a moderate range; and they should not, as a rule, be given to individuals with a history of substance abuse. In my experience, though, OCDers never become addicted to BZDs.

Benzodiazepine medications are indicated when OCD is accompanied by disabling anxiety symptoms, especially severe phobias and panic attacks (shaking, rapid heartbeat, shortness of breath), which are present in up to a third of OCD sufferers. These symptoms should be aggressively treated because, in addition to the direct suffering they cause, they can provoke a marked worsening of obsessions and compulsions.

There is a second indication for BZDs in the treatment of OCD: They may be added to SRI medications to increase their therapeutic effect. Several studies, as well as clinical experience, show that clonazepam (Klonopin) is especially useful as an augmenting agent. Unlike most other BZDs, Klonopin appears to have a direct effect on serotonin that is similar to that of the SRIs.

Additional Augmenting Agents

IN ADDITION TO benzodiazepines such as Klonopin, there are several other medications that, when used in conjunction with the SRIs, may increase anti-OCD effect. These augmenting drugs include buspirone (Buspar), trazodone (Desyrel), fenfluramine (Pondamin), and lithium. All have some effects on serotonin. Any one of them, when added to an SRI, can produce a better therapeutic response. The research supporting the use of these, however, consists primarily of uncontrolled studies and case reports. I must admit that I have had limited success with augmenting agents other than benzodiazepines and occasionally buspirone.

Antidepressants

DEPRESSION FREQUENTLY ACCOMPANIES OCD. Approximately 30 percent of OCD sufferers show symptoms of severe depression at the time they are first treated, and 60–70 percent of OCD sufferers—as opposed to 15 percent of the general population—develop severe depression at some time during their lives. When OCDers show symptoms such as loss of energy, appetite, concentration, and interests, the addition of a standard "tricyclic" antidepressant, such as desipramine (Norpramin) or imipramine (Tofranil), to an SRI can be extremely helpful.

Antidepressants known as monoamine reuptake inhibitors, MAO-Is, are also occasionally used to treat depression in OCD, and sometimes even as primary treatments for OCD. I have not included a discussion of the use of MAO-Is in this chapter, however. Recent research has demonstrated that MAO-Is are less effective in the treatment of OCD than SRIs. Furthermore, the MAO-Is are associated with severe, even life-threatening side effects.

Neuroleptics

THIS POWERFUL GROUP of medications, which includes a number of well-known drugs such as chlorpromazine (Thorazine), haloperidol (Haldol), and risperidone (Risperdal), is used primarily in the treatment of psychotic states. Side effects are a major problem: All neuroleptics can cause tremor and restlessness and can occasionally produce irreversible, abnormal movements of the mouth referred to as tardive dyskinesia. Although these medications have no role in the treatment of classic, uncomplicated OCD, they are extremely helpful in two situations where OCD overlaps with other disorders.

A significant minority of OCD sufferers, perhaps 5–10 percent, have difficulties sorting out what is real and what is not. They may lack insight into their obsessions, insisting, for instance, that their hands truly are contaminated despite all evidence to the contrary. Or, they may have subtle evidence of psychotic symptoms, such as hearing vague sounds or voices. In these situations, neuroleptic medications may be indicated.

A second situation in which neuroleptics are helpful is when OCD is accompanied by troublesome tics—involuntary, repetitive movements such as eye blinks and shoulder shrugs. Here, OCD overlaps with the disorder known as Giles de la Tourette's syndrome, and several controlled studies have proven that very low doses of neuroleptic medications are beneficial.

Experimental Treatments

THERE IS ENCOURAGING evidence that other forms of therapy may be helpful for OCD as well. The evidence, however, is not yet substantial enough to recommend these treatment for general use. Lorin Koran and co-workers at Stanford have been using intravenous clomipramine (Anafranil) in treatment-resistant OCD with some success. Inositol, a natural sugar, has also been shown to be helpful in OCD in a couple of studies, the most recent reported in the *American Journal of Psychiatry* in 1996. It is intriguing that a simple and inexpensive foodstuff might help OCD. I will list another treatment here as experimental, yet in doing so I do it a disservice for the data supporting its efficacy as actually quite strong: brain surgery, which can work in the one-in-a-thousand cases of totally disabling, totally treatment-resistant OCD. I have referred one patient for neurosurgery, and she had a successful outcome. (Interestingly, OCD is at this time the only psychiatric problem for which brain surgery is considered a reasonable treatment option— a clear indication of the largely neurobiological nature of this disorder.)

WHAT TO DO when medication doesn't work? This is generally when the OCD sufferer should review medication treatment with his or her physician and come to a decision. Has anything worked at all? If so, that can be prescribed. If not, medication should be stopped—with the caveat that new medications are being developed constantly, and one of them may well work in the future.

A LOOK AT how medications were used in the cases of Raymond, Sherry, Jeff, and Melissa, whose presenting symptoms were described in Chapter 1 and whose behavior therapy was described in the previous chapter, illustrates the way drug therapy can work in the treatment of OCD.

When Raymond first came to me in the summer of 1993, he was on the verge of a breakdown. Agonizing obsessions of contaminated spills and hours a day of checking compulsions were causing anxiety attacks, deep depression, and finally, an inability to keep up in his work. Raymond welcomed a trial on medications. He was ready for anything that would help.

Although I prefer not to start two different medications on the first visit, the severity of Raymond's condition warranted this approach. I prescribed clomipramine (Anafranil), 50 milligrams at bedtime, and over a week increased the dose to 150 milligrams. I also prescribed lorazepam (Ativan) at 1.0 milligrams three times a day, a dose that was quickly increased to 2.0 milligrams. Raymond noted immediate improvement in his anxiety and ability to sleep. Over the next month, he also began to notice a decrease in the power of his obsessions. Unfortunately, Anafranil caused several side effects including dry mouth and constipation, and when he tried to lower its dose, his OCD and depressive symptoms worsened. We replaced Anafranil with fluoxetine (Prozac), which he tolerated well at a dose of 40 milligrams in the morning.

Raymond continues on Prozac and Ativan to this day. When he cuts down the Prozac, he notices a return of depression and OCD symptoms. When he cuts down the Ativan, which I occasionally encourage him to try, he feels markedly more anxious. The only side effect he notices from his medications is decreased sex drive. We tried adding two different medications, yohimbine (Yocon) and trazodone (Desyrel), to counteract that side effect but have had no luck. Raymond insists it is not a major problem.

Raymond's own conclusions about medications? He told me recently: "The Ativan helps a lot, because when I'm relaxed I can let go of obsessions quicker. Prozac works differently. There's something deep going on with Prozac. It doesn't make me feel any different in any way that I can put my finger on, but when I stop it the obsessions become much worse."

When Sherry came to see me for treatment of her OCD, she was suffering recurring terrifying images of stabbing her husband or driving her car into little children. Sherry was even more anxious than Raymond. Frequent panic attacks—episodes of rapid heartbeat, shortness of breath, and chest pains—could keep her in bed all day long.

Although Sherry had been on medications before, she had many qualms about restarting them. Wouldn't they cause addiction? Couldn't they interfere with her creativity as a painter? And anyway, wasn't using medications a "cop-out"? Upon learning that there were new and specific anti-OCD drugs, however, she did agree at least to give them a try.

A combination of Prozac (20 milligrams in the morning) and Klonopin (0.5 milligrams in the morning and 1.0 milligrams at bedtime) worked well for several months. Sherry's panic attacks vanished and her obsessions seemed less strong and persistent. Higher doses of Prozac caused jitters and vivid nightmares. Even at 20 milligrams interference in sex drive became a problem. This was helped by the addition of a third medication, trazodone (Desyrel) at a dose of 75 milligrams at bedtime. After a year, Sherry's OCD markedly improved, and she was able to cut down her medications. She is now maintained on Prozac at a dose of 10 alternating with 20 milligrams a day, and Klonopin 0.5 milligram as needed.

None of the fears Sherry had about medications materialized. When she first started Prozac, she told me, her husband called every hour to check that she "wasn't out murdering anyone." Yet neither she nor her husband noted any personality changes. As far as medications interfering with her painting, the opposite occurred. "On the medication," she said, "I can get my thoughts together and produce better work." Yet being productive is now no longer such an important issue. For the first time in her life there are moments when her mind is not frantically active, when she can relax and enjoy herself. Reflecting on this change she said one day, "Even if the medication would have ruined my creativity, I'd still take it. It is an incredible gift to live a normal life."

Last year Sherry developed TMJ syndrome, a click in her jaw, and her dentist, speculating that Prozac had been causing her to grind her teeth at night, did not hesitate to suggest that she stop the medication. As she related it, she told her dentist: "I'm sorry, I don't care! You're not taking that away from me."

As for Jeff, his treatment with medications was simpler and less spectacular than that of Raymond or Sherry. He was eager to give medications a try and did well right away on a relatively low dose of sertraline (Zoloft), 100 milligrams a day. After six months in treatment, he was doing very well and he decreased the Zoloft to 50 milligrams. He has since been able to discontinue medication completely.

In the case of Melissa, I strongly recommended starting medications immediately, and she did not object. Melissa's treatment proved somewhat complicated. Prozac was started at a dose of 20 milligrams per day, and she seemed to do well on this, noting a decrease in the intensity of her obsessional questions within the first week or two of treatment. But after six to eight weeks, she complained of disturbing feelings, quite foreign to her, of irritability and even rage. "I got so angry I was snapping out at people and running over curbs," she told me. In addition, she began to have vivid, horrible nightmares—in one dream, rats were eating her feet. We switched to Anafranil (clomipramine), but immediately she felt too groggy. "I can't think straight on this stuff," she said. Sertraline (Zoloft) was then tried, but again, the side effect of vivid dreams emerged after one to two months of treatment. Finally, a combination of a relatively low dose of fluvoxamine (Luvox), 50 milligrams, accompanied by a small dose of clomipramine (Anafranil), 50 milligrams, proved helpful and did not cause side effects.

Melissa is convinced that medications have been very beneficial— that's why she has put up with all the problems they have caused her. Her obsessive questions are not as insistent; she is able to let go of them more easily. Another apparent benefit of the medication is that Melissa has become more assertive. She has experienced the type of beneficial personality change that Peter Kramer talks about in his book *Listening to Prozac*. Before, she wouldn't speak up; once on medication she assertively confronted her sister for the first time in her life. "People notice a complete change." Melissa reported. "I like it."

IS TAKING MEDICATION A SIGN OF WEAKNESS?

LIKE SHERRY, MANY people think that medications are a cop-out, that taking them is to shrink from a personal challenge that should be met. This view is even promoted by some psychiatrists, notably Peter Breggin, author of *Talking Back to Prozac* and *Toxic Psychiatry*. Dr. Breggin, who rails against the use of all psychiatric medicines, including those that are used to treat very serious disorders such as schizophrenia, views all drugs that affect the mind as escapes from the suffering of intense feelings, suffering that should be lived through and dealt with as a means of personal growth. What people should do, Dr. Breggin says, is try to understand the roots of their problems, not escape them through drugs.

The error in this line of reasoning is the assumption that OCD has deep psychological "roots." It is now widely agreed that OCD has little or nothing to do with unconscious conflicts or hidden hang-ups. As discussed fully in Chapter 9, research has now proven that OCD is a discrete, partially genetic, brain disorder. Importantly, OCD is often brought on by life stresses, and they should be addressed in therapy. But far from being an escape, medications are used to treat the direct, physiologic cause of OCD so that, rather than wasting their time looking for imaginary roots to their problems, OCDers can get back on their feet and begin meeting life's real challenges.

I myself have taken an anti-OCD medication on a regular basis for four years now. I had never before taken a psychiatric medication, but at the age of forty-seven I considered the following: (1) I used to have diagnosable OCD; (2) I still had problems with obsessional worries—subclinical OCD, if you will; and (3) I was very impressed with the results of these medications in my practice. Resolving to give myself a trial on an SRI, I found medication to be both helpful and free of side effects. As an example of their benefit, I am now able to drive on long trips comfortably, without my usual excessive dilemmas, such as whether I should be going faster or slower, or whether I should be in the right or the left lane. I function, I would say, somewhat better all-around: sleep a little better, put in a longer day's work. I do not regard my taking medication as a sign of weakness.

Medications, specifically the serotonin reuptake inhibitors, are an indispensable part of therapy for the majority of OCD sufferers. These medications, now conclusively proven to be a specific treatment for OCD, represent a truly remarkable advance in the medical treatment of brain disorders. Relatively free of side effects, easy to take, and apparently safe for long-term use, these drugs can offer dramatic relief from crippling suffering. OCD patients should not hesitate to make use of them, nor should they feel guilty when they do.

6

THE LESSONS OF GROUP:
TEN STRATEGIES FOR
COPING WITH OCD

BEHAVIOR THERAPY AND medications are the two best treatments for OCD, and thus far they are the only ones that have been proven effective in clinical trials. In practice, however, it is obvious that a number of other treatments—including individual psychotherapy, family therapy, and group therapy—can also be helpful. Of these, group therapy is perhaps the most important. I lead OCD groups at both a community mental health center and a university counseling service, and the majority of my patients attend group at one time or another. Most of them benefit markedly. Indeed, for those with relatively mild symptoms, group therapy may be the only treatment necessary.

The type of group I refer to is neither an "encounter" group ("Beth, tell Jennifer why you are angry with her") nor a personal issues group ("Bill, how did your separation affect your self-esteem?"). Instead, what OCD sufferers need is education and support: a group that teaches positive strategies for coping with obsessions and compulsions while providing a sympathetic, enlightened atmosphere to counter the strong negative feelings that accompany the disorder.

Consider the typical OCD sufferer. She is saddled with a problem that no one seems to comprehend, least of all herself. Her symp-

toms, if observed, are likely to elicit ridicule rather than understanding. And instead of sympathy, the attitude most people take
toward OCD is, "Why don't you snap out of it?" Not surprisingly,
she will try to hide her symptoms, fueling feelings such as guilt,
self-doubt, and discouragement.

Group therapy is uniquely helpful because it relieves this burden
of secrecy in a way no other therapy can. In group, the OCD sufferer
makes a remarkable discovery: Those who share the disorder are
likable and responsible individuals. A young woman with tormenting sexual obsessions observed: "The people in group have become
friends who are like family. I look up to them. I admire them so
much. I'm amazed at how well some of them do despite having really bad compulsions. Most of all, though, they understand the pain
of OCD, and nobody else does." The shame of self-tormenting
thoughts and senseless rituals dissipates when it becomes clear that
they are the result of a common, chemical disorder that occurs in
normal—actually, nicer than normal—folks.

Guilt is the most pervasive of the many punishing feelings shoul-
dered by OCDers. Indeed, the tendency to suffer guilt in an exaggerated form is regarded as a cornerstone of the OCD personality.
The following excerpt illustrates how self-blame can be soothed in a
group setting. Included are comments from Melissa, Jeff, and Raymond, whose cases were introduced in Chapter 1.

MELISSA: I was obsessing about being disrespectful to my father. He asked me if I wanted to drive over to State College,
and I said no. Afterwards, I wondered: Was I short with
him? Was I disrespectful? What would people think if they
heard me talk to him this way? It was a terrible time. I felt
so guilty that I almost got suicidal. Finally, two hours later,
I apologized, long after he had forgotten about it.

GROUP MEMBER: When I get breakfast for my kids I have to
wash my hands a dozen times because I think that if I get
sick, the whole family could get sick. Then if the kids miss
school, I wouldn't be able to take care of them. Everything
would be my fault. What I can't stand is the thought that I
would be to blame.

JEFF: I used to feel guilty all the time. I thought I was such a horrible person that I shouldn't even be allowed out of my house. But now I say a couple of things to myself: "Okay, I'm not perfect and I never will be," or, "That's normal, every human being does that once in a while."

RAYMOND: Back when I first started checking everything, it was because I didn't want anyone to ever be able to say that if Raymond had only been more careful, some bad thing wouldn't have happened. My wife said, "Raymond, what's the matter with you? All of a sudden, you're afraid to fail." She was right. We can't be afraid to fail. We just have to accept that we might fail, and be able to deal with that guilt.

Discouragement is another feeling frequently shared in group. A new group member tearfully described changing her baby's diaper over and over, using up whole packages of diapers before finding one that seemed clean enough. "The anxiety is just wearing me down. I am very discouraged. I can't take this much longer," she said. In response, one person shared how he had once been hospitalized for depression from his OCD and how his life had turned around after he got help. Two others emphasized that having compulsions is not a reason for despair; compulsions are part of OCD, and they can be treated. As a result of this discussion, she mustered the courage to keep fighting her disorder and started to make progress.

Self-doubt is yet another common reaction to the rigors of OCD. It often involves the fear of having a complete breakdown. A student who changed her clothes a dozen times a day described her anxieties:

Whenever I walk on the sidewalk I get paranoid that I've walked in dog poop. I know it's crazy, but I think that maybe I got it on my shoes, then onto my clothes, then onto my hands; and then if I touched someone, maybe they could get sick. I know it's far-fetched, but I can't stop thinking these things all day long. I must be losing my mind . . . or going crazy.

One person immediately shared that she, too, had suffered such fears. Another added: "You think that sounds crazy. Let me tell you,

I can top that." And he did, describing a past obsession that he could impregnate women simply by being in the same room with them. The lesson learned from this and similar discussions was that although obsessions are very irrational, OCDers never lose contact with reality; they are never in danger of becoming truly "crazy."

It is hard to overemphasize the relief experienced by OCD sufferers when the burdens of guilt, discouragement, and self-doubt are lifted. An equally important benefit of group, however, is learning coping strategies for dealing with obsessions and compulsions. Here, too, group therapy is uniquely beneficial. I can and do address such strategies in individual therapy, and patients can read about them in books, but neither of these opportunities carries the weight of hearing the experiences of others at firsthand.

It is important to note here the relevance of these coping strategies to behavior therapy. As discussed in Chapter 4, behavior therapy involves three essential steps: recognizing OCD; tolerating obsessions; and fighting compulsions and avoidance. The strategies discussed in this chapter assist in accomplishing these goals. They are aids to behavior therapy. They help people change their attitudes and outlooks, allowing OCD to be recognized more quickly, obsessions to be tolerated more easily, and compulsions to be fought more vigorously.

In each group session, I try to ask each member: What strategy is working the best for dealing with your OCD right now? I ask that the details be spelled out and specific examples provided, so that everyone can understand exactly how the tactic is put to use. The same strategies come up again and again. Some overlap, and others can at first almost seem to be contradictory, but each one is a tried and true method of furthering the goals of behavior therapy. I have reviewed my notes and tapes from six years of group sessions. Here are the ten practical strategies that have been spoken of the most:

STRATEGY NO. 1: IGNORE OBSESSIONS

A STUDENT IN our university health services group was struck by obsessions of loved ones becoming sick. She could only restore them to health with tapping or touching. She was devastatingly embarrassed when, as sometimes happened, her friends made light of her rituals.

> SHELLY: I get these pictures in my mind of awful things happening. Usually, it's my Mom having a heart attack. First I see it taking place really clearly. Then I have the feeling—I know it doesn't make sense, but I definitely have the feeling—that it might come true unless I do some little "thing." So I tap my fingers on the table eight times—always eight—and I feel better. Or else I touch everything on the table. I hate it when someone says: "What did you do that for?" That kills me. It just kills me.
>
> STUDENT: I used to have almost exactly the same obsessions. I would be afraid that something bad would happen if I didn't arrange things a certain way. Like before I went to bed, I had to touch every single thing in my room. But now I just try to ignore those thoughts. I pretend they're some creep who's trying to bother me.

Ignoring obsessions is an ideal coping method. It is, after all, the way most people deal with intrusive, unwanted thoughts. They say to themselves something like, "That sure is a silly thought, I won't pay it any attention"—a fitting response, because ignoring an obsession saps its strength, whereas fighting it only forces it to come back stronger.

OCDers need to look on their obsessions in such a way as to allow them to stay in the forefront of consciousness. That way, habituation can take place and the unwanted thoughts will eventually go away on their own. The perfect attitude might be summed like this: It's okay that I had that thought, and it's okay if it stays. It's no big deal.

Of course, the whole problem with OCD is that a chemical disorder of the brain makes ignoring obsessions very difficult. Often it is helpful to find a metaphor that helps to put an unwanted thought in its place. It may be likened to a wino on a city street, static on the radio, flies at a picnic, or an unwanted suitor (this one works particularly well for college-age women). The response is the same: Once an obsession is recognized, pay as little attention to it as possible.

Ignoring obsessions works best when obsessions are mild. Sometimes OCD sufferers advance to this strategy only after they have progressed in treatment. Sherry, for instance, who once suffered harm obsessions so frightful that she could hardly bear even to bring them to mind, recently told me: "What works now is just to let them happen. Not to knife myself, obviously! But just to let the thoughts come and to let the thoughts go. Ignore them. Treat them as a person I don't want to deal with."

STRATEGY NO. 2: RATIONAL ARGUMENT

GROUP MEMBERS RALLIED around a young homemaker with handwashing compulsions:

EMILY: I'm still washing my hands a lot when I'm around food. Like when I make breakfast. I wash before I take the bread out of the breadbox. Then I wash again before I open the bread, because I touched the breadbox and might have gotten them dirty. Then I wash again before I take the bread out of the toaster, because by then they feel dirty again. Then I wash before I get my juice and again after I've poured it. . . . Get the picture?

GROUP MEMBER 1: Do you really think you will get contaminated? Why don't you argue with those thoughts? You've got to keep telling yourself that they don't make sense.

GROUP MEMBER 2: What I do when I get one of my contamination obsessions is to sit myself down and say to myself: "This isn't logical. It's just another of your obsessions." I psych myself up. Even though I'm worrying about germs I make myself eat by telling myself, "The food isn't contaminated, it's all in your mind." It works. It really does.

GROUP MEMBER 1: Could you give a try to not washing at all while you are making breakfast? Just don't wash, no matter what. Argue back to the obsessions when they happen.

After this discussion, Emily was able to make progress by consistently confronting her obsessions: "I've never heard of anybody getting sick from this; there is clearly no need to wash all the time. Other people don't do this, so I don't need to either."

A nineteen-year-old student named Allison had a number of obsessions when she parked her car, including that the emergency brake was not fully engaged and that the gearshift lever was not in the "park" position. To counteract these fears, she checked the brake over and over and often sat for five minutes or more staring at the gearshift indicator. She stared, she said, in order to insert a clear picture in her mind of the car being in park, so that if she was later surprised by the obsession she could recall the picture and be reassured that the car would not drift downhill and injure someone.

After a couple of months attending group and hearing how other people put obsessions in perspective through rational argument, Allison began to make excellent progress. Remembering what she had learned, she confronted her compulsions by telling herself: "I've checked hundreds of times, and the car has always been in park. I do not need to check again." Or she would say: "This is an irrational compulsion, stop it." Or: "I know this is OCD, and I know that I've got to get going. So do it."

In rational argument, OCDers learn to have discussions, "self-talk," about what is reasonable and what is not. They learn how to stand up to obsessions by logically considering their content. Rational argument is best employed as soon as obsessions hit, before compulsions get started. Sometimes, because compulsions become such strongly ingrained habits, there seems to be no time. Yet there is always a microsecond available to interrupt the split-second program of obsession leading to compulsion with a byte of clear thinking. Slip in a little reason here, and the first step has been taken to bringing OCD under control.

Rational argument is nothing less than the keystone to developing a workable, long-term approach to OCD. It is the strategy that is emphasized the most in group, and it forms the foundation for many of the other strategies that will be mentioned in this chapter. Here are some more quick reminders, gathered from group, useful for putting obsessions in rational perspective.

- I've been in this same situation countless times, and my worst fears have never come true.
- Just because this (urge, image, idea) feels real doesn't mean it is.
- The only way I'm going to overcome my OCD is to learn to live with this fear.
- This silly thought is a result of a hiccup in my brain.
- I'm not going to let this thought rule me.
- I've tried my best, and that will have to be good enough.
- This job doesn't have to be perfect.
- Other people do not need to do this.
- I've done what is reasonable, and that's all I'm going to do.
- Treating my OCD is more important than doing this ritual.
- If it feels like OCD, it is.

STRATEGY NO. 3: THAT'S NOT ME! IT'S OCD

A THIRTY-TWO-YEAR-OLD MOTHER suffered sexual obsessions so intensely guilt-provoking that she would do anything to prevent them from forming in her mind:

> KAREN: I'll be changing my baby's diapers when suddenly I begin to have a bad sexual thought. I don't even know exactly what it is, because I don't let myself think it. I stop it before it gets started. I'll say prayers over and over. I'll watch TV. When nothing else works, I'll even start to imagine killing myself. It's not that I want to hurt myself—I wouldn't because of my baby—but if I put a strong image into my mind of chopping my own head off, it keeps the other thoughts away. Yesterday I spent all day long thinking about that. I absolutely won't let those sexual thoughts come into my mind no matter what. No way.
>
> ANNA: I used to get the same kind of thoughts. I would be changing diapers, and I would worry that I was doing it in a sexual way, or maybe that, somehow, I was enjoying it sexually. Those thoughts used to really bother me. I would do all kinds of rituals to stop them. I drove my husband crazy ask-

ing him for reassurance that they weren't true. What has been most helpful is realizing that they don't come from me. Those thoughts are not who I really am. If I think about it deep and hard, I know I wouldn't do anything sexual to my baby. That's just not me. It's OCD.

Karen employed "That's not me! It's OCD" from that day on. It must be acknowledged that until recently most mental health professionals not only eschewed this strategy but contradicted it. Freud hypothesized that self-tormenting thoughts were due to unconscious conflicts caused by repressed urges, an idea that was accepted by several generations of American psychiatrists and psychologists. As a result, people like Anna were told that, yes, they did have violent, murderous urges deep down inside them and that really the only way to overcome these urges was through years of psychoanalysis. Untold numbers of OCDers were harmed by this mistaken idea.

The leaders in the field now recognize that obsessions do not issue from one's deepest self. They are passing thoughts that gain significance only because of the OCDer's neurochemical inability to process fearful thoughts. Neuropsychiatrist Jeff Schwartz, author of the recent, highly successful OCD book *Brainlock,* emphasizes that OCDers of all ages should remind themselves, "That's not me. It's my brain sending me a false message." Schwartz encourages patients to see OCD as a war. In order to fight it, OCDers must maintain "mindful awareness" of the fact that it is not they themselves but a biochemical disorder that is the cause of OCD's symptoms. Duke's John March, leading expert in the treatment of childhood OCD and author of *How I Chased OCD off My Land,* teaches children to give OCD a name, such as "butt head," "stupid," or "the playground bully." Doing this, he explains, helps children get distance from OCD and motivates them to fight the disorder using behavior therapy.

STRATEGY NO. 4: TAKE CONTROL: STAND UP TO OCD

HEATHER, A JUNIOR majoring in human development and family studies, was tormented by terrible, violent images of being choked—by ropes, belts, and coat hangers. To ward these off, she put her hand to her neck and massaged it, or tried to imagine that she was magically protected by steel shields. On one occasion she reported to group that as soon as she had awakened on the previous Saturday she had been immediately overwhelmed by images of strangulation that drove her to spend all morning clinging desperately to protective rituals. She tried to distract herself by watching TV and listening to music, yet the dreadful images seemed only to increase to new levels of heart-stopping repulsiveness. All she could think was, "Oh, man, what's next?"

At that point, however, Heather remembered what another student had said in group: "You can't let OCD control you; you have to keep up the fight." She said to herself: "I'm not going to have a terrible day. I'm going to take control." She made a list of goals to accomplish, starting with going to the library. As she got started, the obsessions "backed off." She was able to "push through" the fearful thoughts each time they began to recur. The key for her was to boss back her OCD, to be master of the situation.

In individual therapy I can encourage people to take control, to stand up to OCD, but the response is often minimal. Hearing those who speak out of personal experience is infinitely more powerful. A truck driver suffering obsessions that his shoes were full of fleas and mites scrubbed his feet nightly with alcohol, which left them painfully cracked and fissured. Even though it was obvious to him that his compulsive washing was irrational, he told our group that it had simply never occurred to him that he could resist it. He had just assumed that if he did so something terrible would happen. Once encouraged to take control of his rituals, he made surprisingly quick progress. After one month he was able to go a whole week without scrubbing. He reported to our group that as soon as his obsessions would begin, he just said to himself, "To hell with those obsessions; I'm not going to start that washing."

Some of my group members report that they have learned to recognize the "feel" of an obsession. They know it's coming before it is fully formed because they detect a familiar, foreboding. Being able to detect an obsession in this way is extremely valuable because the quicker OCD is confronted the better. A group member said she stopped rituals in their tracks by saying firmly, "Stand up to OCD. Don't even get started!"

STRATEGY NO. 5: WHATEVER HAPPENS, HAPPENS

ONE DAY A freshman, Lindsay, who had been attending group for about a month, and a senior, Linda, who had been attending off and on for two years, reviewed for a new group member what had been working for their OCD:

> LINDSAY: I've had obsessions since seventh grade, when I started waking up in the middle of the night afraid that I would go crazy and knife my parents. But my latest obsession is the thought of jumping out the window. I live on the fifth floor in the dorms, and the idea comes into my mind of running over to the window and throwing myself out. I absolutely do not want to do this, but a few weeks ago it got to the point where I was just breaking down and crying. I was on the phone every night with my parents. I was getting friends to tell me, "You're all right, you're not going to do it." I was repeating to myself, "I won't do it, I won't do it," all day long. Sometimes I even told myself: "You're on the first floor, you're on the first floor"—even when I was on the fifth floor! I thought I was going to have to drop out of school. But I'm doing a lot better this week.
>
> LEADER: What's been working?
>
> LINDSAY: Like we talked about here, I'm telling myself: "It is possible that I could jump out the window. I might get a brain tumor that would affect my brain, and I'd go crazy, and I'd do it. It's a one-in-a-billion chance, but it's possible. It could happen to anyone. I have to accept that." This lessens the anxiety. The thought just doesn't seem as frightening.
>
> LINDA: I tell myself the same thing. That's my number one way of coping with OCD. Like I have this obsession that I'm going to have a bad day. It makes me terribly scared. Last

year before I could leave my room I had to look in the mirror with a certain expression on my face and say to myself, "I'm going to have a good day." I had to repeat that over and over until I got it just right, and that could take a long time. It was wacky! But I fought that one and I won. Now, I say to myself: "Oh, well, I'm going to have a bad day. Bad days are part of nature. Everyone has them."

LEADER: You say to yourself that you might have a bad day, or you say that you will have a bad day?

LINDA: I tell myself that I am definitely going to have a bad day. You have to accept that it will happen. You have to be okay with it. If you do that, you can get past the obsession. Another of my obsessions is that I'm afraid of rejection. I'm zoning out all day and thinking the weirdest things to counter these obsessions about rejection. So now I just say, "Let the worst happen. Let them say, 'Who the hell are you? You're a moron!' I can deal with it."

LINDSAY: I can see you doing that with your obsessions, but I don't think I can do that with mine. What works for me is to recognize that although it's a one-in-a-million chance, it could happen to me, or to anybody, and I'd have to accept it.

Whether viewing it as Lindsay did that the chance of a feared event's happening is slim but real, or as Linda did that the feared event is definitely going to happen (not many people take this stance), the result is that the anxiety-producing thought, the obsession, is held in the mind and tolerated, leading to a dissipation of the terror it causes.

This is a venerable approach. Whatever happens, happens, has been recommended by philosophers for over two thousand years. Epictetus, a famous Greek, put it this way: "We must not try to anticipate or to direct events, but merely to accept them." Marcus Aurelius, the most celebrated of the Stoic philosophers, said, "Accept everything which happens, even if it seems disagreeable." In the twentieth century, the famous philosopher Bertrand Russell, as well as the highly influential clinical psychologist Albert Ellis, have both emphasized the advantage of a worldview that includes whatever happens, happens.

This strategy, however, can be difficult to pull off. Sometimes patients are loath to accept even a remote chance that a particular obsession might occur. Whatever happens, happens, is especially difficult with obsessions involving violence against loved ones, such as a mother's thought to knife her baby, and with obsessions involving strongly held religious beliefs, such as the thought of losing salvation. On the other hand, whatever happens, happens, is especially helpful when obsessions center on uncertainty. In the case described above, Lindsay's tormenting thoughts centered not so much on the act of jumping as on the doubt she had that she might do it. Saying, "It might actually happen and I have to accept the possibility," cut to the heart of her uncertainty.

Raymond, whose case was introduced in Chapter 1, caught on to this coping strategy after about a year of attending group. Encouraged by a sermon given in his church, he reasoned that since whatever happened was God's will, he should be willing to accept anything. He imagined and "accepted" that he had hit someone with his car, that his son had contracted AIDS, and that everyone in his town had died from an epidemic that he could have prevented had he only taken notice of a spill of infected scrub water. This caused a marked decrease in the strength of his obsessions.

Soon, Raymond became an enthusiastic advocate of this strategy. One day in group when a young woman shared her obsessive fears that the food she was serving her husband was contaminated, he offered her some rather blunt advice: "Look, you're going to have to say to yourself: 'I'm going to cook; and if he dies, he dies.' "

STRATEGY NO. 6: REMEMBER OTHER OCDERS

A GREAT BENEFIT of group therapy is receiving advice from other OCD sufferers as to what is reasonable and what is not. An undergraduate student was besieged by fears that the food she bought was tainted. She threw away loaves of bread unopened, fruits never touched, and hoagies and pizzas that never made it out of the bag.

These compulsions were demoralizing, embarrassing, and expensive:

> MARIA: My roommate was really mad at me this week. We ordered a pizza from Domino's, and when it came I got so nervous I threw the whole thing right in the garbage. "It doesn't look very good," I said. She about died. Then I had to run out and buy another one. I know I shouldn't do it, but I just can't stop. When I look at the food, it just doesn't look right. Or else it doesn't feel right. I know I shouldn't throw food away . . . but you know, maybe some of it really is contaminated. They're not very careful in some of these places.
>
> GROUP MEMBER 1: Look, if we allow ourselves to believe that, we're all in big trouble. Everybody orders pizzas. Nobody gets sick. You need to stop going back to buy food. You need to break that compulsion.
>
> GROUP MEMBER 2: I used to work as a bag boy at a supermarket. For one thing, nobody got sick. For another, okay, some of the food probably has germs, but you can't tell that from looking at it or feeling it. Anyway, you can't see or feel germs. You just have to make yourself eat the food like everyone else.

This feedback from group members she knew and respected allowed Maria to curtail her costly compulsions. When compulsions threatened, she was able to resist them by telling herself: "Remember what the people in group said. They wouldn't lie to me. I just have to trust them."

Vince, a truck driver, found it useful when struck by a severe obsession to visualize the face of each person in his OCD group. He brought to mind exactly what had been talked about in the previous session and remembered, too, how silly it all sounded. Then he reminded himself that he would be in group next week discussing his obsessions and how ridiculous he would sound. Then he said to himself, "Why not realize right now how silly these obsessions are, and learn to live with them?"

Another group member was strengthened by his desire to be encouraging to others. He once shared that what worked for him was remembering the despair and hopelessness of a young woman who had cried the week before in group. He said to himself, "I'm going to beat my OCD. I'm going to be able to tell that girl that we don't need to be ruled by this disorder."

Group members often report that the simple act of being understood by their fellow sufferers is immensely consoling. Among other things, it helps them deal with the criticisms and bad advice offered by those who do not understand the disorder. Melissa, whose case of religious obsessions was introduced in Chapter 1, had many friends at church who were quite opposed to the idea that her prayers represented compulsions. She spent hours on the phone with her own sister explaining what she had learned about obsessions and compulsions, but to no avail. Her sister would counter, "It's good to obsess about God. You should stick with the Bible and stop the shrink." After much strong persuasion from group members that her sister was completely out of touch with this situation, Melissa was able to accept the reluctant conclusion of most OCD sufferers: There are some people who will never understand OCD, no matter how clearly you explain it to them.

STRATEGY NO. 7: TRUST IN GOD

MELISSA'S CASE ALSO demonstrates that although religion is a frequent topic of obsessions, religion is also one of the greatest helps for dealing with OCD. Melissa, whose faith never waivered while fighting her excessive scruples, recently told our group: "The coping method I use now always starts with: 'God, help me to accept your grace on this matter.' " For Melissa, the difference between religious symptoms and religious faith was clear. Indeed, untangling the two is seldom difficult. Religious obsessions and compulsions are unpleasant, repetitive, senseless, and have an alien quality. True faith is meaningful, exciting, and issues from our deepest sense of self.

Typical of the comments of many people in OCD group is that of a young mother tormented by knife obsessions after the birth of her first child: "This is the most helpful thing: I pray and put my trust in God every day to heal my mind and help me deal with these thoughts."

A born-again Christian student explained that, when walking along the street, an image would flash into her mind of the person walking in front of her stumbling and falling. She would have to "undo" the image immediately by imagining the person standing upright again. Yet even as she would attempt to do this, the person would "fall" once more. As she aptly put it, "Since I know what I don't want to see, I keep on seeing it." Soon more rituals would be called on to chase away the obsessive images, such as exhaling deeply and tapping her fingers together. After four months in group she began to make progress. She reported to us: "What works is to stop and turn to God and leave the situation in his hands. My trust in God has to be stronger than the compulsions, though. If it's not, the compulsions win."

A particular dilemma occurs when devoutly religious OCD sufferers are struck by blasphemous obsessions while praying. One member of our community mental health center group, when saying grace before a meal, was struck with the shocking thought that she was praying to the devil instead of to God. Another member of the same group had the heart-stopping image that she was performing a sexual act with Jesus. Yet intrusive, blasphemous thoughts such as these are no different from any other type of obsessions. They should never stop a person from praying—that would be avoidance. Like harm obsessions or contamination obsessions, these sorts of agonizing religious obsessions can be overcome by recognizing their senselessness and finding ways to tolerate them.

A group member with violent obsessions once shared a prayer that he found very helpful. I will include it here, since it is the best prayer I have heard for OCD. It is found in the classic fourteenth-century text, *The Imitation of Christ*:

My Lord and God, do not abandon me; remember my need, for many evil thoughts and horrid fears trouble my mind and terrify my soul. How shall I pass through them unhurt? How shall I break their power over me? You have said, "I will go before you. I will open the gates of the prison." Do, O Lord, as you have said, and let Your coming put to flight all wicked thoughts.

STRATEGY NO. 8: LIMIT OR POSTPONE A RITUAL

A JUNIOR MAJORING in education suffered from severe, chronic OCD. As a freshman, she had had to take a medical withdrawal because of disabling symptoms. Now she was once more falling behind in her studies, and quite discouraged, she was again considering dropping out of school. Particularly oppressive were harm obsessions involving friends and loved ones and mental rituals that could occupy her mind all day long. One day in group, when asked how she was doing, she told us tearfully:

LAURA: My OCD is getting bad, again. It's the same routines over and over—I mean like all the time, all day long. I have to imagine dozens of different faces; I have to clearly picture a face and have a positive thought at the same time I'm doing it or something bad will happen to that person. First I do family members, then close friends, and then acquaintances. This involves everybody that's important to me. There must be twenty or thirty different people. While I'm doing it, other pictures come into my mind, "interrupter people," who mess things up. Then I have to start over. I can't even read a book.

STUDENT 1: Can't you fight them? You need to remind yourself that those people are going to get along fine without your thinking about them.

LAURA: Nothing works. The thoughts are too strong.

GROUP LEADER: (after a pause) Can anyone else relate to this?

STUDENT 2: I used to have the same rituals. I couldn't go to sleep until I clearly visualized the faces of all the members of my family—and I've got a big family—with a certain expression on their faces, and all this had to happen while I was lying a certain way and saying a certain prayer. But a big problem happened when I came to college: I didn't see these people for months at a time, and I would lose their images in my head. That drove me nuts. Like nuts. I would lie there and get so mad at myself that it gave me insomnia.

GROUP LEADER: What was helpful to you to break those compulsions?

STUDENT 2: I told myself, "You've got to stop this. You're a big girl, now."

LAURA: I can tell myself to stop, but the thoughts come back even stronger. I'm like totally gone.

STUDENT 1: Laura, maybe you can try this. Don't stop the ritual all together, just cut down on the number of faces you are imaging. Maybe that will work. Just visualize the five most important people, then stop for a while.

To my surprise, Laura benefitted from this suggestion. When it was brought up, I had thought it overly simple. In fact, I was ready to write Laura another medical withdrawal. This experience clearly demonstrates one of the great benefits of group therapy: People who are actively fighting OCD have insight that others lack into what works.

Limiting a ritual also worked for a middle-aged woman in our community mental health center group who suffered from compulsive reading and hoarding. Picking up *Good Housekeeping,* for instance, her eye would catch an article on aging. Even though the subject was boring, she would feel that she had to read the article so that she wouldn't miss something important for her family's health. Attempting to do so, however, she would find that she wasn't able to attend fully to the article. She would then have to reread it. Invariably, she would never gain certainty that she had sufficiently absorbed the article's information, and she would have to save the magazine so that she could refer to it later. Stacks of magazines lay in piles on her floors and littered her attic. Group members helped her break her compulsions by suggesting that she throw them away a half-dozen at a time. It worked. She was able to accomplish this by telling herself, "There are so many magazines here that throwing away a few of them isn't going to matter."

Postponing rituals, a similar strategy, can also be quite effective.

Another middle-aged woman suffered from handwashing compulsions that left her sinks clogged with soap and her hands chapped and occasionally bloody. Group members gave her the homework assignment of resisting the urge to wash her hands for ten minutes after using the toilet. This caused her tremendous anxiety, but she did it—holding up her hands like a surgeon, fearful to touch anything at all. Over subsequent weeks she stretched the interval to twenty minutes, then thirty, and finally to two hours, after which the obsession lost its strength. She did it by telling herself, "I've just got to hold off for a few more minutes, then I can wash."

Melissa once reported that when no other strategy worked, postponing did. When faced with an agonizing need to analyze a conversation over and over, it was all she could do to put off the compulsion by telling herself, "Just wait for twenty minutes, and then think about it. There will still be plenty of time to call and apologize if I need to." By the end of the twenty minutes, her need to review the conversation was no longer powerful, and she could use reason to deal with it.

STRATEGY NO. 9: LEAD AN ACTIVE LIFE

A MIDDLE-AGED CARPENTER who had been tormented by fears that his house was infested with insects told our group:

> Keeping busy is good for me. If I let myself sit around I start thinking about those termites. I imagine them in the wall, in the attic, in the floor, everywhere. I start walking around looking for little piles of their sawdust. So I work on my car, clean the house, buy groceries, start my mother-in-law's wood stove—whatever needs to be done is better for me than watching TV. If I just sit around I start to dwell on things.

A young woman with handwashing and cleaning compulsions who worked as a hospital aide noted, "The best thing I've found is to schedule my days so that each hour is accounted for. When I have things to do, I don't obsess so much."

I was skeptical of the utility of "lead an active life" when I first started specializing in OCD. A person should learn to be able to enjoy free time, I thought, and not be driven to activity. But I didn't know much about OCD back then. The fact is that the strategy of keeping active can be extremely helpful.

A man with severe OCD shared a reminiscence that was both touching and edifying. During his twenties, when his OCD was at its absolute worst, the only thing that kept him out of the hospital was keeping busy by helping others. Every day he would go his relatives' houses and ask if anyone needed anything done. He would fix a furnace, mow a lawn, chop firewood, anything at all. He became a sort of legend in his family for his good works. Yet, he told us, all this activity served a dual purpose. It kept his mind occupied so that he was not constantly tormented by obsessions; and, at a time when he was filled with agonizing self-doubt, it made him feel good about himself.

What helps OCD sufferers the most is being involved in tasks that are challenging and creative, tasks that provide a sense of accomplishment. Perhaps that is why Winston Churchill, who suffered tormenting obsessions himself, once said: "Those whose work and pleasures are one are fortune's favorite children." The child in the excellent movie *The Touching Tree* (available through the OC Foundation) discovers that his OCD is completely quieted when he acts on stage. A good strategy for anyone, but especially for OCDers, is to find a creative endeavor, a mission, and be devoted to it 100 percent.

STRATEGY NO. 10:
ACCEPT OCD AS A CHRONIC DISORDER

IN A GROUP discussion not too long ago, members talked of the advantage of developing a realistic, long-term view of OCD:

GROUP MEMBER 1: I just accept that I'm going to have OCD forever. But I also know that it's not going to stop me from living my life. When I get a bad obsession, I tell myself,

"You've gone through this hundreds and hundreds of times, and you'll go through it hundred and hundreds more. It's not going to ruin you. The less attention you give it, the better."

GROUP MEMBER 2: I've learned to live with OCD, too. What really helps is knowing that the symptoms will come and go. Even if I'm having a hard time now, I know that I've done very well in the past and I will in the future, too.

RAYMOND: It's helpful for me to tell myself, "I have OCD, and I'm probably going to have it the rest of my life. So I better just deal with this obsession as best I can, because there's no escaping from it."

GROUP MEMBER 3: I'm not ashamed of having OCD any more. I think positively about it. For some reason God made me with a bizarrely creative mind. He must have known what he was doing.

People with moderate to severe OCD usually have some symptoms all their lives. Recognizing and adapting to this can be a crucial step in therapy.

THESE TEN STRATEGIES are the ones most frequently mentioned in my group therapy sessions, but many others work well. Relaxation methods such as self-hypnosis and transcendental meditation can be helpful, especially if put to use immediately when a person is hit by an obsession. OCD experts Jeffrey Schwartz and John March recommend "mindful awareness," a Buddhist Vipassana meditation technique that involves focusing attention carefully on the various movements of the body and mind. Mindful awareness results in increased psychological distance between the self and obsessions, an excellent way to build tolerance to obsessions and make progress in behavior therapy.

Some of my OCDers report that they can "trick" themselves out of performing compulsions. A student who touched the table six times to "prevent" her mother from having an accident would say to herself at the last minute, "If I touch the table, my mother *will* have an accident." This stopped her ritual in its tracks. Another strategy fairly popular among my group members is the "split screen" technique: Allow the obsession to occupy a part of your mind; get on with your life in the other.

Humor deserves special note. Sherry once noted, "If I'm having a bad knife obsession, I'll tell my husband about it, and he'll begin to hum the tune from *Jaws* when the shark is ready to bite somebody. I crack up. The obsession seems so ridiculous it doesn't bother me anymore." John March once treated a boy who suffered obsessions of stabbing his mother by having him sing, to the tune of "The Farmer in the Dell," "I'm going to stab my mother, I'm going to stab my mother. . . ." When it works, humor is an excellent way to increase psychological distance from obsessions.

What works best of all is to try different strategies and see which ones are most helpful. Sometimes a particular method is effective for a few months and then loses its power. Other times, the same strategy retains its effectiveness for years. At the very least, starting a strategy fosters hope and brings focus to the fight against OCD.

Lastly, OCDers should keep a watchful eye that a useful strategy does not itself turn into a compulsion. This snare occurs when a strategy is no longer used as a method for dealing with obsessions and compulsions but rather is simply repeated over and over without variation. In other words, the strategy becomes a ritual to chase away unwanted thoughts, rather than a method to learn to live with them.

In the case of Melissa, for instance, the strategy of bringing reason to bear on an obsession turned into a ritual when she started to spend hours going over the minute details of conversations. Similarly, praying turned into a compulsion for her when prayers ceased to be acts of worship and turned into magical incantations. The strategy of relying on other people backfired as well when she started to call family and ministers many times a day, not to learn anything new but just for reassurance.

In practice, fortunately, it is not difficult to tell when a helpful strategy has turned into a ritual. Patients themselves are usually easily able to spot the self-defeating, clearly excessive nature of a compulsion. It is helpful to remember that a useful strategy changes the way a person looks at, or thinks about, obsessions and compulsions, allowing them to be more easily tolerated. A ritual causes no change in perspective; it only chases obsessions from the mind.

To recap, many OCD sufferers insist that group therapy is the most helpful of all the treatments that they have received. It lifts the burden of secrecy. It addresses, in a way more powerful than individual therapy, negative feelings such as guilt, self-doubt, and discouragement. And group therapy allows OCDers to learn at firsthand, from the people who really know, the strategies that are successful in the battle with OCD.

OCD IN THE FAMILY

ONE OF THE most poignant cases of OCD I have treated is that of Jerry, who was a close friend of mine in sixth grade. Growing up, Jerry lived only a block away; we enjoyed playing golf, chess, and ping pong together. He was a dark-complected, handsome boy with greasy black hair, every strand of which was plastered perfectly in place by an excessive amount of hair cream. Shy and rather nervous, Jerry was always eager to have my friendship. A memory that strikes me vividly: Jerry and I are sitting in my living room playing chess, laughing heartily as we sing along to a record about a rebellious cannibal boy who refused to eat people. We play this tune over and over, having a great time. The song must have struck some deep chord, both of us being, like the cannibal boy, peacemakers and timid by nature. In junior high school, though, Jerry and I developed new friends. Or at least I did. I found out what happened to Jerry when he visited me as a patient thirty years later.

It will be instructive to tell Jerry's story primarily from the standpoint of his mother, Mrs. Kaufmann. She is a short, wiry, intense woman who I have remained in contact with over the years, even as I lost track of Jerry himself. I sometimes would ask Mrs. Kaufmann how my old friend was doing, but it was only after Jerry came to see me that she would openly discuss his OCD. By then she was able to look back on the tough times with impressive objectivity and forgiveness—for herself, for Jerry, and for the professionals who had only made matters worse.

It was when Jerry started kindergarten, in 1952, that she realized she had a problem on her hands. Jerry was never on time for school; indeed, he could not be made to be on time. The car pool would arrive; he would be assembling blocks. "Come on, we're waiting," she would yell, rushing him along. But Jerry wouldn't move—as if he didn't hear her. Soon she would be shouting, "You're going to be late, hurry!" Yet it was only after several minutes of escalating screams and threats that Jerry finally arrived at the car. This happened every single day.

At first Mrs. Kaufmann assumed it a case of stubbornness, or perhaps intentional disobedience. As the behavior continued, however, she became convinced there was something deeper. She went to Jerry's kindergarten teacher, seeking advice, perhaps a referral to an expert. But she was told only that Jerry was fine and that his stubbornness would pass. This was the first in what would become a long series of incorrect or harmful professional opinions.

In the years between kindergarten and seventh grade, there were constant problems. Mrs. Kaufmann remembers one teacher scolding that Jerry would flunk unless he got his homework in on time and another who threatened legal action because of Jerry's habitual tardiness. Jerry also began to show inordinate concern with his appearance and to spend excessive time in the bathroom. Yet, despite all this, Jerry remained a relatively happy child throughout those years. He performed fairly well in school, had several good friends, played golf regularly, and swam competitively for a YMCA team.

When Jerry himself looks back on those years, the only OCD symptom he remembers clearly is hair-combing rituals. He would spend ten to fifteen minutes every morning parting his hair, starting from the back and working to the front, separating out each strand, carefully combing the shorter strands to the right, the longer ones to the left, taking special care that the part was neither too high nor too low and that it formed a perfectly even line with a slight ellipse. It was a painstaking ritual, and he did not enjoy it. Yet if he skipped it, he would feel that his hair was "not quite right," and he would become overwhelmingly anxious.

In seventh grade Jerry took a sharp turn for the worse. He remembers it as the time when he lost his friends. Terrors of contamination began to haunt him, as well as ill-defined fears of death. Rituals snaked their way into all areas of his life. OCD took over. Before he could play golf, he now had to spend half an hour cleaning his clubs; each shaft, each head, each grip, each groove, carefully scrubbed with a stiff bristle brush, soap, and scalding water. When he finally got on the course, he had to address the ball for minutes at a time, waiting until his fingers felt just right in the overlap grip, his shoulders and feet exactly aligned, before he could swing the club.

Jerry's dawdling quickly irritated his golfing friends. "What are you doing, counting the dots on the ball? Let's get going!" they would say. His behaviors soon stamped him as too different to remain a part of the group. First he was teased and then deliberately avoided.

How did I treat him? It seems odd that I can remember vividly the good times that Jerry and I shared, yet have only a hazy recollection of these months. I do remember that I felt embarrassed for Jerry. I also remember, however, that I didn't stick up for my friend. Yes, I even began to think that perhaps Jerry *was* a little too different. Before long Jerry quit playing golf and then dropped out of competitive swimming. Isolation and loneliness set in.

Mrs. Kaufmann remembers seventh grade as the time when Jerry's "breakdown" occurred. Before that he had lived a normal life; afterward he couldn't. First his hand washing became severe, and every day she needed to apply lotion to his reddened, chapped hands. Then Jerry began to wash his own clothes and the furniture in his room, too. On one occasion, Mrs. Kaufmann found Jerry putting all the clean towels from the closet through the washing machine. "Enough!" she screamed. "Don't touch my linen closets again!" Soon Jerry was regularly changing the filters of the water system for the house and spending his allowance to buy new ones. When Mrs. Kaufmann discovered a large stash of soap hidden in Jerry's closet, she decided to try "a test." She took all his soap and announced that he was no longer permitted to use any soap at all. Jerry screamed and cried; he "fell apart." She knew then that she absolutely had to get help.

She took Jerry to see a psychologist at nearby Penn State, but after six sessions Jerry quit going. Jerry's parents were told nothing, and nothing helpful was accomplished.

Mrs. Kaufmann was left to deal with the OCD herself. Her husband, a successful businessman, traveled extensively during those years and was home only on weekends. Feeling sure that her husband, indeed, could not accept Jerry's problems, Mrs. Kaufmann kept secret their seriousness. Jerry, for his part, effectively hid most of his symptoms from his father. By an unspoken agreement, the mother and son kept the disorder to themselves.

Mrs. Kaufmann could make no sense of it. Sometimes she thought he performed rituals in order to avoid work, such as when he stayed in the bathroom for an hour rather than cleaning up his room. Other times, she thought he was doing them for attention, such as when he would insistently demand that she take him to the store to buy countless items that he said he needed for his homework. Most often, though, Jerry's behaviors seemed too strange and self-defeating to be purposeful. So she blamed herself. "He was my child, he wasn't normal, therefore it was my fault," she recalls thinking. She often went to bed crying.

Just as she could find no coherent way to make sense of Jerry's rituals, Mrs. Kaufmann could find no satisfactory way to deal with them. She tried reasoning with Jerry, explaining to him that unless he became more productive and stopped the rituals, he was not going to be able to compete in the world. She tried being more strict. ("I became a nagging mother, and I'm not proud of it.") Frequently she ended up going along with the rituals: driving Jerry where he said he needed to go, putting up with his lateness, and tenderly applying cream to his chapped hands.

Throughout junior and senior high school, Jerry's compulsions took up at least one to two hours every day. Ordering or "just so" rituals became a major problem. Jerry recalls that he would sit for an hour lining up the books on his bookshelf, pushing them back a few at a time, checking them, then nudging them forward again, so that there was not a bit of waviness in the line. Washing rituals became quite complex. Wearing heavy rubber gloves, using scalding water, he would scrub his face, hair, and genital area until they were red and sore. For each washing, he needed clean sponges, which created a logistical problem. Routinely exhausting the supplies of sponges in nearby stores, he would anxiously check the shelves each day, waiting for them to be restocked. Homework prompted many different rituals, including compulsive shopping for paper, pencils, compasses, slide rulers, and other school supplies. On one occasion, Mrs. Kaufmann had to cancel the family's lines of credit when she found that Jerry was charging over a hundred dollars a month for such items. These were miserable years for both mother and son.

Jerry graduated in the bottom third of his high school class, despite having an impressive IQ measured later at 124. He then took a try at college. In retrospect, he never had a chance. Away from home for the first time, beset by compulsive rituals, separated from his only source of love and support, he quickly became severely depressed and suicidal. The college psychologist recommended hospitalization. The Kaufmanns asked where it would be best to send him. The answer was the internationally renowned Menninger Clinic in Topeka, Kansas.

Jerry was admitted to Menninger on June 16, 1969, and discharged on May 16, 1970. The records from his hospitalization show that on admission his diagnosis was "obsessive-compulsive disorder" and his prognosis was "guarded." Eleven months later, when his debt-ridden parents could no longer afford the cost of his care, which now stood at $50,000, Jerry was discharged, his condition "unchanged." His rituals were no better, his prognosis was still "guarded." The treatment provided Jerry—the same as for all patients at Menninger at that time—was state-of-the art Freudian therapy. Deep-seated parent–child conflicts were presumed to be the underlying cause of all major psychiatric disorders, and the therapist's job was to make the patient aware of these and help him deal with them. In Jerry's case, OCD was attributed specifically to "a symbiotic relationship with a potentially devouring mother."

"I took it very personally," Mrs. Kaufmann told me. "I said to myself, 'Okay, kid, you really did it this time.' I went to pieces." It took many years and the help of a therapist before she was able to rid herself of a persistent sense of personal failure.

After Menninger, Jerry continued to suffer severe OCD. Washing and cleaning rituals occupied two to three hours every day. Out in the world, even though a personable and bright man, he could not hold a job. A marriage also failed. Jerry moved back home.

In the 1980s, hearing of new and better therapies for OCD, Jerry came to see me for treatment. Progress since then has been rather slow; Jerry has continued to suffer moderate to severe symptoms. Presently, however, his life is in an upswing: He is holding down a full-time job, has been "dating" his exwife, and is optimistic about his future.

ONSET IN CHILDHOOD is common for obsessive-compulsive disorder. Recent studies indicate that half of all cases start before age eighteen—a considerably higher percentage than that seen in any other major psychiatric disorder. Given that 1–2 percent of people suffer OCD at some time during their lives, as many as one person in a hundred will develop it early on.

If this were an infectious disease, it would be considered an epidemic. The magnitude of the OCD problem, however, goes unrecognized. A 1988 study of 2,000 New Jersey adolescents found eighteen to have OCD, but only four cases had been diagnosed.

OCD can, indeed, begin at an extraordinarily young age. A case has been described of an eighteen-month-old boy who anxiously arranged and rearranged his toys all day long. A patient of mine started to have symptoms at age three, repeatedly circling around trees certain numbers of times. His repeating rituals worsened over the next few years to include entering and leaving rooms, turning on and off the TV, and compulsively swallowing in sets of three, six, nine, or a dozen times.

Approximately one OCDer in twenty develops clear symptoms by age six. A student touchingly recalled the start of her OCD in first grade. Every day she would keep the other children waiting at the bus stop while she ran across the street and stepped up and down on the curb. She was ridiculed by other children, misdiagnosed by a school professional as autistic, and referred to a low-functioning "special ed" class. Not until college was she diagnosed as having OCD.

A few differences stand out between the early childhood form of OCD and that seen later on. Very young children most frequently perform ordering and counting rituals, whereas washing and cleaning are more common after six or seven. Another contrast is that young children typically do not appreciate the inappropriateness of their compulsions, whereas older OCDers, as a rule, have this insight. Lastly, epidemiological studies show that boys outnumber girls in childhood and adolescent OCD by a ratio of up to two to one. This disparity may be related to OCD's frequent association with a disorder of primarily male children, Tourette's syndrome.

The prepubertal years are the most common time prior to adulthood for the arrival of OCD symptoms. A ten-year-old's OCD looks essentially the same as that seen in a person of forty: contamination obsessions predominate, and after that obsessions involving danger to self or loved ones, need for symmetry, sexual fears, and scrupulosity. A typical case is an eighth-grade girl who suddenly found herself with an overwhelming fear of contracting AIDS. She would spend an hour washing herself in the bathtub each night before bed and would not allow herself to be touched until the next morning. In school she made frequent excuses to go to the restroom to vigorously scrub her hands. She would refuse to use the school toilets because they were too "dirty" and as a result developed severe constipation.

The onset of OCD in childhood or adolescence tends to predict a chronic course. In the largest systematic followup of pediatric OCDers treated with medications and behavior therapy, researchers found that after two to seven years only 11 percent were free of significant obsessions and compulsions, and 70 percent required ongoing medication treatment.

There is one pernicious aspect of childhood OCD that is often overlooked: Severe symptoms can seriously impede social development. Researchers studied seventeen OCDers between the ages twelve and seventeen with marked obsessions and compulsions. They found a general lack of peer acceptance, along with shortcomings in skills fostering cooperation and intimacy, such as initiating conversations and inviting others to join them. The unfortunate results of bypassing the intensive social learning experiences of adolescence are illustrated by Jerry's case.

The Burden Shouldered by Parents

BRINGING UP A child with more-than-mild OCD is always an imposing task. Parents become frustrated that their child cannot be reasoned out of rituals and angry when he or she will not stop them. They blame themselves for their child's symptoms, assuming they are somehow responsible. They often dread that their child may be developing some sort of a psychotic disorder.

The burden is partly lifted when parents find good professional help. They come to realize that OCD is a biological disorder, limited in its severity, and that they are not responsible for it. Further, they are provided much-needed structure for dealing with the disorder at home. But parents never get completely off the hook. Behavior therapy presents its own dilemmas, such as deciding when a child is showing attention-seeking behavior and deciding when to enforce behavioral limits. Furthermore, obsessions and compulsions make children moody and irritable. On top of that, because OCD children are unusually bright, loving, and dependent, parents tend to identify closely with them and to suffer their setbacks with great anguish.

In a survey of OCD parents conducted in 1993, the Obsessive-Compulsive Foundation found that more than 80 percent reported significant disruption of family life, particularly the loss of normal closeness in family relationships. Major problems identified in OCD sufferers were depression, lack of motivation, and inconsiderate behavior. Major problems for family members were excessive arguing and being drawn into rituals. Parents' greatest concerns were the future well-being of the OCDer and how they themselves could get back to enjoying life normally.

Parents of OCDers must, indeed, strive to lead a normal life—this is crucial for both parents and the affected child. In order to do this, it is necessary to maintain a rational view of OCD and to avoid becoming overly involved in a child's symptoms. The OC Foundation has several pamphlets that can be helpful, including, "Learning to Live with OCD," by Barbara Van Noppen, "Obsessive-Compulsive Disorder in Children and Adolescents," by Hugh Johnson, and "A Survival Guide for Family," published by Obsessive Compulsives Anonymous. This last suggests that parents keep reminding themselves, "We didn't cause our child's OCD, and we can't cure our child's OCD."

Early Warning Signs

ALL CHILDREN HAVE at least a few rituals. Toddlers come to expect routines in feeding and bathing; four- and five-year-olds show rituals involving bedtime stories and the careful arrangement of their toys. How is a parent to decide whether these behaviors indicate OCD? A 1990 study, "Childhood Rituals: Normal Development or Obsessive-Compulsive Symptoms?" determined the following general guidelines.

Normal rituals begin at age two and begin to fade by five or six, whereas OCD rarely begins earlier than five and then progressively worsens. Normal childhood rituals commonly involve orderliness and superstition (especially "lucky numbers"), whereas OCD usually entails washing, checking, or repeating. Normal rituals are accepted by children as normal, whereas OCD is regarded as something that sets them apart. And normal rituals can be skipped without a problem, whereas omitting an OCD ritual causes marked distress.

The factor of overriding importance in deciding whether any type of childhood rituals should be taken seriously is whether they are interfering significantly in a child's life. If rituals are detracting from a child's ability to learn, have fun, and develop social relationships, they may well represent clinical OCD and should be evaluated. It should be kept in mind that OCD children, like adults, will usually attempt to hide their rituals. Here are some of the early signs to look for.

- Large blocks of time spent alone in the bedroom or bathroom.
- Excessive time taken to perform simple tasks.
- Overconcern for minor details.
- Routinely staying up late to finish homework.
- Strong emotional outbursts in reaction to trivial matters.
- Avoidance of certain activities.
- A need for constant reassurance, particularly about cleanliness.

TREATING OCD IN CHILDHOOD AND ADOLESCENCE

BACK IN THE days when Jerry developed OCD, mental health professionals, especially psychiatrists, sometimes did more harm than good. Back then, parents were blamed for many psychiatric problems that have since been identified as clear-cut neurobiological brain disorders. When I started psychiatric training in 1971, Tourette's syndrome, now known to be genetic, was attributed to parental rejection. Autism, now recognized as a severe biochemical disease of childhood, was attributed to the psychological effects of a chillingly remote "refrigerator mother." Schizophrenia, now also known to be a biochemical brain disease, was ascribed to a "schizophrenogenic mother" who "double-binded" her child by simultaneously requesting one behavior while nonverbally reinforcing its opposite. And OCD, it was hypothesized, was due to "an overdose of parental perfectionism." Inestimable damage was done to both parents and children by these erroneous psychodynamic theories.

What would have happened, one might speculate, if Jerry had developed OCD in the 1990s rather than the 1950s, and if he had received good treatment? In all likelihood, his life would have been dramatically different. Behavior therapy and the SRI medications, the same two treatments that are effective in adults, are also markedly helpful in children and adolescents. The largest study to date on the treatment of severe OCD in this age group found that combined treatment with behavior therapy and medications resulted in half of the patients being markedly improved and four fifths significantly so.

SRI medications have been used in the treatment of childhood OCD for approximately a decade. Whether used singly or in conjunction with behavior therapy, most children are significantly helped by these agents. Clomipramine (Anafranil), the most studied SRI in children, has been proven to reduce OCD symptoms an average of 30 percent—usually sufficient to make OCD tolerable. Placebos, sugar pills, on the other hand, have little effect. All the SRI medications in current use for the treatment of adult OCD—fluoxetine (Prozac), sertraline (Luvox), paroxetine (Paxil), and fluvoxetine (Luvox)—appear to be equally effective in children.

In treating childood and adolescent OCD, the SRI medications should be prescribed cautiously. There is insufficient data at this point to completely rule out the possibility that they may cause damage to the developing nervous system. Medication treatment should not, however, be sacrificed out of excessive and irrational fears. The SRI medications have been used by tens of millions of people, so far have proven very safe, and are highly unlikely to possess an undetected major toxicity. A great deal more damage is done, in my opinion, by doctors and parents who withhold SRI medications than by those who employ them. Given the problems in social development that can occur as a result of childhood OCD, it is especially important to treat this age group aggressively. If any of my three young children developed obsessions and compulsions that interfered with learning, having fun, or developing social relationships, I would first try behavior therapy, and then if the symptoms were not adequately controlled I would quickly start medications.

Fortunately, behavior therapy has proven to be very effective in children. The general approach used is similar to that with adults, the goal being exposure to obsessions and prevention of compulsions. In treating children, a key point to emphasize is the separation of individual identity from OCD symptoms. This emphasis allows children to feel good about themselves even when suffering bad symptoms, and it sets the stage for actively fighting the disorder with behavior therapy. Helping a child gain distance from OCD can be accomplished by presenting the disorder as a "short circuit," or a "jammed" area of the brain that keeps on sending messages when it shouldn't—something the child is not responsible for but he or she can fix by resisting the performance of rituals. John March and Karen Mulle's excellent book on the treatment of childhood OCD, *How I Chased OCD off My Land,* suggests asking the child to give OCD a name, such as "germy," or "schoolyard bully." The child is then encouraged to look on behavior therapy for OCD as a battle with a bad guy. The therapist is the coach and the parents are cheerleaders. This approach works so well that OCD is often controlled after just a few sessions. A recent case illustrates how easily many children with OCD can be treated.

The Case of Darren

"HE COMES TO the table with his hands raised like a surgeon!" Darren's mother complained, shooting a glance at her slightly embarrassed but otherwise serene eight-year-old. She further explained that her son spent ten minutes washing his hands before each meal and that he excused himself from the table mid-meal to wash them some more. Because of his reddened and cracked hands, an appointment had been scheduled with a dermatologist.

Other embarrassing behaviors prevented the family from eating out. If served a hamburger, Darren insisted on holding it in a napkin and ate only the part that never touched the napkin. French fries and potato chips he took directly from the plate with his mouth.

The strange behaviors were not limited to mealtime. Darren had also stopped playing with all his battery-operated toys, announcing that he might get sick from them; and he quit riding his bike after his wheel came too near a battery.

Darren's mother assured me that he had never before had any type of mental, or physical, problems. His development was entirely normal, and he was doing well in school. He was an especially loving child who still enjoyed spending hours in his mother's lap. This mother was in shock. She had no idea what was going on.

When I questioned Darren as to why he was behaving in this strange manner, at first he fidgeted and said he didn't know. But when I pressed him for an answer, he allowed, "I'm scared I'll die or get sick from eating something." In a hemming and hawing manner, he also added, "My mind is telling me that I will be sick from batteries. I can't get that out of my head."

In doing therapy with Darren, I took care to conceptualize OCD not as an embarrassing personal weakness but rather as a short circuit of the brain that was not his fault. I emphasized to him that if he didn't actively resist this brain problem, it would only get worse. Darren, like most children, easily grasped this idea. Next, I encouraged Darren to look on this problem as a war and to pick suitable names for OCD and himself. The battle was soon joined between OCD, the "bad guy," and himself, "a Texas Ranger." Darren's job was to fight the bad guy by not performing the rituals. A family meeting was held, with Darren present, to agree on how much help family members should give. His mother assisted by coaching him on his eating, timing him in the bathroom, and sitting with him while he gradually exposed himself to batteries.

All that proved necessary was to meet with mother and child for a total of five sessions. Quick progress was made with the presenting rituals and also with two new obsessions that cropped up, a fear of guns and a fear of bees. Once they caught on to the behavior therapy strategy for combating OCD, mother and son carried it out in efficient, military fashion. By the end of the fifth session, Darren's rituals were so diminished that they were in need of no further treatment. It never became necessary to use medications. Darren's case is not unusual—such positive outcomes are more the rule.

Dealing with OCD at Home

BROADLY SPEAKING, OCD parents err in one of two ways: assisting with rituals or becoming angered by them. Both of these responses are completely understandable; indeed, they are the common and natural reactions to OCD. Yet, indulging a child's rituals actually reinforces the habits, while taking a hard line on OCD increases stress, which also exacerbates the problem. Parents become drawn into a vicious cycle: Their natural responses to OCD symptoms—even if well intentioned—produce the contrary effect of making rituals worse.

A student in my OCD group, Aileen, recalls the moment during her seventh-grade year when she woke late at night with a start, consumed by the thought that she could grab a knife and stab her parents while they slept. For a week, she fought to get the terrifying idea out of her mind, but it only got worse. Finally, she tearfully confessed it to her parents. "Don't worry," they reassured her. "You, of all people, would never do anything like that." But the next night the obsession returned and she had to ask again. Reassurance quickly became a ritual, and soon Aileen was spending one full hour every day telling her mother her fears. When her mother tried to curtail the litany, Aileen would beg to be heard, and her mother would always give in. Severe reassurance rituals continued throughout junior and senior high school, greatly interfering in the lives of both Aileen and her mother.

Another student, Danielle, remembers when at age twelve she started to scrub her skin raw in response to irrational fears of dirtiness. "It was like I was in another world when I was in the bathroom," she recalls. "First I had to get every bit of dirt off, and then I had to get all the soap off, and I could never be sure if I got it all." Every night she spent two hours in the bathtub. Her mother's response was to yell, "Stop it! What's the matter with you!" Danielle's most painful memory of childhood was of lying in the bathtub and hearing her mother, in the next room, ridiculing her to others. "I can't believe how long she takes in the bathroom!" her mother would laugh. Danielle soon developed severe problems with depression and self-esteem. Finding refuge with the drug crowd, she "outdid them all" with her use of alcohol and marijuana. Later she required extensive drug rehabilitation.

The successful approach to OCD involves avoiding the extremes of indulgence and disapproval. Rather than reacting with anger, or worse yet ridicule, parents should take a sympathetic attitude and avoid any personal criticism of the child. They should encourage a discussion about worries. Parents can gently inquire, for instance, "You seem to be doing things over and over. Lots of people do this because they are afraid something bad will happen. Have you been worried about something?"

Supporting the child, however, does not mean enabling rituals. The goal is for parents to completely stop participation in any of a child's compulsions. A critical step in behavior therapy is establishing a mutually acceptable contract between child and parent regarding how to respond to rituals. It might be agreed, for instance, that when the child is involved in excessive hand washing, the parent should intervene and help the child to stop.

"OCD and Parenting," a pamphlet available through the OC Foundation, makes the following general suggestions for dealing with OCD children.

- Create an atmosphere in which the child is comfortable talking about feelings, especially worries.
- Don't give in to demands to provide unnecessary reassurance or to cooperate with other rituals.

- Encourage the child to take reasonable risks.
- Demonstrate, by example, that anxiety is "no big deal."
- Work on co-parenting; don't allow the child to "divide and conquer."

What About Siblings?

THE TRUTH IS that brothers and sisters are seldom sympathetic toward OCD. A nine-year-old girl teased her twin brother about his counting rituals: "Why do you do that? That's really weird!" A female college student who suffered reassurance rituals in junior high school recalls, "My brothers and sisters were terrible. They were flat-out mean. I would ask my sister if the house was safe, and all she would say was, 'Won't you ever shut up and stop bothering me?'"

In cases of severe childhood OCD, siblings must be brought into treatment, educated about the nature of OCD, and coached on helpful ways to respond. In cases of milder OCD, when the sufferer has been successfully hiding his or her symptoms, it may be best to leave siblings out.

THE SPOUSE WITH OCD

I FIRST MET Matt when he accompanied his wife, Tina, to her third visit with me, on an evening in March. A big, slow-moving twenty-five-year-old dressed in work clothes and rugged boots, Matt had just finished up another twelve-hour day as a self-employed trucker in the logging business—one of the few booming industries in the Appalachian mountains of central Pennsylvania. It was a new job for Matt, a bold step to have taken with a pregnant wife at home, but it was turning out well. His income was already double what it had been working at WalMart.

I asked Matt to tell me about Tina's problem: what he had observed, what he thought was causing it, and how he dealt with it. Matt spoke in a careful and deliberate manner, pausing frequently to look at the floor while he searched for the exact words to express himself.

The major difficulties had begun six months ago, right after the birth of their first child. Before that, during two years of dating and another of marriage, Matt had recognized that Tina worried excessively, fussed abnormally about small details, and was overly concerned about cleanliness. He had concluded, in fact, that she was "basically lazy" because of her inability to keep to an orderly work schedule. Yet he had adjusted to these shortcomings. He badgered Tina, reasoned with her, and, when all else failed, put up with her. This, he figured, was all part of being married. But now the situation had worsened immensely. Now, he could no longer deal with it. "I want to be honest with you, Doc," Matt said. "I'm a decently patient person, but I'm ready to leave."

Matt told me of the expectations he had held. He and Tina agreed they would have a "traditional marriage": She would stay home with the children; he would be the breadwinner. When he arrived from work, she would have supper ready. But it wasn't working out that way. She was worrying all day long, doing "next to nothing," and nothing he said made any difference. Not only that, but her worries no longer made any sense. "I want a normal marriage," Matt lamented, "where people fight about money, not about crazy stuff."

Worst of all were Tina's almost constant fears of contaminating the baby. What if she changed his diapers incorrectly? What if she cleaned his crib insufficiently? What if rust from the can opener poisoned the formula, or if, when screwing on the cap of the baby bottle, she pushed too hard and caused pieces of glass to land inside? To make sure the baby bottle nipples were clean, Tina would stand over a pan of boiling water, repeatedly dunking the nipples down into the water for a half an hour or more, until they were, as Matt put it, "gummy and half decomposed." Then, after taking them out, she would fear that the paper towel she set them on had in the meantime become dirty, necessitating that she put the nipples back into the boiling water and start over. Sometimes, Tina brought Matt into this ritual, insisting that he do the boiling. Her fear of spreading germs caused her to wash her hands many times an hour, and her skin was now chapped and red. The hot water, Matt complained, was almost constantly in use. He knew this for sure because it immediately came out scalding whenever he turned on a spigot.

Obsessions of harm were also severe for Tina. What if the light switch was not quite off and as a result a fire might start? Tina would compulsively turn the switch on and off until she had attained an adequate feeling of certainty, only then to think, What if she had by now played with it too long? She would call Matt to check—even in the middle of the night. "It drives me up the wall," Matt said in exasperation. "I feel like garbage the next morning." Another daily obsession: What if the stove wasn't turned all the way off? "We'll be in the car halfway to Altoona," Matt explained, "and she'll insist that we turn around and check the stove." Yet even returning to check could not quench her uncertainty; she would continue to ask Matt repeatedly what would happen if the stove was not turned off.

It was the endless requests for reassurance that bothered Matt the most. As soon as he pulled his car into the driveway, he was met with a barrage of confessions, concerns, and requests for reassurance. Tina would yell out, "Guess what happened to me today?" The baby had walked on the carpet where it was dirty, had come too close to an ant trap, or had touched the formula with his finger. She had turned the light on and off too many times, changed the diapers the wrong way, or contaminated the soup. She had to get these worries off her chest, they weighed her down so badly; and she wouldn't quit until everything had been told. She would beg Matt to listen to her; and if he refused, she would yell at him: It was his baby and he needed to know!

Overwhelmed, Matt responded in different ways, depending largely on his own mood. Sometimes he would hear her out, nodding, giving her the comfort she wanted. Sometimes he would attempt to demonstrate to her that there was no problem. "If the light switch were on fire, you'd see smoke coming out of it," Matt would say. "Do you see any smoke? Okay, you've answered your own question." Increasingly, though, Matt was blowing up in anger.

A particular compulsion developed which crystallized Matt's conviction that he could not stay married to Tina in her present condition. Tina would have the thought—even though she was on birth control and had not missed her period—that she was pregnant and that she was sitting in a posture—bent over too far, back not straight, or leaning to one side abnormally—that was harmful to the baby inside her. Tina knew full well that this was bizarre. Still, it seemed so real and her fear was so great that she would wiggle, stretch, move back and forth, and get up and down repeatedly so that no harm would come to the baby she feared was inside her. And she would have to tell Matt all about it.

By the end of that session it was clear that Matt was very pessimistic about the situation. Tina was downcast. But I was quite hopeful. I explained to the two of them that Tina's severe OCD symptoms had been triggered by the unique stresses of being a new mother and were being exacerbated by marital discord. There was every reason to believe that with behavior therapy, medications, family meetings, and time, her symptoms would greatly improve.

Fortunately, in addition to being admirably honest and straightforward, Matt truly wanted to save the marriage. At my request, he accompanied Tina to several of our early sessions. I had two goals for Matt: to understand about OCD and to help with behavior therapy. Learning that Tina had a "chemical disorder" was a revelation to Matt. Finally, he could make some sense of it all. Yet he was still often critical. Tina wasn't getting the meals ready in time, or keeping up with the checkbook, or getting the housework done. He would also complain that she was not putting enough effort into her behavioral assignments. "You have to get off your butt and try some things," he would say. I tried to point out that although Tina might be lazy, it was not the cause of her rituals, and furthermore, anyone having OCD plus a new baby would be worn out. Matt never acknowledged the truth of that, but at least our sessions provided a place for Matt to vent his frustrations, and as therapy progressed he became more sympathetic.

As for behavior therapy, like most OCD family members, Matt was delighted to learn that it is best not to participate in rituals. The three of us took a careful look at the situation and agreed on a realistic approach to limiting his involvement. In some instances Matt was able to cease participating immediately. He stopped washing the baby's hands and turning the car around to check the home. For other rituals it was best to remove Tina from the situation. Matt took over making formula, and they bought a timer for the lights. Still other rituals had to be negotiated as therapy progressed. Tina's reassurance compulsions were a special problem. We tried to set limits: Tina could have half an hour when Matt got home to vent her fears to him, or ten minutes every hour after dinner. Yet Tina, inevitably, would badger Matt for reassurance until he either became angry or gave in. Fortunately, however, her reassurance rituals gradually lessened to a degree that they were tolerable.

By the end of four months of behavior therapy, medications, and family meetings, Tina had progressed from full-time to part-time OCD. Since then she has continued to make further gains. The family is now stable.

I asked Matt what was most beneficial to him in our treatment. "It was a big relief," Matt said, "when I finally understood exactly what was going on. She couldn't control her OCD, but we could treat it, and I could live with it in a normal way."

I then asked him the best methods he had found for handling Tina's OCD.

First of all, I keep straight the difference between her compulsions and her laziness. When she doesn't do the housekeeping and bookkeeping, I can ride her about it. That's laziness. But her fears about dirt, electricity, or germs are in another category—that's the OCD. Then of the compulsions, there are certain ones I can buck her on, and others I can't. For instance, I always make her turn off the lights and take care of the baby's stuff—she'll complain a little bit, but she'll do it. But I still have to give reassurance sometimes. I've learned that it's better for me to just say, "It's okay," than to cause a scene.

What advice would Matt give a friend whose spouse had OCD? "I'd tell him to go and see a good doctor. Seriously, that would be the most important thing. Learn what OCD is. Get medications. After that, go along with the rituals to some extent in order to keep the peace. And don't scream, that only makes it worse."

As can well be imagined, being married to an OCD sufferer can turn into an ordeal even worse than having a child with the disorder. A recent study published in the *Journal of Sex and Marital Therapy* reports that more than 60 percent of OCD marriages are significantly troubled. Another study finds that 80 percent of OCDers' spouses become involved in their rituals. Interestingly, other studies, seemingly in contrast to these findings, indicate that OCD marriages are on the average just as happy as non-OCD unions. What this suggests is that the agreeable personality characteristics of OCDers often make up for the problems caused by their rituals.

The most crucial factor in determining adjustment in OCD marriages is the severity of the sufferer's obsessive-compulsive disorder. "Full-timers," those who spend virtually every waking moment fighting obsessions or carrying out rituals, do poorly in marriage. Males who fall into this category, in fact, tend never to marry at all. Women full-timers usually do get married but then end up either divorced or in chronically maladjusted relationships. The strains of being married to a full-time OCDer can be almost unimaginable. A husband or wife can become a tyrant in the household, ruling family members according to the dictates of obsessions. I once treated a woman who prevented family members from using the bathrooms in their own house; they had to use a gas station's, instead.

"Part-timers," on the other hand, usually have normal marriages. Mild to moderate OCD is no harder on a marriage than the same degree of depression, and is probably not as bad, because of the OCD sufferer's special facility to hide rituals and function normally despite them. As for intimacy, it used to be thought, on the basis of Freudian theories, that OCD sufferers were almost always sexually maladjusted. Psychoanalysts contended that the obsessional's excessive need for control caused avoidance of sexual contact because of fear of failure to perform. But two recent studies document that there is no particular problem with sexuality in OCD marriages.

The distinction between full-time and part-time OCD points up the importance of therapy, because what effective treatment most often accomplishes is that very sort of partial reduction in symptoms, a change from overwhelming to manageable OCD.

How a spouse deals with OCD can contribute greatly to whether therapy is successful; in particular, this often determines whether the gains of therapy continue after treatment. A 1993 study by Gail Stektee of the Boston University School of Social Work found that patients with severe OCD who benefited from treatment were significantly more likely to relapse when spouses were critical of their condition, taking the attitude that the suffer *should* be able to control rituals on his or her own. At the same time, the study showed that when spouses expressed support, initiated rational discussions about rituals, and urged confrontation with feared obsessional situations, OCD sufferers maintained treatment gains.

In my experience, perhaps one fourth of OCD spouses, for whatever reason, will have nothing to do with their partner's disorder. They will attempt to ignore OCD, and when that is not possible, they will convey an attitude of disgust. They will discourage psychiatric treatment and refuse any discussion. Although such a response is unfortunate, it doesn't have to be devastating. A number of my patients with severe OCD have been able to do very well in treatment despite getting nothing but a cold shoulder from their spouses. Raymond, whose case was presented in Chapter 1, is an example.

Yet it is invaluable for a spouse to actively support treatment. OCDers are so guilt-prone and overly responsible that they can easily be turned away from therapy by the slightest intimation that they are wasting money, depriving the family of their time, or getting addicted to medications. Often it is extremely helpful for a spouse to take an active role in behavior therapy, helping the OCDer to carry out exposure and response prevention tasks. This sort of involvement does not require a great sacrifice of time or effort. Behavior therapy is such a powerful treatment that just a little help can make a great difference.

The most important step for any family member to take is becoming educated about the disorder. Talking to someone about OCD isn't enough. So much has changed in our conceptualization of OCD over the last decade that even mental health professionals may not be up to date. The Obsessive-Compulsive Foundation is an excellent source of up-to-date books and pamphlets on OCD. The foundation also sponsors numerous conferences. Perhaps the best introduction to dealing with OCD in the family is the pamphlet, "Learning to Live with OCD," which contains the following helpful guidelines for all family members.

GUIDELINES FOR OCD FAMILY MEMBERS

1. Avoid personal criticism and angry outbursts. Deal with OCD as you would deal with diabetes. The sufferer should not be blamed for the symptoms.

2. Support therapy. Make it clear that treatment is worth the cost. If the OCD sufferer hasn't yet seen a competent therapist, take whatever steps are necessary to find one (see Appendix D).

3. Be a medications advocate. Medications may be rejected out of a belief that taking medication is a sign of weakness, out of a fear of addiction, or out of an obsession that the medication is contaminated. All are equally false. "Talk up" medications, because they are usually a key to successful therapy.

4. Renegotiate regularly how family members are to deal with OCD. Address specifics, such as when and how to intervene to stop rituals, as well as how family members can keep their lives normal.

5. When confronting rituals, keep communications clear and simple. It is seldom helpful at this point to enter into a debate on the irrationality of a ritual. It is usually best just to say, "What I think is that this is an OCD ritual and it shouldn't be performed."

6. Recognize "small" improvements. Don't overlook the strong effort necessary to make even a little headway against OCD. Verbal praise is a strong reinforcer—particularly for OCDers, who tend to be permanently entrenched people-pleasers. Let the OCD sufferer know that his or her hard work is noticed.

7. Be sensitive to moods and to sources of stress. Although it is extremely important to set limits on rituals, it is just as important to know when to back off. Bad feelings make OCD worse. Flexibility is the key.

8. Avoid day-to-day comparisons. OCD runs a waxing and waning course, and comparing current symptoms to a day ago, or a month ago, or even a year ago, means little. Furthermore, overly sensitive OCDers often take comparisons as criticism. Limit comparisons to noting how much improvement there has been since the rituals were at their very worst.

9. Avoid comparing an affected family member with another OCD sufferer. Some OCDers have the equivalent of lifelong insulin-dependent diabetes, which will always cause symptoms, whereas others have the equivalent of mild, adult-onset diabetes, which is easily cured.

10. Keep the family routine as normal as possible. Disruption tends to occur when family members are either drawn into rituals or become overly protective toward the OCD sufferer.

8

MAKING SENSE OF
SENSELESS SYMPTOMS

OBSESSIONS AND COMPULSIONS seem uniquely puzzling. How can intelligent people allow themselves to be upended by thoughts that they know are senseless? And how can they waste hours and hours performing silly rituals?

No other psychiatric symptoms are so mysterious. The imaginary voices heard by a young man with schizophrenia can be seen, without stretching the reasoning capacities too much, as a breakdown in a mechanism in the brain that separates true sensory perceptions from daydreams and fantasies. Similarly, the loss of capacity for enjoyment, decline in interests, and hopeless withdrawal of major depression can be seen as a failure in the mechanism that controls the amplitude of mood swings. The attacks of shaking, rapid heartbeat, and shortness of breath characteristic of panic disorder can be readily understood as excessive discharges of the body's "fight or flight" response.

But the senseless rituals and self-tormenting thoughts of obsessive-compulsive disease have defied a satisfying explanation. Particularly enigmatic are harm obsessions, such as Sherry's terrifying impulse to stab her daughter, an idea that would not seem to have anything whatsoever to do with a normal mental process, however broken or distorted. Puzzling, too, are destructive compulsions, such as Raymond's hours a day of checking. If Raymond recognizes it's senseless and harmful to check so much, why can't he stop?

Freud, who called OCD the most fascinating of all mental disorders, admitted that it was also the one he never mastered. "I must confess," the great psychoanalyst wrote in his celebrated 1909 article, "Notes upon a Case of Obsessional Neurosis," "that I have not yet succeeded in completely penetrating a severe case of obsessional neurosis. . . . If we endeavor to penetrate more deeply into its nature, we still have to rely upon doubtful assumptions and unconfirmed suppositions." Esteemed British psychiatrist Sir Aubrey Lewis went so far as to suggest, "It may well be that obsessional illness cannot be understood without understanding the very nature of man." OCD has a self-destructive aspect that eludes analysis in terms of a normal, mechanistic process gone awry.

In Western culture, the time-honored explanation for obsessions and compulsions has been that they are caused by attacks from the Devil. The psychologist and philosopher William James noted, "The lives of the saints are full of blasphemous obsessions, ascribed invariably to the direct agency of Satan." This view, it must be admitted, does have a certain logic, since obsessions are, it is true, experienced as coming from outside of us and forcing themselves upon us. In any case, it was not challenged until the late 1700s, when psychiatric disorders first began to be approached from a medical standpoint.

Early medical theories on the cause of OCD involved a certain "psychic energy," which was thought to flow through the nerves just as blood flows through the veins. The most authoritative psychiatric textbook of its day, Henry Maudsley's *Pathology of the Mind,* published in 1895, described obsessions and compulsions as resulting from "lowered energy in the inmost elements of the mental organization." OCD was due to "sluggish molecular processes" that caused a "lack of nervous vitality." Maudsley attributed the problem to heredity.

At the turn of the century, the great French psychiatrist Pierre Janet published the most complete work ever written on obsessions and compulsions, the extraordinarily detailed and insightful two-volume *Les obsessions et la psychasthenia.* Janet hypothesized that OCD was caused by a selective loss of psychic energy in the highest mental functions, those dealing with will and attention. Such advanced capacities required more mental energy, he suggested, than lower functions such as emotions, memories, and muscle movements. Janet likened the various mental capacities to different types of machines: the more complicated, the more energy required to run them. Thus when mental energy ran low, a condition Janet termed *psychasthenia,* the capacities of will and attention were affected first. The result was excessive doubt and a loss of control over voluntary behaviors—symptoms of OCD. Janet's observation that uncertainty is central to OCD was particularly astute. In France, OCD is sometimes still referred to as *la folie de doute,* the doubting disease.

Yet it was Sigmund Freud's psychoanalytic hypothesis of obsessive-compulsive disorder that became widely accepted in America. Freud published fourteen major papers on OCD, more than on any other topic, and he left us the most complete and famous case history of the disease, his 1909 analysis of "Rat Man," which will be discussed in Chapter 11. Like his predecessors, Freud espoused the idea of psychic energy. To Freud, however, it was not an insufficiency in this regard that caused OCD; rather, it was that energy became bottled up in the unconscious and could not get out. Freud taught that OCD began in childhood when a boy or girl instinctively wanted to behave in a sexual or aggressive manner but was prevented by a parent from doing so. The resulting parent–child conflict, if not satisfactorily resolved, resulted in "repression" of the conflict, as well as of the conflict's energy, into the unconscious. This energy, needing to be discharged, was finally released later in life through pathological attachment to various thoughts and behaviors, turning them into obsessions and compulsions.

By the time I was in medical school, most psychiatrists favored a derivative of Freudian theory referred to as "ego psychology." Developed by Heinz Hartman, George Vallient, and others in the 1950s and 1960s, ego psychology emphasizes the present rather than the past and stresses the importance of unconscious defense mechanisms—dynamic, basically adaptive mental devices that serve to keep people from being overwhelmed by conflicts between instincts, internalized prohibitions, and the real world. Ego psychology attributes OCD's symptoms mainly to troubles with three defensive mechanisms: intellectualization, where an instinctual wish is let into consciousness without accompanying feeling; displacement, where feelings are redirected from the object that caused them to another situation or person; and reaction formation, where a person's behavior is diametrically opposed to an unconscious impulse.

None of these theories, in my opinion, gets to the heart of OCD's mysterious, self-defeating nature. Those of us who have suffered OCD know from our own experiences that obsessions have less the feel of defensive maneuvers than of enemy attacks. In that sense, none of these medical hypotheses account for obsessions and compulsions as well as attributing them to Satan.

Fortunately, the last twenty years have seen a burst of scientific research into the nature of obsessions and compulsions. Much of the work has been carried out by clinical and experimental psychologists using behavioral, rather than psychoanalytic, or Freudian-based, approaches. In general, what behaviorists study is that which can be readily observed and measured. Behaviorists avoid the unconscious—in fact, many do not believe it exists. These studies do not provide a final answer to the mystery of OCD, or even a single unifying theory for obsessions and compulsions, but the results from four very different areas of research do offer clues that, when taken together, add up to what I think, and my patients by and large agree, is an objective view of OCD that is useful and makes sense.

CLUE 1: INTRUSIVE, UNACCEPTABLE THOUGHTS ARE COMMONPLACE

TO LAY A foundation for making sense of OCD, it is first of all necessary to understand that the thoughts that plague OCD sufferers are not, by themselves, abnormal. In 1978, psychologist Stanley Rachman of the University of British Columbia, the world's leading authority on obsessions and coauthor of the 1980 text *Obsessions and Compulsions* and the 1992 reference *Obsessive-Compulsive Disorder: The Facts,* asked 124 students, hospital workers, and nurses: "Do you ever get thoughts or impulses that are intrusive and unacceptable?"

Fully 80 percent answered yes, they had such thoughts, usually at least once a week. Dr. Rachman and his coworkers then transcribed these "unacceptable thoughts" on paper and compared them with the obsessions of OCD patients. Guess what? The experts could not tell the difference between the unacceptable thoughts of average people and the obsessions of OCD patients.

Take a look at a sample taken from Rachman's classic study. These are intrusive, recurrent thoughts that people recognize as inappropriate and that they do not want to think. Yet most of us have at least one or two of them regularly. I've had four of these myself. See anything familiar?

THE MOST COMMON UNACCEPTABLE THOUGHTS

1. Urge to jump onto the rails when the train is approaching.
2. Urge to disrupt peace in a gathering.
3. Identifying with a person being executed.
4. Image of family being greatly harmed by chemicals.
5. Urge to be violent toward small children.
6. Image of walking along and suddenly discovering you're naked.
7. Image of accident occurring to a loved one.
8. Urge to jump in front of a bus.
9. Urge to commit "unnatural" sexual acts.
10. Urge to jump from the top of a tall building.
11. Urge to crash the car when driving.
12. Idea that harm has befallen someone near and dear.
13. Wishing that someone close to you will be harmed.
14. Urge to commit a robbery.

The remarkable conclusion is this: The large majority of people experience thoughts that are exactly the same in content as obsessions. This has now been verified by over a dozen studies. For instance, a 1992 study detailed the percentages of all people who report fifty-two different types of unacceptable thoughts. Here is a sampling:

- 55 percent of us have impulses to run our cars off the road.
- 42 percent of us have urges to jump from high places.

- 25 percent of us have ideas that our phones are contaminated.
- 13 percent of us have images of exposing ourselves in public.
- 13 percent of us have thoughts to fatally stab friends.
- 8 percent of us have unwanted impulses to stab family members.

Almost everyone experiences unwelcome thoughts—the guy walking down the street, the woman in front of you at the supermarket—it's just that for most people these thoughts cause no problems. They are normal, and that single fact is for OCD patients often the most comforting insight gained from months of therapy.

CLUE 2: INTRUSIVE, UNACCEPTABLE THOUGHTS ARE MADE WORSE BY TRYING NOT TO THINK THEM

A WELL-KNOWN EXPERIMENT makes clear an important mental law. The Russian novelist Leo Tolstoy wrote that when he was a child, his older brother once dared him to stand in a corner until he could stop thinking of a white bear. The difficulty involved in carrying out this challenge impressed the young Tolstoy greatly. Indeed, trying not to think of a particular object sets into motion a frustrating, and intriguing, mental procedure. Wherever you are, just stop reading, and for the next thirty seconds, TRY NOT TO THINK OF A WHITE BEAR.

Done? Were you able to do it? Not likely. Psychologist Daniel Wegner devotes an entire, fascinating book (*White Bears and Other Unwanted Thoughts*) to the implications of this test. In a 1987 experiment at Trinity University in Texas, Wegner studied two groups of students. One group heard a talk about white bears, the other was told not to think about them. As you might guess, the group told not to think about white bears had bear thoughts throughout the day, whereas the other group rapidly forgot about bears. Not only that, but in a second phase of the experiment, when the two groups were both instructed to think white bear thoughts, the group who had previously been told not to think such thoughts had many more thoughts of bears.

Other experiments have demonstrated similar outcomes. Researchers in England instructed a group of subjects to stop thinking

troublesome, intrusive thoughts by switching their attention to another thought; then they compared these results with those of a
matched group instructed to endure such thoughts. Later in the day,
the group that had tried to avoid the intrusive thoughts experienced
a much stronger recurrence of them.

The point is, when you try not to think a certain thought,
whether by putting it out of your mind or by forcing your attention
to something else, you only end up, eventually, focusing on it more
intently. This psychological law explains a number of seemingly
paradoxical findings: that people who try not to think about a de-
ceased spouse take longer to get over their loss; that surgery patients
who try not to think about an upcoming operation can become
more upset afterward; that dieters who try to escape thoughts about
food can be the most likely to go on binges and become overweight;
and that incest victims who actively block out thoughts of their
traumas are those most tormented by intrusive memories.

Why do our minds bring back painful thoughts against our will?
Studies of post-traumatic responses offer a hint. Pilots returning
from combat missions, it has been shown, often replay a battle over
and over in their mind's eye before they can let it go. People who
have witnessed a terrorist attack frequently suffer intrusive thoughts
and nightmares until they adjust. Rape victims develop flashbacks
until psychological healing occurs. It is clear that instant replays of
traumatic events are somehow necessary for our adapting to them.

The landmark studies on post-traumatic thoughts were done by
psychiatrist Mardi Horowitz at the University of California in 1977.
Students were shown grisly movies of industrial accidents, such as
machine operators getting their fingers sawed off. Afterward, the
students had intrusive unpleasant images of the accidents, images
that recurred over and over, until gradually they began to lose their
unpleasantness and fade away. Horowitz concluded from his experiments that some sort of "mental processing" is necessary for us to
come to terms with traumatic memories.

Horowitz hypothesizes that this processing is carried out through
a computerlike, match-mismatch mechanism for assimilating and
accommodating new information. When the memory of a traumatic
event comes to mind, it is compared with preexisting wishes and

fears and appraised in relation to coping capacity. If there is a match, if the memory harmonizes with preexisting associations about the self and the world, then the memory is quickly stored. But if there is a mismatch, if the post-traumatic memory does not fit with existing information, then a process is initiated by which additional associations are formed, integrating the new information with the old.

Horowitz's theory is used to explain a number of current therapies for post-traumatic stress syndrome. The widely publicized technique EMDR, eye movement desensitization and reprogramming, for instance, utilizing the idea that REM sleep is the prime time for processing of post-traumatic memories, seeks to speed up the processing by inducing eye movements similar to those of REM sleep. EMDR's founder, psychologist Francine Shapiro explains: "When a trauma occurs, the processing mechanism gets disrupted. By inducing the eye movements, we accelerate the processing."

Most experts now agree that obsessions, like post-traumatic thoughts, repeat themselves again and again in order to be further processed. If you try to bypass this mechanism, to skip out on the replay of a painful thought, the result is that the thought is brought back again, and even stronger, so that next time you'll let the processing be done. Harvard's Pitman concludes in a 1987 review article, "The core problem in OCD is the persistence of mismatch." It is a person's inability to complete the processing of intrusive, unacceptable thoughts that lies at the heart of OCD.

Thus, an obsession is a struggle between a part of the brain that wants to dismiss an unacceptable thought from consciousness and another part that wants to process it further. The word "obsession" is, after all, derived from "to besiege." It's a battle.

CLUE 3: OCD SUFFERERS EVALUATE UNACCEPTABLE THOUGHTS WITH AN EXAGGERATED SENSE OF PERSONAL RESPONSIBILITY

WE HAVE SEEN that it is normal for unacceptable thoughts to come to mind and also normal for them to recur and to increase in strength when people try not to think them. What, then, makes

OCD sufferers turn these "normal" thoughts into self-tormenting obsessions? What makes them the people who fall into white-bear traps?

Evidence mounts that a basic abnormality of OCD sufferers lies in the way they evaluate their thoughts. Pioneering researchers in cognitive psychology, including psychiatrist Aaron Beck and co-workers at the University of Pennsylvania, demonstrated in the 1960s and 1970s that there is an automatic, almost instantaneous, evaluative process lying outside our awareness that assigns different levels of importance, or attentional value, to intrusive thoughts. Researchers applying cognitive psychology's findings to the development of obsessions have concluded that, as Stanley Rachman put it, "Intrusive, unacceptable thoughts become unduly significant only to the extent that the affected person attaches special meaning to them. The majority of people dismiss or ignore their unwanted thoughts and regard them as dross. However, once a person attaches important meaning to these unwanted thoughts, they tend to become distressing and adhesive."

Most people seem to approach their intrusive, unacceptable thoughts with an attitude something like: "There's another nutty thought. I'm not going to let it bother me." Dr. Rachman tells the story of a memorable subject, a young female psychology student who routinely experienced "outrageously promiscuous and violent unwanted images and urges." Although they may have been shocking to the examiners, these ideas didn't trouble the young woman at all. "Her tolerance for thoughts and impulses that most people would regard as antisocial or immoral," the researcher noted, "was seemingly unlimited." But that's not the way it is for OCD sufferers.

In the last decade, research by psychologist Paul Salkovskis of Oxford, England, and by other scientists in Cambridge, England, as well as in Canada, Australia, and the United States, has identified a single, specific abnormality in the way OCD sufferers evaluate their intrusive, unacceptable thoughts. As mentioned in Chapter 3, OCD sufferers tend to take excessive personal responsibility for the bad things they think might happen. Salkovskis puts it this way: "Obsessions occur when patients interpret the occurrence and content of an intrusive thought as an indication that they might be responsible for harm to themselves or others unless they take action to prevent it."

This theory—referred to by Rachman in a 1992 review article, "Obsessions, Responsibility and Guilt," as the most significant advance in our understanding of OCD in a decade—seems so logical it's a wonder nobody thought of it before. Consider the most common obsessions: contaminated hands, a stove left on, a forbidden sexual attraction, blaspheming God. All involve a negative consequence that might come about if the thinker doesn't act to prevent it. Significantly, obsessions never involve fearful consequences that are beyond peoples' control, like earthquakes and floods. And most compulsions—washing over and over, checking excessively—can be easily seen as irrational acts resulting from a need to take action personally in order to prevent a negative outcome.

Only a few relatively uncommon obsessions seem to fall outside the area of personal responsibility for harm: a song, for instance, that keeps coming back into the mind despite repeated attempts to cast it out. Here, the OCD sufferer manages to turn what is initially innocuous into a cause for alarm. And although there are compulsions, such as counting, tapping, and arranging objects symmetrically, that are not obviously associated with preventing any sort of harm to self or others, most of these are driven by obsessions whose theme of preventing harm is readily recognizable. For instance, I see a young woman who, ever since childhood, has been compelled to tap her fingers in a ritualized manner at least several times every day because of a feeling, recognized by her as irrational, that if she doesn't, harm will come to her parents.

Salkovskis' insightful hypothesis explains a number of puzzling aspects of OCD. Betsy, a homemaker and mother of three who suffered from depression and obsessive-compulsive disorder, was one of the first patients admitted to our new mental health unit at Centre Community Hospital in State College. After a week on the unit, she developed an irresistible compulsion to set off fire alarms and detonated an ear-piercing whistle several times a day. Betsy explained that a picture would flash into her mind of a cigarette starting a chair on fire and igniting a blazing inferno. She knew it was unreasonable to pull the alarms, and she apologized every time she did it; yet she could not be reasoned out of her compulsions. Eventually the fire alarms had to be relocated.

That case will forever stick in my mind because, as director of the new mental health unit, I was that very week making promises to hospital administrators, and to the staff of the coronary care unit on the floor below, that our patients would never cause problems for the hospital. Our nurses and counselors, I assured everyone, could handle even the most agitated and boisterous patients without disturbing a single soul. But I hadn't reckoned on Betsy's irrational feelings of responsibility.

Why did she continue to set off the alarm when she knew there was no fire? Salkovskis' hypothesis helps us understand how the personal responsibility Betsy felt for preventing a possible disaster robbed her of a sense of perspective, took away her ability to assess the situation clearly. Betsy felt that if a fire did start, admittedly a one in a million chance, she would be responsible for the deaths of many people. She felt this as a deep, gut-wretching guilt comparable in intensity, perhaps, to a rage that overwhelms reason.

The prominent role of feelings of responsibility and guilt in the genesis of obsessions helps explain another puzzle, which is why OCD sufferers have so much trouble expressing, even feeling, anger. People with OCD, as discussed in Chapter 4, tend to be timid and nervous, seldom hot-blooded or impulsive. The key is that: while anger is blame directed outward, a person with an excessive sense of personal responsibility directs blame within, producing guilt. OCD sufferers are hard-wired to feel a lot of guilt and little anger.

But back to Betsy. Why did she wait a week before she started setting off those fire alarms? Actually, it is a common pattern. OCD symptoms are often mild during the initial part of a hospitalization. Salkovskis' hypothesis, again, helps us to understand why. When Betsy first arrived on the unit, a strange place full of strangers, she took little responsibility for what happened. But as she made friends and became familiar with our unit, she slowly began to feel more and more accountable, and this soon led to obsessions.

Typically, OCD sufferers do well in new places. On a short vacation, there may be a complete absence of symptoms. In a related way, OCD sufferers often fare much better when the responsibility for a troubling task is given to another person. Clinically, it can be helpful to transfer responsibility for, say, checking the doors at night to a spouse. Conversely, OCD sufferers do most poorly when personal responsibility is magnified. For this reason, the birth of a child, particularly a first child, sometimes sets off the illness.

Putting together clues one, two, and three allows us to make some sense of obsessions. Intrusive, unacceptable thoughts are not the problem. Rather, it's the way they are evaluated. A pathologically elevated sense of personal responsibility causes the OCD sufferer to bring certain thoughts back into consciousness again and again. Recognizing them as senseless, he or she tries not to think them, but in doing so, he or she falls into the white-bear trap, and the thought dismissed comes back stronger. It is a vicious cycle that escalates normal intrusive, unacceptable thoughts into pathological, self-tormenting obsessions.

WHAT ABOUT COMPULSIONS? Can sense be made of senseless rituals? Compulsions follow from obsessions—they are safeguards, attempts to neutralize, to put at ease, the irrational ideas, images, and urges for which OCD sufferers feel excessively responsible. As Salkovskis notes, "Compulsions are attempts to put things right, and avert the possibility of being blamed." Yet since compulsions don't work, and since they are time-consuming, demoralizing, embarrassing, and sometimes physically painful (as in the case, for instance, of excessive hand washing), why do people continue to perform them?

One fact that has long been clear both clinically and experimentally is that compulsions are made stronger because in the short run they do lessen anxiety. Behavioral psychologists refer to this as "negative reinforcement." OCD sufferers who are, for example, tormented by intrusive, unacceptable thoughts that the gas jet is left on will be temporarily relieved after checking it a certain number of times. And even though they recognize that the checking is senseless, the next time the same obsession hits they will check again.

Yet, it seems improbable that negative reinforcement by itself would be strong enough to build up, against a person's will, unbreakable and harmful habits. Furthermore, the principle of negative reinforcement does not explain why compulsions are so eerily stereotyped, performed exactly the same time after time. As psychologists Ricciardi and Hurley note in a 1990 review, "[The principle of reinforcement] cannot adequately explain the mysterious order that surrounds the apparent disorder within OCD."

CLUE NO. 4: COMPULSIONS CLOSELY RESEMBLE FIXED ACTION PATTERNS IN ANIMALS

FEMALE CANARIES REARED from birth in cages containing manmade nests of felt will at certain times in their breeding cycles start methodically gathering any pieces of string that are placed in the cages and systematically weaving them together into nests. All female canaries will do this, whether they are raised in the wild or in complete isolation, and they will always do it exactly the same way. This is referred to as a nest-building ritual. Cats lick their faces and paws in just the same manner many times a day, an example of an auto-grooming ritual. Male fiddler crabs perform elaborate movements, invariable in form and timing, with one of their two claws before mating: a courtship ritual. Other common animal rituals involve defensive shows, elimination behaviors, and food gathering and burying. All are "fixed action patterns," behavioral sequences that are always carried out in exactly the same way and that, once started, are carried out to completion.

Nobel Prize–winning Austrian zoologist Konrad Lorenz first described such fixed action patterns more than fifty years ago. He observed that these rituals of behavior are performed at specific times: when they are helpful for the animal. They are adaptive, indeed essential, behaviors, as they allow important sequences of movements to be carried out automatically in a myriad of situations, enabling quick, appropriate responses. Lorenz concluded that fixed action patterns are instinctive, behavioral programs stored in the brain that are incorporated into the genetic makeup of animal species through the process of evolution.

Of great interest is the fact that fixed action patterns may be set off when they shouldn't be, especially in stressful situations. For instance, in experiments where rats are given inescapable foot shock, they may start auto-grooming—clearly a maladaptive response. Similarly, dogs under stress may, for no apparent reason, start compulsively licking their paws, a sometimes injurious response that can lead to painful, raw sores, a veterinary ailment called acral lick dermatitis.

Do human beings have fixed action patterns? An untold number. Not only do we perform the equivalent of nest-building, auto-grooming, and many other animal rituals, but also, it turns out, many simpler muscle actions that were previously assumed to be chain reflexes are actually fixed action patterns, as well. Swallowing, for example, far from a simple reflex, involves a brain program that intricately times and coordinates contractions of at least eleven different muscles.

Experts speculate that compulsions represent our own inappropriately discharged fixed action patterns. This theory is advanced by Dr. Judith Rapoport, among a number of other leading experts. In a paper titled "Hand-washing People and Paw-licking Dogs," Rapoport suggests that both people and dogs groom themselves on the basis of fixed action patterns that are hard-wired into the brain and that compulsive hand washing in people and excessive paw licking in dogs occur when auto-grooming rituals are inappropriately activated. I like the simple way Harvard's Roger Pitman puts it. There are two primary brain systems that drive behavior, Pitman says, an advanced memory system, which incorporates rational thinking, and a primitive habit system of fixed action patterns. Compulsions occur when the habit system overrides the memory system.

What evidence supports this hypothesis? As mentioned, the similarities between human compulsions and animal fixed action patterns are striking, both in form and content. Both are carried out in uniquely stereotyped manners that, once started, have to be executed to completion. Both involve the same basic issues: showering, bathing, and toothbrushing compulsions correspond to licking and biting auto-grooming rituals; hoarding and collecting compulsions bear similarities to nest building; and checking compulsions resemble fixed action defensive behaviors.

But there is further evidence beyond these surface similarities. Research reviewed in the next chapter proves beyond a doubt that the brain chemical serotonin is in some way involved in causing compulsions. Recently, at least three different research groups have found evidence that changing brain serotonin levels in animals results in changes in fixed action patterns. Furthermore, some veterinary diseases that are secondary to excessive fixed action patterns, such as acral lick syndrome in dogs and feather-picking disorder in birds, respond to the same medications, the serotonin reuptake inhibitors, that are effective in the treatment of OCD.

Even more impressive evidence for the link between compulsions and fixed action patterns comes from studies showing that both responses are generated in the basal ganglia, a small, grapelike cluster of cells located in the center of the brain. Research linking OCD to the basal ganglia, reviewed in the next chapter, is so strong that some experts now simply refer to OCD as a "basal ganglia disease." Animal studies in this area are also robust. Studies by a number of scientists, including noted brain researcher Paul MacLean, involving electric brain stimulation, selective surgical procedures, and drug experiments, prove the basal ganglia's role in the development of fixed action patterns. For instance, electrical stimulation of the nerve fibers leading to the basal ganglia increases fixed action patterns, whereas lesions to the basal ganglia can completely eliminate them.

The striking similarities of appearance in compulsions and fixed action patterns, the prominent role in both of the brain chemical serotonin, and the fact that both are generated in one small area of the brain add up to convincing evidence. Judith Rapoport concludes that compulsions most likely represent the inappropriate triggering of genetically programmed, fixed action patterns that are stored in the basal ganglia of the brain.

IT IS NOW possible to make some sense out of OCD's mysterious, self-defeating thoughts and senseless rituals. Consider Sherry, the young mother described in Chapter 1 who developed terrible obsessions to stab her child. We may theorize that her obsessions began when her imagination, quite normally, was generating intrusive thoughts about bad things that might happen. The thought came to her of stabbing her baby. Next came the OCD sufferer's basic irrationality: Sherry felt excessively responsible for the harm that she might cause. An idea that others would have quickly dismissed as irrational and irrelevant filled her with panic. She tried to stop thinking it but got caught in a white-bear trap: by pushing the thought away before her mind had fully processed it, she only guaranteed that it would come back even stronger.

Or consider the needle obsessions and mental compulsions I developed while in medical school. There I was, a stressed-out doctor in training with an overactive sense of personal responsibility, thinking about inserting needles into peoples' veins. My imagination was throwing up various intrusive thoughts, and up comes one that the probe might slip in my hand and jab me. Soon, I was seeing an image of the needle jumping from my fingers and plunging through my skin. It didn't make sense, and I knew that. Needles don't jump. Nevertheless, the silly image caused a genuine feeling of sharp pain and was distracting. I tried to put it out of my mind. It kept coming back. I had an obsession.

In my brain, a basal ganglia behavioral program was activated. My mind's eye featured a second image: me gently rubbing a soft, white, impenetrable cream on my hand. Now the needle couldn't harm me. It worked! Little did I know that I had now put into action a fixed-action grooming ritual, negatively reinforced because it temporarily rid me of the distressing needle thought. Now I had a compulsion, too.

I didn't know what to make of those obsessions and compulsions in medical school. I didn't even figure out that I had diagnosable OCD. Mental compulsions were not recognized back then, and my whole approach to the problem was to think about it as little as possible (an odd lack of curiosity for a psychiatrist, perhaps, but an OCD sufferer's normal minimizing and secreting of symptoms).

Little was understood about OCD back then, but now OCD sufferers can be helped to make sense of their senseless rituals and self-tormenting thoughts. Inasmuch as people with severe obsessions and compulsions are often demoralized by their symptoms, frequently fearing that they are going crazy, making sense of symptoms can be crucial.

9

OCD AS A BRAIN DISORDER

TWENTY YEARS AGO, even members of the medical profession had a hard time accepting the idea that OCD was a bona fide medical disorder. The difficulty was that OCD, like many other psychiatric disorders, was thought to lack a physical cause. No matter what psychiatrists said, the average physician could not be altogether convinced that a problem without a demonstrable biological basis should be included in the proper domain of medicine.

In those days, OCD stood in apparent contrast to, say, coronary artery disease (CAD), the common cause of heart attacks. CAD's symptoms, such as chest pain and shortness of breath, were caused by physical changes in the body that could be *observed,* fatty tissues that clogged the coronary blood vessels. OCD, on the other hand, was caused, according to the authoritative *Comprehensive Textbook of Psychiatry,* by "a defensive regression of the psychic apparatus to the preoedipal anal-sadistic phase." The exact meaning of those Freudian terms was a mystery to everyone but psychiatrists, but it was clear that they did not refer to any sort of biological process. Coronary artery disease was a true medical disorder; OCD was something else.

But times have changed. Over the last two decades, our understanding of OCD has been revolutionized by a series of fascinating and totally unexpected research findings. It is now absolutely clear that OCD is caused not by vague conflicts in the unconscious but rather by measurable chemical abnormalities that occur in specific regions of the brain. OCD, it turns out, is every bit as much a biological process as CAD. No one should any longer doubt that OCD is a distinct medical disorder.

Viewing OCD in this way has profound personal and social implications for those who suffer from it. Talcott Parsons, founder of the field of medical anthropology, described these implications in the 1940s. Parsons noted that in every culture people who suffer from physical disorders are dealt with in a special manner. They are relieved of their normal duties, taken care of. They are not blamed for their condition. Their treatment is, all in all, very different from that accorded to people who are recognized as otherwise defective: slackers, weaklings, or criminals.

Yet, many OCDers still think of themselves in just those terms. A few even turn themselves in as criminals! This is because OCDers are so prone to guilt. I once asked Tina, whose severe OCD was discussed in the last chapter, what aspect of her treatment had been most helpful to her. She said that it was learning that she had a "chemical disorder." Before this, Tina had unmercifully blamed herself for her condition. Her husband had only made matters worse by nagging her, assuming that if she tried harder she could overcome her ridiculous fears. A great weight was lifted from Tina's shoulders when she learned that her problems were in fact due to a physical problem. The new explanation resonated at a deep level: The symptoms were not her fault. It is of the utmost importance for OCDers, along with their families and the general public, to fully grasp this fact.

BRAIN IMAGING AND OCD

EVIDENCE THAT CONCLUSIVELY proves OCD's physical, biological basis comes from a number of divergent fields of study, including radiology, pharmacology, neurochemistry, neurology, and genetics. The strongest evidence, if one assumes that seeing is believing, is from the burgeoning field of brain imaging.

Before 1980 there was no way to measure regional biochemical reactions as they occur in the brain. Indeed, it was not even known whether such measurements were possible. Today, however, techniques such as positron emission tomography (PET), single-photon emission computed tomography (SPECT), and magnetic resonance imaging (MRI) can perform continuous surveys of chemical reactions in the brain and then display them on a screen. The development of these brain-imaging techniques represents the greatest advance in neuroscience in the last decade.

In both PET and SPECT, investigators label a substance with a radioisotope, inject it into the bloodstream, and then observe where the isotope shows up in the brain. Sophisticated radiation detectors provide the pictures. In PET, to date the most widely used technique, the labeled compound is usually sugar, the sole source of brain cell nourishment. The areas that light up on the PET scan screen are the brain regions that are absorbing the most sugar, those that are working the hardest.

The technology used in MRI is somewhat different. In this case the brain is imaged by measuring the energy that is emitted by subatomic particles. There is a clear advantage to MRI in that it involves neither radiation nor the drawing of blood. In addition, it is proving to be the most sensitive and versatile of the new brain-imaging techniques.

Using PET, SPECT, and MRI, researchers can see where in the brain the neurons are firing, which region is transmitting the most messages. If a person is scanned while studying a book, the visual center in the back of the brain lights up on the screen. If attention is turned to music, auditory centers located not far from the ears are highlighted. Solving a puzzle causes the frontal lobe to stand out. With the movement of a hand, activity is shifted to the motor cortex located at the top of the brain. Different perceptions, different feelings, different ways of thinking, show up on the screen like storms on a satellite weather map.

Since 1987, more than a dozen studies have looked at the local biochemistry of the brain in patients with obsessive-compulsive disorder. The researchers who have done the bulk of this work are Judith Rapoport and Susan Swedo at the National Institutes of Mental

Health, Lewis Baxter and Jeffrey Schwartz at UCLA, and Michael Jenike and Scott Rauch at Harvard. What they have discovered is that in OCD sufferers two areas of the brain light up abnormally: the basal ganglia, a core of cells at the center of the brain resembling a small cluster of grapes; and the orbital frontal region, a large area behind the forehead. The unusual excitations of these two regions are apparent even in OCD patients at rest and are intensified when OCD patients are engaged in compulsive rituals. Furthermore, these abnormalities are diminished, indeed sometimes disappear, when OCD is effectively treated with either medication or behavioral modification. No other psychiatric or physical disorder involves simultaneous abnormalities in these two brain areas. What is observed is a unique, visible, pathological condition of the brain directly related to OCD's symptoms: convincing proof that OCD is truly a neurobiological disorder of the brain.

In addition to regional biochemical abnormalities, there is mounting evidence of significant structural abnormalities in the brains of people with severe OCD. Using MRI, which can depict brain structure in great detail, investigators have observed anatomical irregularities in the ventricular system, frontal cortex, and basal ganglia in both adults and children with OCD.

The most interesting of these findings was reported in 1996 by researchers at Harvard, who examined serial MRI cross-sections of the brains of a group of OCD patients and controls, a painstaking procedure that takes over thirty hours per subject to complete. The crucial observation: The brains of OCD patients had significantly more gray matter (brain cells) and significantly less white matter (myelin and connective cells) than did the brains of control subjects. This makes a certain amount of intuitive sense: OCD sufferers, it seems, think too much. There is also speculation that OCD may reflect a failure in brain maturation. For reasons not yet determined, we are all born with an excess of brain cells; as the normal brain matures, however, it streamlines, losing unnecessary cells. OCD may involve a lack of this normal "pruning."

NEUROCHEMICAL ABNORMALITIES AND OCD

FROM A STATISTICAL point of view, the strongest evidence for OCD having a biological cause comes from studies involving the brain chemical serotonin. These studies number a hundred or more, and their findings are conclusive.

Serotonin is a neurotransmitter, one of over a hundred different substances found at the junctions of brain cells whose job it is to carry messages from one nerve cell to another. Serotonin is manufactured near the connection of the brain and the spinal cord by a cluster of uniquely specialized cells that stretch out from the base of the brain to distant parts of the cerebrum. Serotonin's involvement in OCD is immediately suggested by the fact that these cells project especially to two areas: the basal ganglia and frontal cortex.

The best evidence linking serotonin abnormalities to OCD comes from medication studies. Some thirty-two controlled trails involving thousands of patients have shown that medications which specifically affect serotonin activity—Anafranil (clomipramine), Prozac (fluoxetine), Luvox (fluvoxetine), Paxil (paroxetine), and Zoloft (sertraline)—are vastly superior to both placebo and all other psychiatric drugs in the treatment of OCD. In the largest of these studies, active medication was found to benefit 84 percent of OCD patients, while the corresponding number for placebo was 14 percent. These are extremely significant treatment results, similar, for instance, to the effectiveness of penicillin in the treatment of pneumonia. The ineffectiveness of placebo in these studies is in itself a strong indicator that OCD is a specific, biological disorder, since most psychiatric conditions respond to placebo at a rate of 20 to 30 percent.

Other studies add to this evidence. mCPP, a drug that affects serotonin in a manner opposite to Anafranil, has been shown by investigators in Israel and the United States to make obsessions and compulsions worse, unless a person first receives Anafranil, in which case it has no effect. Still other studies have demonstrated a link between OCD and two hormones that exert an indirect effect on serotonin activity, oxytocin and vasopressin.

A dozen studies have attempted to directly gauge serotonin activity in OCDers. Some studies have measured levels of serotonin and its by-products. Others have used more complicated techniques, such as assessing the binding of serotonin to blood cells, or measuring levels of the hormone prolactin (thought to be a general indicator of brain serotonin activity) in response to a dose of d-fenfluramine (a serotonin-releasing agent). The results of these studies demonstrate with certainty that OCD is associated with some sort of abnormal serotonin activity.

The exact nature of the abnormality, however, has proven frustratingly elusive—nothing so simple, it appears, as an increase or decrease in the total amount of serotonin in the brain. The leading theory at this time proposes that serotonin receptors (the molecules on the surface of brain cells that receive and bind serotonin) may be abnormal in OCD.

NEUROLOGICAL DISEASES AND OCD

A NUMBER OF neurological diseases caused by damage to the basal ganglia are accompanied by obsessions and compulsions indistinguishable from those found in OCD. Research into the relationship between OCD and these disorders, especially when taken in conjunction with the other findings discussed in this chapter, suggest that OCD itself is caused by some sort of a primary basal ganglia abnormality. Currently, this is the leading theory on the cause of OCD.

Given these connections, shouldn't OCD be removed from the purview of psychiatry and put into the field of neurology? The idea has some merit, especially given the stigma many people attach to the word "psychiatric." In truth, after two decades of intensive brain research, the line between neurology and psychiatry has become permanently blurred.

Gilles de la Tourette Syndrome
OCD BEARS A close relationship to the unusual neurological disorder known as Tourette's, a genetic disorder of the nervous system

characterized by sudden jerks and twitches called tics. Simple tics, such as eye blinks and neck stretches, occur in 10 percent of children and not uncommonly in adults. Tourette's, in contrast, is characterized by complex, highly abnormal tics. In its extreme form, a person so afflicted may, for no apparent reason, repeatedly stop in his tracks and make a series of quick jumps while walking down the street. Another may spin around, take a couple of steps backward, then abruptly turn forward again. Most attention-getting of all are the vocal tics: muffled grunts and even explosive, involuntary shouts of profanities.

OCD resembles Tourette's in several ways. The most obvious is the subjective likeness between tics and compulsions, respective hallmarks of the two disorders. Both are experienced as senseless, repetitive acts that a person does not want to do but must do in order to relieve tension. Both are preceded by intrusions: In the case of OCD these are unwanted thoughts; in Tourette's they are uncomfortable sensations. Epidemiological studies, too, confirm a close association between OCD and Tourette's. At least 40 percent of people with Tourette's also have OCD, and about 10 percent of people with OCD have Tourette's. Such an association would be impossible if the two were not related in some way.

Anatomic and neuroendocrine studies further strengthen the connection. A 1996 National Institutes of Health study found that Tourette's symptoms could be traced to abnormally sensitive neurochemical receptors in the basal ganglia.

Lastly, a genetic link between OCD and Tourette's has now been confirmed by family and twin studies. These findings lead some experts to speculate that OCD and Tourette's are different expressions of one genetic, neurobiological disease.

Autoimmune Neurological Disorders

TODAY'S MOST EXCITING frontier of OCD research stems from a remarkable finding reported in 1997 by psychiatrists Susan Swedo, Judith Rapoport and colleagues at the National Institutes of Mental Health. What the NIMH researchers have discovered is that childhood OCD is frequently associated with group A beta hemolytic streptococcal infections—strep throat!

This research had its start a decade ago with the study of OCD's link to Sydenham's chorea, a now rare disease of childhood that was seen frequently before the age of antibiotics. Once known as Saint Vitus' dance, Sydenham's is characterized by the sudden onset of neurological symptoms ranging from mild clumsiness and a tendency to drop objects to unrestrained flailing of the arms and delirium. Sydenham's, it has been discovered, is an autoimmune disease. As with rheumatic fever, infections with streptococcal bacteria lead to the production of antibodies that double-cross the body: They kill not only streptococci but normal cells as well. In rheumatic fever, the heart is attacked; in Sydenham's chorea, the brain. Brain-imaging studies of people suffering Sydenham's chorea demonstrate inflamed, bulging basal ganglias.

OCD has long been known to bear a relationship to Sydenham's, which is characterized by obsessions and compulsions in over half of all cases. Exploring this relationship, Swedo and colleagues asked this question: Could some routine cases of childhood OCD be caused, like Sydenham's, by autoimmune damage to the basal ganglia? They were astounded by the finding. It now appears possible that up to 25 percent of childhood OCD may, indeed, have this origin. On the horizon is the remarkable possibility that large numbers of children with OCD may be effectively treated with penicillin. University centers are already screening childhood OCDers for anti-streptococcal antibodies and treating some cases with antibiotics. The NIMH researchers, whose offices are located not far from the National Zoo, have given a name to these immune system disorders that attack the basal ganglia: pediatric autoimmune neurobiological disorders associated with streptococci, or PANDAS.

It is interesting to note that Saint Therese of Lisieux, the Christian luminary who was discussed in Chapter 3, may well have had PANDAS. Therese suffered severe bouts of sore throat all of her life and finally died at twenty-four of a respiratory illness. As a child, just prior to developing obsessive-compulsive disorder, Therese was confined to bed for a period of two months with a disorder of intermittent delirium she later referred to as "my strange sickness." The saint's aunt remembered, "the little girl was seized with a nervous trembling, followed by seizures of fright and hallucinations that were repeated several times a day." The family maid recalled that Therese had "propulsive seizures during which she made wheel-like movements that she would have been absolutely incapable of making in a state of health." The doctor called on to treat the disorder diagnosed St. Vitus' dance.

Von Economo's Encephalitis and Huntington's Disease

TWO ADDITIONAL DISORDERS of the basal ganglia are associated with OCD. Von Economo's is the name given to cases of brain infection that developed with the worldwide flu pandemic of 1917 to 1926. It's symptoms were rigidity, tremor, and obsessions and compulsions, counting rituals being particularly common. Huntington's disease, the cruel neurological illness that struck folk singer Woody Guthrie, starts in midlife with twitches and jerks and then inevitably progresses to dementia and death. In its early stages, Huntington's commonly includes obsessive cleaning and checking rituals. In both Von Economo's encephalitis and Huntington's disease, brain damage is restricted largely to the basal ganglia.

BRAIN TRAUMA AND OCD

DIRECT DAMAGE TO the basal ganglia can be another cause of OCD. In one reported case, a previously healthy fifty-six-year-old woman with no history of nervous or psychiatric problems was hospitalized following a stroke. For two days she recovered well; then she developed the urge to count things over and over: lines on the wall, dots in the ceiling, and stitches in her hospital gown. She couldn't stop. A psychiatrist was consulted for treatment of OCD. Several dozen similar cases of brain injury leading to sudden OCD—some involving head trauma, others carbon monoxide poisoning—have been studied. In each instance, X rays, CAT scans, and MRI studies of the brain have shown that the physical injury was limited to the basal ganglia.

Minor brain damage, often caused by childhood infections, birth injury, or genetic factors, is also statistically correlated with the development of OCD. Such subtle brain injuries are usually recognized by the presence of neurological "soft signs," minor abnormalities affecting movement, coordination, and sensation. In a 1990 study, thirty-four of forty-one patients with severe OCD were found unable to rapidly point their fingers back and forth from one object to another in a normally coordinated manner, whereas only nine in the control group showed the abnormality. OCD patients are also more likely than others to have slight deficiencies in memory and in planning and organizational skills, as demonstrated by neuropsychological testing. OCD patients also often show minor irregularities in vision.

IN SUM, SUFFICIENT evidence has now accumulated that no unbiased observer can seriously doubt that OCD is a true medical disorder. Does this mean that only physical processes are involved in the cause of OCD? Obviously not. Consider again the example of coronary artery disease. Its direct, or proximal, cause is the biochemical abnormality referred to as atherosclerosis. However, many factors contribute to the development of this abnormality, including elevated cholesterol, high blood pressure, and psychological stress. These, in turn, are affected to varying degrees by a person's genetic makeup, the genes they were born with. In considering the root causes of OCD, genetics and stress are especially important.

THE GENETICS OF OCD

OUR UNDERSTANDING OF how our genetic makeup interacts with the environment in which we live has grown immensely over the last twenty years. To grasp the implications of the genetic model for OCD, a few basic principles should be kept in mind. It is well known that a person inherits one set of genes from the mother and another from the father. Together, these two join in the formation of a cell, which then starts dividing. With each division, the genes form exact replicas of themselves. The cells, on the other hand, begin to turn out differently.

It has been clear for several decades now that the reason for this type of cell differentiation is that only a small portion of the gene serves as the architectural template for each cell. What has recently been discovered is that the part of the gene that serves as a template is regulated by signals from the outside world. We now know that the genetic plans are not, as many people have thought, fixed and unchanging. Rather, they are regulated, *fine-tuned,* by experience.

The part of the gene that regulates eyesight, for example, is uncovered shortly after birth, ready to go to work as a blueprint for the visual system. Yet, animal studies show that in order for sight to develop there is a critical period during which perceptions from the outside must start coming in through the eye. If an animal is left in darkness during this interval, the gene controlling vision is covered up, and the opportunity to develop sight is forever lost. A more complicated illustration: Suppose a person is genetically coded to be timid but is raised in a turbulent household where he is continually exposed to dangerous, unpredictable situations. In this case, the plans for timidity languish, and other half-hidden blueprints for aggression and decisiveness are opened up. A person who starts with an inclination to timidity will not necessarily end up that way. Genetic inclinations are adjusted by feedback from life circumstances.

Of the evidence that proves OCD to have a strong genetic influence, family studies are most prominent. Although research of this type cannot provide the absolute final word on genetic cause—that will have to wait for the identification of a specific OCD gene—the results from these studies are already very convincing.

Over a dozen reliable studies, for example, show that on average, if a person has OCD, the chance that a parent, child, brother, or sister will develop the problem is 10–25 percent—much higher than OCD's overall lifetime incidence of 1–2 percent. In a well-controlled 1995 study, investigators from Yale and Brown universities interviewed all the available parents, siblings, and children of 100 OCD patients, finding that fully 10 percent of these relatives had definite OCD, and another 8 percent had possible OCD. Reviewing all the studies in this area, a team of scientists from four American universities recently concluded that of all anxiety disorders, OCD and panic disorder are the two that run most strongly families.

The results of such family studies, admittedly, can be misleading. Environmental problems such as neglect and abuse, which can run in families for generations, might drive people to obsessions. In order to establish genetic cause with greater certainty, scientists study pairs of twins.

The key to twin studies is the fundamental difference between identical and fraternal twins. Identicals, formed at the union of one sperm and one ovum, have matching genes. They're clones of each other. Fraternals, on the other hand, result from different sperms meeting different ovums—they're no more alike genetically than ordinary brothers and sisters. To find out whether a trait is genetic, researchers determine how often it is shared by pairs of identical twins, then they compare that to how often it is shared by fraternals. When a trait is found more often in both identicals than in both fraternals, the discrepancy proves some degree of genetic cause.

In Huntington's disease, the causative factor is a single mutant gene. If one identical twin is affected with Huntington's, the other will be affected, too; among fraternals, the disease is shared only 50 percent of the time. Huntington's is rare—a 100 percent genetic illness. Compare it to generalized anxiety disorder, a broad term for excessive nervousness and worry. Here the incidence in identical twins equals that in fraternals exactly; such anxiety is not genetic at all. Or consider, again, coronary artery disease. A recent study in Norway found that if one identical twin has CAD, the chance of the other twin having CAD is 66 percent, whereas if one fraternal twin has CAD, the chance of the other twin having the disease is 25 percent. CAD, then, is one of many diseases that are *partially* genetic in origin.

In the case of obsessive-compulsive disorder, ten different studies have reported on a total of fifty-one OCD patients with identical twins; thirty-two of those twins were found to also have OCD (63 percent), while 19 (37 percent) did not. One of the best studies in this area was a 1982 trial that located fifteen OCD patients who had identical twins and another fifteen with fraternals; on interviewing the siblings, 87 percent of the identicals were found to have OCD, while for the fraternal twins that figure was 47 percent. In sum, the results indicate that OCD is a partially genetic disease with a heritability factor that is, in fact, very similar to that of CAD. David

Fogelson, psychiatrist at UCLA's Neuropsychiatric Institute, has concluded: "A good guess is that OCD is 60 percent genetically caused."

In order to appreciate the scope of the genetic influence in OCD, it is helpful to note that the personality factors associated with OCD—timidity, introspection, and a tendency to depression—have been shown themselves to be genetic to varying degrees. Timidity has been well researched. Tests show that even in the first year of life, the fear of strangers develops more similarly among identical twins than fraternals. Harvard psychologist Jerome Kagan, the world's expert in this area, has followed infants' levels of fearfulness from birth to adulthood, finding that although environment does play a part, timidity is, in fact, a largely inherited trait. Introversion is also strongly genetic, as the English psychologist Hans Eysenk first suggested in the 1950s. A 1992 report by Heath and co-workers in St. Louis on 2000 twins concluded that genetic factors account for 73 percent of the variance in introversion. The tendency to develop severe depression also has a strong genetic component.

Other personality traits that predispose to OCD are also thought to be partially genetic. Robert Cloninger, whose biochemically based personality theory was discussed in Chapter 3, views the traits of novelty seeking, harm avoidance, and reward dependence as independent, genetic factors that lead to OCD. A 1996 article in *Nature Genetics* has supported this view, reporting the discovery in both Israel and the United States of a specific gene that regulates the trait of novelty seeking.

One important result of the genetic research on OCD, however, is often overlooked. In pointing out percentages of genetic influence, these studies also demonstrate that a large part of the cause of OCD is, indeed, environmental. Heritability of 60 percent still leaves 40 percent for life experiences. This 40 percent may determine whether or not the disorder becomes severe.

STRESS AS A TRIGGER OF OCD

EXPERTS AGREE THAT stress plays an important role in the development of OCD. Thus far, seven studies have addressed this issue, with the best work coming from India, where Sumant Khanna and co-workers compared patients with recently developed OCD to a matched control group. In the year prior to developing the illness, the OCD patients experienced more than twice as many stressful events as the control group, particularly episodes of sickness and death in their families.

Stress may lead to OCD by a number of mechanisms. As discussed in Chapter 8, researchers have demonstrated that traumatic experiences must be replayed again and again in our minds until they are processed—matched and integrated with previous life experiences. It is probable that the repeated appearance of minor posttraumatic thoughts secondary to life stresses can start a vulnerable person on the way to experiencing true obsessions.

Researchers have also found that the physiologic state of anxiety itself may lead to obsessions. Studies by Colin MacLeod and co-workers in Australia have demonstrated that highly anxious students have more trouble than others ignoring various types of threats, a finding that has been confirmed by half a dozen other investigators. MacLeod concludes that when we are anxious, an automatic mechanism of the mind opens the door to increased numbers of intrusive, worrisome thoughts.

The important role of life experiences in the development of OCD was certainly true in my own case. My obsessions and compulsions started during my first year of medical school and ceased to be a significant problem once I was finished with the late nights of studying and the long days under scrutiny. A friend provided me with still another example of the effect of stress on the development of obsessions. Soon after her husband died, she began developing for the first time in her life a number of compulsive behaviors: She checked her doors and appliances many times a day to make sure they were safe and frequently had to leave work and run home to see about the electric blanket. She knew this checking was unnecessary and it bothered her, but she could not control it until a year had passed after her husband's death. In a group for grieving widows, she found that three of the other six women had also developed minor compulsions.

In the cases of my patients, the pattern is similar. I find that their obsessions usually come along—commonly accompanied by other symptoms of anxiety, such as loss of sleep, nervousness, and exhaustion—when health, marital, and job problems pile up.

It is when a person is highly stressed, dealing with life's more acute difficulties and challenges, that he or she is most likely be hit by self-tormenting thoughts.

THE RESEARCH REVIEWED in this chapter demonstrates beyond a doubt that OCD is a biological, medical brain disorder with both genetic and environmental determinates. It is worth re-emphasizing that although OCD's symptoms are directly caused by biochemical brain changes, that does not mean that OCD is merely a matter of biochemistry. Attitudes, behaviors, and life events play a major role. More than biological factors must be addressed.

One current concern of vital interest to OCD sufferers and their advocates is parity in insurance coverage. If OCD is a medical condition, shouldnt it be insured in full? Fearing the high cost of coverage, insurance companies have been dragging their feet on this issue for years, but there is reason for cautious optimism. In 1997 the state legislature of Colorado passed a health insurance parity bill mandating that every policy provide coverage for the treatment of biologically based mental illness that is no less extensive than the coverage provided for any other physical illness. The bill pertains specifically to four psychiatric disorders, one of which is OCD. Similar bills have been introduced in twenty-six other states, and a parity amendment has been introduced to the Kassebaum–Kennedy health insurance legislation of 1997 by U.S. senators Wellstone and Domenici.

FROM HYPOCHONDRIASIS
TO SEXUAL ADDICTIONS:
OBSESSIVE-COMPULSIVE
SPECTRUM DISORDERS

AS RECENT DISCOVERIES from many different areas of brain research have greatly expanded our knowledge of OCD, interest has been kindled in syndromes that bear similarities to OCD, usually referred to as "OCD-related" or "OC spectrum" disorders. All manifest themselves in either intrusive thoughts that resemble obsessions or repetitive behaviors akin to compulsions. For the most part, these disorders are not especially well understood, and how closely they actually resemble OCD is controversial. Some appear to be quite similar to OCD; they may even be the same disorder. Others, however, seem fundamentally different.

Two of these syndromes, in particular, can appear almost identical to OCD: hypochondriasis (unfounded preoccupations with medical illnesses), and body dysmorphic disorder (preoccupations with deformed appearance). It is quite possible that in the future some cases of both of these will be considered as OCD. Two other syndromes show essential similarities to OCD but also have significant differences: trichotillomania (pathological hair pulling), and anorexia nervosa. Then there are a number of disorders involving a loss of impulse control, such as impulsive stealing and sexual addictions, which are also often included in the OC spectrum.

HYPOCHONDRIASIS

IN 1724, THE EMINENT physician Daniel Turner, author of the first English textbook on dermatology, recorded a case of a man with the irrational fear of having syphilis. Dermatologists of that era were keenly interested in syphilis, then the most dreaded of all diseases, because lesions of the skin were often its presenting symptom.

Dr. Turner recounts being visited one evening by "a tradesman in good business, of a thoughtful temper . . . who sat down and fell into tears, wringing his hands." The patient had been going from doctor to doctor complaining of a multitude of aches and pains, fearful that he had contracted syphilis. Unable to feel reassured by doctors who told him he had no serious disease, he had seen a number of charlatans, who treated him with strong doses of laxatives and salivants (medications that cause the mouth to water copiously). Subsequently, he misinterpreted the powerful side effects of these drugs, such as nausea and dizziness, as further proof that he did, indeed, have a grave illness. A vicious cycle of anxiety-related complaints and iatrogenic symptoms was in motion.

On examining the patient, Dr. Turner determined that although the tradesman complained of symptoms of his "head, his nose, and all parts of his body," he had absolutely none of the characteristic symptoms of syphilis. Furthermore, he had not been to a prostitute, then considered the most likely source for contracting the disease. "I now plainly perceived it was all a delusion," Dr. Turner relates. "I told him he had been abused not by a girl, but by his quack doctors; and that he was free entirely from any such disease, and stood in no need of my assistance."

Despite such an excellent consultation (we present-day physicians should be so honest and direct), the patient continued to seek out different doctors and to go downhill. Eventually he became bedridden and developed the idea that, since advanced syphilis can cause the loss of body parts, his nose might fall off. At that time he called again for Dr. Turner, and while holding tightly onto his nose, angrily told him: "You never would believe I had the distemper, but it is now apparent, for my nose, if I were not to support it, would drop off this instant."

Dr. Turner relates that he reassured the patient of the integrity of his nose by means of a dramatic demonstration: "Ordering a candle to be brought near, with much difficulty I persuaded him to take away his fingers, when immediately with my own fingers taking fast hold thereof, I raised his head from the pillow, and saying never a word, I let the same drop down again." When the patient saw that his nose was not in Dr. Turner's fingers, but rather still on his face, he became "convinced of his mistake."

But soon the insight gained was lost and his worries returned in full. Dr. Turner then had a talk with the family: "I called his wife aside . . . and advised her to provide some place for him where he might be kept out of harm's way." Following this advice, the patient and his family moved to a country village. His condition improved somewhat, yet he continued to be disabled by his fear of illness. He spent a great deal of time, Dr. Turner notes, examining his nose in front of a mirror.

In discussing the case, Dr. Turner points out the distinguishing feature of hypochondriacs: Despite being free of disease they cannot be convinced that they are well. He also issues the warning that because these patients seem satisfied only when being tried on a new course of medication, they are easy prey for quack doctors.

In the eighteenth century this malady was diagnosed, like OCD, as a type of melancholia, or depression. Now it is classified as a separate disorder. In the current diagnostic manual of American psychiatry (DSM-IV), hypochondriasis is defined as an intense preoccupation with having a serious illness that persists despite medical reassurance. It is estimated that from 5 to 9 percent of patients seen by family doctors suffer from the condition, and perhaps, up to 2 percent of the general population.

Does hypochondriasis belong in the OC spectrum? It closely resembles OCD in involving insistent, irrational fears that lead to repetitive checking and reassurance seeking. On closer inspection, however, it differs from OCD in several important ways. First, the hypochondriac's concern is for the present, whereas OCDers worry about the future. Second, the hypochondriac generally has some minor but real physical symptom, such as a skin blemish or stomach cramp. Finally, and perhaps most importantly, the patient with hypochondriasis almost always has less insight into the inappropriateness or senselessness of his concerns than an OCDer.

Despite all these differences, some cases of hypochondriasis seem almost identical to OCD. Recently a twenty-one-year-old student came to see me because of an intense fear of having AIDS. Well dressed, personable, and highly anxious, he shared with me that a month before he had noticed a "bump" on his neck. Afraid he might have cancer, he went to the student health center, where he was examined and informed that he had no serious disease. A few days later, however, when the lump seemed to change in texture, he needed to be reassured with a second opinion.

The next week, after studying in the library, he left a can of chewing tobacco behind. Returning a short time later and putting a pinch under his lip, he was immediately besieged by the fear that someone with AIDS might have "done something with it." Again he presented to the health center. This time, however, neither a physical examination nor blood tests could put his mind at ease. He started reading everything he could find about AIDS and making calls to the Center for Disease Control in Atlanta. Then he found a lump on his lip. A dentist told him that this was merely a cold sore, but thoughts of having a malignant disease now started to torture him every minute of the day.

This student's problem had the "feel" of genuine OCD—his obsessions being intrusive thoughts of disease, and his compulsions being repeated requests for reassurance. Further history revealed that he had a number of minor compulsions, including regularly checking appliances three or four times to make sure they were off. And just like OCDers, he was a very conscientious student, prone to anxiety and feelings of guilt when he did not perform up to expectations.

He was helped by the standard OCD treatments. Using the behavior therapy technique of exposure in the imagination, he rehearsed having various dreaded diseases and having to live or die with them. He also benefited from the SRI medication fluoxetine (Prozac) at a dose of 20 milligrams a day.

Yet, there are other cases of hypochondriasis that do not have the feel of genuine OCD. Not long ago I was asked to consult on a fifty-three-year-old woman who was in the hospital for chest pains. She had been hospitalized for these pains at least once a year for the last fifteen years. She came to the emergency room so frequently that all the staff there knew her by her first name. She had had hundreds of electrocardiograms, as well as three cardiac catheterizations. No heart disease had been found.

On interview, she described in the minutest detail the sharp pains that bored inwardly to her lungs then outwardly to encompass her ribs and arms. They would immobilize her, sometimes cause her to fall in her tracks. Usually they were accompanied by a fluttering of her heart and a feeling of faintness. She spoke in an intense and dramatic manner and talked on and on with hardly a pause. I felt smothered by her strong personality and nonstop talking.

This patient's thoughts of illness were not intrusive, fearful, or unwanted. On the contrary, she used them to relate to people and to gain attention. She refused to consider the possibility that a nervous disorder could be playing a part in her symptoms, and she saw no reason for me to visit her a second time.

The difference between these two cases illustrates a major short-coming in our current concept of hypochondriasis. In reality, hypochondriacal symptoms are probably related to several different syndromes, OCD being only one among them.

BODY DYSMORPHIC DISORDER

DR. TURNER'S TRADESMAN, the one who feared having syphilis, gradually became obsessed with the condition of his nose, and finally with the unlikely idea that his nose would fall off. In hindsight, this man may have developed a second psychiatric disorder: body dysmorphic disorder (BDD).

BDD is the excessive preoccupation with a slight or imagined defect in appearance. BDD sufferers exaggerate the slightest wrinkle, scar, blemish, or vascular marking of a body part (nose, face, and skin are most common) and become terrified that this minor imperfection represents a serious abnormality.

A senior in high school with a typical case of body dysmorphic disorder was referred to me by her dermatologist. She presented as a plain and shy young woman, dressed unflatteringly in dirty jeans and a T-shirt. Self-consciously, with little eye contact, she told me her story.

> I've been messing with my skin, and I don't have the self-control to stop. I spend an hour in front of the mirror every night. Mainly it's my nose. I'm always thinking that the pores are infected because they look too large. So I squeeze out all the moisture from every single pore. I'm saying to myself, "You shouldn't do this. You really shouldn't do this." After I leave the bathroom, I feel all kinds of guilt. The most terrifying part of the day is when I get up in the morning and have to look at my skin. Sometimes I have some pretty bad bruises on my face, and I worry that they might turn into permanent scars.
>
> My looks are on my mind almost all the time. My hair doesn't look good no matter what I do, so now I keep it short. I cut every strand exactly, precisely the same length. I think about my lips a lot. They seem too big, like they are swollen, so I put a lot of cream on them, and sometimes they get cracked. Then there's funny dots under my eyes that other people don't have. I put a lot of cream on them, too. My cuticles around my nails don't look right, either. I work on them a lot—often until they bleed. Then there's a curve in my spine that really bothers me. I wonder if I can get that fixed. I look so bad. No one will ever want to marry me.

Body dysmorphic disorder, "imagined ugliness," can lead to shame, disabling avoidance, and severe depression. In one study, fully 98 percent of BDD patients reported significant social impairment because of embarrassment over their appearance, 32 percent were housebound, 83 percent had suffered major depression, and 29 percent had made suicide attempts. One patient refused to drive a car because she feared her ugliness would be so shocking to other drivers that it would cause an accident.

A major complication of this disorder is unnecessary plastic surgery. A 1993 study of fifty BDD patients found that twenty had been operated on at least once for their "defects"; and one patient had had fifteen operations. Occasionally, BDD sufferers obsess about other people's looks. I once treated a teenager with BDD who had managed to badger her family into getting a surgeon to operate on her sister's nose.

Until the 1970s, this syndrome was variously considered a form of phobia ("dysmorphophobia"), hypochondriasis ("beauty hypochondriasis"), or obsessive-compulsive disorder. Pierre Janet, the great turn-of-the-century French psychiatrist, viewed BDD as closely related to OCD. Most twentieth-century psychiatrists have followed his lead.

The unwanted thoughts of BDD, after all, fit quite well the definition of obsessions. They are always intrusive, recurrent, resisted, and usually recognized as excessive. Also, more than 90 percent of BDD patients develop compulsions, most commonly mirror inspections, camouflaging perceived defects, comparisons to other people, and reassurance seeking. A 1997 study by by OCD experts Fugen Neziroglu and Jose Yaryura-Tobias compared the clinical characteristics of OCD and BDD. The conclusion was that BDD is best conceptualized as a variant of OCD.

Preliminary research supports the use of exposure and response prevention techniques in BDD and a few studies indicate that, like OCD, it also responds preferentially to SRI medications (although not as robustly as OCD). I personally have had good results using behavior therapy and SRI medications with BDD patients.

Two differences have been noted between body dysmorphic disorder and OCD. BDD patients show higher levels of associated depression, social withdrawal, and low self-esteem than do OCD patients. This is not surprising in view of the fact that BDD deals with physical appearance, a matter of great importance to self-esteem. More puzzling is the repeated finding that, as with hypochondriasis, BDD sufferers tend to have less insight into their disorder than OCDers. It is not clear why this is so, although it may be simply that when obsessions involve our own bodies it is especially hard to gain a distanced perspective on them.

TRICHOTILLOMANIA

REPETITIVE, EXCESSIVE PLUCKING or pulling out of hair was first described as a psychiatric disorder in 1889 by the French physician Hallopeau. He gave it a name that means "hair pulling insanity." The features that he noted remain, with a few minor changes, our diagnostic criteria: noticeable hair loss, not due to a medical condition, that causes distress; an increasing sense of tension before pulling out the hair; pleasure or relief afterward.

Trichotillomania and OCD are similar in many ways. Both involve repetitive, uncontrollable behaviors that disturb people's lives. Furthermore, both hair pulling and many of the typical rituals of OCD are related to grooming, a connection that has led OCD expert Judith Rapoport to speculate that both trichotillomania and OCD may involve an abnormal release of genetically coded grooming tendencies (see Chapter 8). Another similarity between trichotillomania and OCD is that in both disorders patients keep their problem a secret. Hair pulling, like OCD, was in the past thought to be uncommon but has now been found to be widespread. A recent survey of 2500 college students found that more than 1 in 200 had diagnosable trichotillomania.

The following excerpt from my first interview of a student with typical trichotillomania illustrates the similarities between this disorder and OCD, as well as a number of important differences. Katie, a twenty-five-year-old unmarried elementary schoolteacher, had returned to college to pursue a master's degree. She came to our clinic early in her first semester, depressed and discouraged. I asked her to tell me about her problem.

> KATIE: I pull out my hair all the time. I have no hair at all up here (pointing to the top of her head). I've pulled my hair back so people can't notice. If I were to comb it forward you would see that it's totally bald. When I was in college, it was just a little patch. Now, it's the whole top of my head.
> PSYCHIATRIST: You do a good job of camouflaging.

KATIE: I've had a lot of practice.

PSYCHIATRIST: What bothers you the most about the hair pulling?

KATIE: It's just that . . . I don't want to be bald. I'm always thinking people are staring at me. I can't go swimming. I'm always wearing hats or bandanas. I hate if somebody's standing behind me, like in an elevator. I can't have normal relationships. The last time I had a boyfriend, he picked me up at my apartment, took one look at the floor, and said, "Boy, somebody's going bald around here." I just about died. Now, I'm too ashamed to have a boyfriend.

PSYCHIATRIST: For how long has hair pulling been a problem?

KATIE: I've done it since adolescence. It was my terrifying secret. Nobody knew but my mom, and the two of us never discussed it. I always wondered if anyone else ever had it. This is actually the first time in my life that I've ever told anyone about it.

PSYCHIATRIST: I notice you haven't pulled any hair as we've been talking.

KATIE: No, I never do it in front of anyone, but at home it's terrible. For hours I'm telling myself, "Quit it, quit it, quit it." But I stop for a minute, and then I'm doing it again. I have to keep my hands busy, playing Nintendo or something, or else my hands are up there pulling. Half the time I don't even realize I'm doing it. Sometimes I wonder if I do it in my sleep.

PSYCHIATRIST: Does it feel pleasurable to pull out a hair? Or does it hurt?

KATIE: Well, neither, really. It's just . . . my scalp will itch a little bit. And it relieves the itch when I pull a hair out.

PSYCHIATRIST: Do you have any thought that comes into your mind prior to the hair pulling? Do you think the hair is dirty? Or that a hair follicle is infected, or anything like that?

KATIE: No, I just get a tingling or a feeling like a pinch or something. It happens on one certain area of my scalp. Then I pull a hair and it relieves it. Sometimes I'll get the itch on

a big area. Then I have to pull in a whole circle before I can
quit.

PSYCHIATRIST: Do you feel the itch now?

KATIE: Yes, but I'm resisting pulling

PSYCHIATRIST: Is there anything else that plays a part in hair
pulling?

KATIE: I like it better—this is going to sound weird—if the
hair has a little tuft on the end.

PSYCHIATRIST: Why is that?

KATIE: It feels good to pick it off.

PSYCHIATRIST: Do you ever eat it?

KATIE: Oh, my God, I've never told that to anyone in my
whole life!

PSYCHIATRIST: Don't feel embarrassed. People with trichotillomania often do that.

KATIE: I feel like I'm gross. I don't want to do it. I try not to do
it, but I still do it

PSYCHIATRIST: Why do you do it? Does it taste good, or is
there some other reason?

KATIE: No, it doesn't taste good! I don't know why I do it.

Katie told me that she had several minor rituals, such as repeating sentences in her head and counting syllables over and over in
multiples of ten, but these never caused her any trouble. She also admitted to severe depression, with low energy, poor sleep, and occasional suicidal thoughts. Yet she insisted, "Hair pulling is the big
problem. I'd be fine if it weren't for that."

Katie's case is typical. Trichotillomania occurs primarily in
women, by a ratio of at least three to one. It usually starts in adolescence and is kept a secret for a long time. The scalp is the most frequent site of pulling, although often other body areas, such as
eyebrows and genitals, are involved. Stress often makes hair pulling
worse. In Katie's case, returning to school seemed to have brought
on a crisis. And oral behaviors such as rubbing, licking, or eating
hair are common; they are reported by approximately half of patients with trichotillomania.

Yet there are clear differences between the rituals of trichotillomania and those of OCD. First, hair-pulling rituals are not preceded by obsessions, or recurrent unwanted thoughts. Second, a certain amount of pleasure generally accompanies hair pulling, while OCD, in contrast, is never pleasurable in *any* way. Finally, the rituals of trichotillomania are often done absentmindedly, automatically, whereas OCD's compulsions are performed with focused attention.

Thus, the symptoms of the two disorders overlap and yet are distinct. Similarly, neurophysiological studies suggest that while trichotillomania and OCD are related, they are not the same. A 1997 imaging study performed by researchers at Harvard, for instance, demonstrated that trichotillomania, like OCD, does involve a demonstrable abnormality in the brain's basal ganglia; the specific area within the basal ganglia found to be affected, however, was different than that detected in OCD.

Effective treatments for the two disorders, likewise, differ in important ways. The SRI medications that work well in OCD are also effective for trichotillomania, but the response is less vigorous. An excellent 1989 study using clomipramine (Anafranil) in the treatment of trichotillomania showed a very positive result, but since then studies using other SRIs have been less encouraging. Katie did benefit markedly from sertraline (Zoloft) at a dose of 150 milligrams per day, but that may have been mostly due to its antidepressant effect.

Behavior therapy, too, is useful in trichotillomania. Since there are no obsessions in hair pulling, however, the exposure and response prevention techniques that are useful in OCD are ineffective. What does work is "habit reversal": (1) closely monitoring when hair pulling occurs; (2) identifying the precursors to hair pulling, such as studying or watching TV, tingling or itching of the scalp, and touching or straightening hair; (3) increasing awareness of these precursors; (4) learning a relaxation method such as deep breathing; and (5) interrupting the response of precursor leading to hair pulling by using relaxation methods.

Studies suggest that habit reversal is effective for trichotillomania, although not as effective as exposure and response prevention for OCD. Katie carried out habit reversal for only a short time, then lost her motivation. That is the usual problem. For some reason, patients usually don't follow through with this technique. I must admit that I have not had great success with habit reversal. My impression, however, is that clinics which specialize in this technique do an especially good job. A list of such clinics may be obtained from the OC Foundation or the Trichotillomania Learning Center.

ANOREXIA NERVOSA

THERE IS ANOTHER psychiatric syndrome involving preoccupations with appearance that bears similarities to OCD. Richard Morton, M.D., personal physician to King James II of England, is credited with first describing this disorder in 1689 in a book on diseases that cause wasting away of the body:

> Mr. Duke's daughter in the eighteenth year of her age fell into a total suppression of her monthly courses from a multitude of cares and passions of her mind. Her appetite began to abate, and her digestion to be bad; her flesh also began to be flaccid and loose, and her looks pale. . . . She wholly neglected the care of her self for two full years, till at last being subject to frequent fainting fits, she applied herself to me for advice.
>
> I do not remember that I did ever in all my practice see one that was so much wasted. There was no fever, but on the contrary a coldness of the whole body; no cough, or difficulty of breathing; nor an appearance of any other distemper. . . . Only her appetite was diminished and her digestion uneasy, with fainting fits. . . .
>
> I did endeavor to relieve by the outward application of aromatic bags made to the region of the stomach, also by the internal use of bitter medicines . . . but after three months she was taken with a fainting fit and died.

"Grief, fears, cares, and too much thinking" were, according to Dr. Morton, the cause of this disorder, which he named "nervous consumption." Later the name was changed to anorexia nervosa, meaning "loss of appetite due to nervousness." This term, however, is not accurate, since there is often, in fact, no loss of appetite. Probably the best designation for this disorder (but few would favor again changing the name) is the German *pubertaetsmagersucht,* meaning "adolescent pursuit of thinness."

Morton noted, astutely, that anorexia "flatters and deceives the patient." It flatters in that a young women who is mildly overweight feels a great sense of accomplishment when she starts to diet. It deceives in that as normal dieting turns into starvation the sufferer begins to think that she looks better as a skeleton than as a healthy human being. In anorexia, the normal sense of body image becomes unhinged. Even as a patient becomes seriously ill, she pushes herself to lose even more weight by such measures as inducing vomiting, abusing laxatives and diuretics, exercising prodigiously, and absolutely refusing to eat.

To me, anorexia nervosa is the most puzzling of all psychiatric disorders. The girls and young women who contract it (it rarely strikes men) seem almost psychotic. Their lack of ability to reason and their extremely distorted body image suggest to me some major biological brain abnormality. Yet no such major brain irregularity has been found so far.

In my psychiatric training at the University of Iowa, I worked on a hospital ward with a program devoted to the treatment of anorexia nervosa. At that time, we used a strict behavior modification program to foster weight gain: A patient was granted privileges such as radio, TV, letters, guests, and passes only as she put on weight. The program always worked for weight gain, but many of our patients relapsed as soon as they were discharged.

The treatment now favored for anorexia nervosa is cognitive therapy: working to help a patient gain an understanding of, and then to actively refute, her distorted attitudes and beliefs, especially self-image. Exposure and response prevention techniques, so helpful for OCD, do not work in this disorder. The SRI medications may be somewhat helpful, but generally the results are not impressive. The psychiatric therapies for anorexia nervosa remain, on the whole, disappointing.

There are obvious overlaps between anorexia nervosa and OCD. The anorexic's preoccupations with weight loss and body image resemble obsessions, and her rituals of repeated weighing, checking in mirrors, measuring body parts, and hiding food look very much like compulsions. Furthermore, the two disorders often occur together: Up to a third of anorexia nervosa patients also have OCD. As a result, the two disorders have often been assumed to be closely related. In the 1940s, psychiatrists considered changing the name of anorexia nervosa to "obsessive-compulsive neurosis with loss of weight."

A closer look, however, reveals that there are more differences than similarities. Most conspicuous is the mystifying lack of insight possessed by anorexia nervosa sufferers in regard to their condition. Whereas OCDers fight to put obsessions out of mind, anorexics welcome their distorted ideas. Whereas OCDers consider their obsessions to be unwanted and alien, anorexics look on their preoccupations as one of the most meaningful parts of their innermost selves.

IMPULSIVE STEALING AND SEXUAL ADDICTIONS

OFTEN INCLUDED IN the OC spectrum are a handful of disorders characterized by irresistible urges to engage in behaviors that are unethical, immoral, or self-destructive, such as stealing, setting fires, pathological gambling, and random sexual acts. The people who suffer from irresistible urges differ from others who behave in the same manner in this way: They truly do not want to carry out the acts that get them in trouble.

Terminology is a problem. Sometimes these disorders are referred to as compulsions, as in "a shoplifting compulsion," but strictly speaking this is an incorrect use of the word. Often, too, these disorders are referred to as addictions. This label is more appropriate, in that these are destructive habits in which a person's well-being is sacrificed for a short-term excitation. But the best term for these behaviors is the one used in the diagnostic manual of American psychiatry (DSM-IV): impulse control disorders.

Impulsive stealing has been recognized as a psychiatric disorder for many centuries. The most famous French psychiatrist of the 1800s, Jean Esquirol, named it "kleptomania" (stealing insanity) and defined it as a disorder in which "voluntary control is profoundly compromised: the patient is constrained to perform acts which are dictated neither by his reason or his emotions—acts which his conscience disapproves of, but over which he no longer has willful control."

It is important to note that the great majority of people who steal do not have this disorder. A recent study of 50 apprehended shoplifters found that only 4 percent could be diagnosed as having kleptomania. (The rest were, presumably, simply criminals.) Another recent finding is that up to 30 percent of people with kleptomania have OCD. Stealing would seem to run counter to the overly conscientious nature of OCDers, but this is sometimes not the case.

Alex, a tall, gangly postal clerk with a broad face and a stubby ponytail, came to see me early in 1996 after being arrested for shoplifting. A very outgoing and friendly man, Alex tended to talk endlessly and without pause on any subject, so that I had interrupt him frequently in order to gather a history.

Alex explained that he came to see me because he had a problem he couldn't solve. It had started about a year and a half before. While on vacation, browsing in a department store, he had had the sudden impulse to steal a souvenir. In "sort of a dreamlike state," as he put it, he simply hid the item under his arm and walked out. Once safely in his car, he experienced "a wonderful feeling, like a rush, like a kid opening presents on a Christmas morning."

The next day he awoke feeling very ashamed. The shoplifting had been intoxicating, but the guilt he felt was "a terrible hangover." Despite strong feelings of remorse, however, shoplifting slowly developed into a regular habit.

"I'll walk into J.C. Penney," Alex told me, "and when no one is looking I reach down under the checkout counter and pull out a plastic bag. I walk around putting items in the bag like a kid on a shopping spree. On the way out I even joke with the sales people. Or I'll go into a convenience store to buy cigarettes, and before I know it I steal a hoagie for lunch.

"It's out of control," he added. "Shoplifting has become a way of life. I've tried my best to stop, but I can't. I'm addicted to it."

When I questioned Alex about his past history, I found that as a young man he had suffered mild to moderate OCD characterized by obsessions to jump off buildings and bridges. I asked him how his present impulses compared to his past obsessions. He replied: "My thoughts to jump off bridges were terribly frightening. The shoplifting thoughts are much different—they give me a high."

Alex's last comment points out a major difference between impulsive shoplifting and OCD. Although both involve repetitive behaviors that a person doesn't want to do, shoplifting and the other impulse control disorders involve a certain thrill, whereas there is no gratification or pleasure involved in OCD.

The crucial differences between impulse disorders and OCD can again be made clear by contrasting two common sexual problems. On the one hand, there are repulsive sexual thoughts that a person fights to get out of mind. One example would be the unwanted homosexual thoughts of Jeff, described in Chapter 1. Another, the ultimate blasphemous thought of a surprising number of OCD women, is that of having sex with Jesus. Such thoughts are typically fended off through compulsions such as repeated prayers. This is OCD.

On the other hand there are impulsive sexual behaviors that cannot be controlled. Not long ago I treated a student who came for help because she had become a "sex addict." Almost every night she went to bars and picked up men. She would take them back to her apartment and aggressively initiate sexual relations, getting a thrill out of staying in total control of the situation. One day, however, she realized that she didn't want to do this any longer. She tried to stop but found she could not. Invariably, she gave in to irresistible urges to pick up men. This is an impulse control disorder.

There is a way in which impulse control disorders and OCD are the exact opposites: One involves giving in to an urge; the other, fighting it off. Consider my own obsession to stab myself with a needle. Fortunately, I did not have the rare impulse control disorder known as impulsive self-mutilation and prick myself. Rather, having an average case of OCD, I conjured up mental compulsions to counter the obsession.

Because of this inverse relationship, it has been suggested that impulse control disorders and OCD may represent over-excitation and under-excitation of the same brain system. This hypothesis has received some support from studies on violent, impulsive criminals, who appear to have decreased brain cell activity in the same general area where OCDers show hyperactivity. Thus, the two disorders could be related in the same way as hypothyroidism and hyperthyroidism are—at opposite ends of a single spectrum of physiologic activity. Against this hypothesis, however, is the puzzling fact that some people have both disorders at the same time. Whether impulse control disorders and OCD belong in the same spectrum is not yet clear. What is very clear, however, is that they are very different problems.

In the treatment of impulse control disorders, habit reversal techniques are sometimes helpful, but exposure and response does not work at all. What was helpful for Alex's impulsive shoplifting was to make him more aware of the times and circumstances when he was most likely to shoplift and to rehearse ways of overcoming the urge to steal. In addition, practical steps that limited the opportunities for shoplifting were very beneficial, including taking a companion and wearing tight clothes when shopping. Overall, however, the treatment of impulse control disorders is much more difficult than that of OCD.

SRI medications can be quite helpful, but the therapeutic effect often seems to wear off. Occasionally, SRI medications actually make impulse control disorders worse. I myself saw a patient whose impulsive shoplifting started shortly after he was put on Prozac. The anti-anxiety effect of the medication took away his ability to resist the urge to steal. Treatment consisted of getting him off his SRI.

It is well to note that none of the OC spectrum disorders has been studied nearly as extensively as OCD itself. In the 1996 edition of the authoritative text *Psychiatric Diagnosis,* the authors caution that "only about a dozen" psychiatric problems have yet been studied in sufficient detail to demonstrate that they are valid and reliable medical diagnoses; that is, that they represent homogeneous disorders that can be clearly recognized, and that do not change into anything else. OCD is included on the list, but hypochondriasis, body dysmorphic disorder, trichotillomania, and the impulse control disorders probably contain several independent syndromes within their boundaries, some of which may be related to OCD, some not.

We will be in a better position to judge which disorders are closely related to OCD when advances in research allow psychiatric syndromes to be classified on the basis of pathophysiologic cause rather than symptoms, an evolutionary step that most fields of medicine took long ago. These advances now appear tantalizingly on the horizon.

11

SPIRITUAL DIRECTORS AND GREEK DOCTORS: A HISTORICAL PERSPECTIVE ON OCD TREATMENT

WHEN I WAS in training in the early 1970s, neither behavior therapy nor medications were used as treatment for OCD. The great majority of psychiatrists favored psychoanalysis and other closely related forms of psychotherapy. Behavior therapy, although known to be helpful in the treatment of phobias, seemed too superficial for complex problems such as obsessions and compulsions. And although medications were used to treat the severe anxiety that often accompanies OCD, they were to be avoided if possible since they were thought to interfere with the ability to participate fully in psychotherapy.

Within fifteen years, however, psychoanalysis was out and behavior therapy was in. Medications were no longer considered a hindrance to therapy but rather a first-line treatment. These changes were part of a general about-face in psychiatry away from Freud's theories. Psychiatrists were thrown into an identity crisis. It seemed our profession had suddenly abandoned a time-honored course and lurched out in totally different directions.

Yet a closer look reveals that, at least in the case of OCD, what actually happened was that psychiatry simply circled back to its origins. An examination of available historical reports shows that from antiquity to relatively recently the two primary treatments for OCD have been behavior therapy and medications.

BEHAVIOR THERAPY

ALTHOUGH BEHAVIOR THERAPY was not embraced by the field of medicine until the twentieth century, its essential techniques—exposure and response prevention—were, indeed, widely used in prior centuries. As has been pointed out previously, because OCDers show a strong aversion to seeing physicians, psychiatrists have drastically underestimated the true incidence of OCD. Who have OCDers turned to for help? In Western cultures, people who suffered from obsessions and compulsions have turned primarily to the clergy.

This makes sense considering that OCD, more than any other mental disorder, has seemed to deal directly with spiritual matters. Obsessions, which tend to take as their subject whatever provokes the most fear, very frequently used to take the form of direct, blasphemous thoughts against God. Past accounts suggest, in fact, that obsessions dealing with blasphemy were once the most common type, a conclusion supported by studies showing that even now obsessions with religious content predominate in devoutly religious communities. Compulsions, too, often took the form of muttering prayers, making religious gestures, and repeatedly confessing sins.

Many of the manuals for religious counselors of past centuries contain sections on how to deal with the tormenting thoughts and repetitive behaviors we now recognize as obsessions and compulsions. What is astonishing is the depth of psychological insight shown by some of the spiritual directors. Although they classified obsessions and compulsions as types of religious temptations, they did not recommend treating them by religious means, such as fasts, penances, or prayer. Rather they recommended what can be easily recognized as behavior therapy.

SPIRITUAL DIRECTION IN THE MIDDLE AGES

ONE OF THE earliest reports of the treatment of severe obsessions by exposure and response prevention is related by Saint John Climacus (570–649). He tells the story of a religious brother who was overcome by intrusive, blasphemous thoughts:

> A certain monk was troubled for twenty years by horrible temptations to blasphemy. He rejected them with abhorrence and vehemence, arming himself against them by fasts, watchings, and great austerities. Yet because he adopted an unsuitable method, his temptations, far from showing any diminution, daily grew more harassing. At length, being quite at a loss to know what to do, he took counsel of a holy monk. Not venturing to tell him by word of mouth the wicked and detestable thoughts that swarmed in his mind, he gave him a paper to read containing them, remaining meanwhile prostrate with his face upon the ground, deeming himself unworthy to raise his eyes.
>
> The wise old monk read the paper, and quietly spoke as follows: "My son, I take upon myself all the sins which these temptations have led you, or may lead you, to commit. All I require of you is that for the future you pay no attention to them whatever."
>
> At these words the temptations vanished from the mind of the monk, simply because he was made free from the alarm which gave occasion to all his fancies.

This advice seems simple—as behavior therapy always does—but contains a wealth of insight. First of all, the wise old monk recognized that these temptations were not of the normal variety to be fought by spiritual means. Instead, these thoughts were what we now know as obsessions, the key psychological truth of which he articulated clearly: It is the alarm, or fear, that attends such thoughts that keeps them coming back. What he recommended was a psychological approach: Learn to ignore these thoughts. As for compulsions, or "watchings," the wise old monk deemed these "unsuitable methods" for dealing with such thoughts. Good behavior therapy.

Later in the Middle Ages, the anonymous author of the classic Christian text *The Cloud of Unknowing* suggested similar strategies for dealing with obsessions.

> If it happens that certain thoughts or impulses concerning sins . . . are always inserting themselves in your awareness . . . I would like to tell you something, according to my experience, about some spiritual tactics by which you can put them away.
>
> [The first is] you are to do all that lies in you to act as though you did not know that they are pressing upon you very hard. Try to look over their shoulders, as it were, as though you were looking for something else.
>
> [Another is] when you feel that you can in no way put down these thoughts, cower down under them like a poor wretch and a coward overcome in battle, and reckon it to be a waste of time for you to strive any longer against them. Feel as though you are hopelessly defeated.

The reader may recognize two of the more popular present-day strategies for dealing with OCD, as discussed in Chapter 6: ignoring obsessions, and imagining the worst and accepting it (the behavior technique of flooding).

In order to prevent giving a grossly inaccurate picture of the treatment of OCD in the Middle Ages and Renaissance, it should be acknowledged that, undoubtedly, most people were not counseled with such insight and understanding. It is clear from both civil and church records that harm and blasphemous obsessions were often taken as signs of demonic possession and that some people with OCD were brought to trial for witchery. In *Mystical Bedlam,* Michael MacDonald points out that "few of the people who thought they were possessed by the devil suffered from insanity or displayed spectacular symptoms. Most of them complained of anxiety, religious fears, and evil thoughts."

A 1584 case of apparent OCD in which the sufferer was almost burned at the stake is recorded by a justice of the peace of that time, Reginald Scott of Kent, England. Scott writes of Mrs. Davie, "a good wife," who was brought before him after she admitted to having evil thoughts to harm her family. The prosecutors wanted her torched, but Scott ruled, "She hurt no one except, by her imagination, herself. . . . Anyone who looks closely at the thoughts, words, and actions of this woman will perceive that she is not a scheming witch, but a poor deceived, melancholy woman. . . . No one in his right wits would believe her." Other OCDers were surely not so fortunate in those who would judge them.

But at least in some levels of the Christian church, progress continued to be made in understanding the peculiar tormenting thoughts we now know as obsessions and the strange repetitive actions called compulsions. Richard Baxter (1615–1691), an English minister very famous in his own time, offered advice for OCDers in his *Christian Directory* that is so good it can hardly be improved upon. Baxter suggests: (1) Take less notice of your troublesome thoughts. They are like troublesome scolds. If you answer them, they will never be done with you. But if you let them talk, and take no notice of them, they will become weary. (2) Trust not your own judgment, but commit yourself to the direction of an experienced guide. (3) Be sure that you keep yourself constantly employed as far as your strength will bear.

ENLIGHTENED SPIRITUAL DIRECTION

PERHAPS THE MOST insightful discussion of OCD from centuries past is that of John Baptist Scaramelli, a Jesuit who wrote in 1753 a popular instruction manual for spiritual directors, *The Directorium Asceticum*. Scaramelli devotes a hundred pages to obsessions, compulsions, and their treatment, anticipating modern concepts and approaches.

He first points out that certain temptations come into the mind that, unlike other temptations, are detestable to both the rational and the animal part of our being. These temptations, which include certain blasphemous and abominable thoughts, are not dangerous in themselves. They can, however, cause great turmoil and spiritual desolation. Scaramelli astutely notes that "the more these thoughts are driven away, the more they return to the mind, because resistance to them only stirs them up and imprints them more deeply." As for how to deal with such thoughts, Scaramelli emphasizes:

The priest should tell the sufferer first that he does not commit a sin by having such thoughts. Then he should order the sufferer not to act against the thoughts, for it is unwise to struggle or to enter into hand-to-hand combat with these. The sufferer should allow them to pass through his mind, without giving ear to them. He should fix his attention on what he is doing—to go on praying if at prayer; talking if in conversation; working if occupied. In a word, the sufferer should deal with these temptations just as if an idiot were to whisper them in his ears: he should go on without giving notice to them.

Scaramelli gives an especially comprehensive account of scruples, obsessions that take the form of tormenting religious doubts. He likens scruples to "a kind of pitch—the more we handle them by thinking and talking about them, the more they stick." He advises, therefore, "It is best to take no notice of them . . . and to keep fully occupied." Aware of the shortcomings of many religious counselors, he wisely advises the scrupulous to "avoid people of narrow conscience; and seek out the advice of not just any priest, but of an experienced, spiritual master."

Scaramelli deals at length with compulsions. He describes mental compulsions, which he refers to as "interior acts," such as people repeating prayers and saying certain words over and over. He also describes behavioral compulsions, "exterior acts," such as people shaking their heads, pressing their hands upon their bosoms, and rolling their eyes strangely. The result of all of these, Scaramelli notes, is that "the more the thoughts are driven away the more they return to the mind." Scaramelli highlights the particular problems of endlessly repeated confessions and prayer rituals. Of the latter he notes: "Some persons are greatly distressed in reciting vocal prayers, fancying they have omitted portions, or not pronounced the words plainly, so that they repeat again and again the same words, without, of course, ever gaining any peace or satisfaction from so doing." The advice he gives is to stop the rituals: "Such people should be commanded to go forward in their prayers, and they must be forbidden ever to repeat any portion."

Scaramelli's approach is distinctly psychological. Of obsessions and compulsions, he notes, "Their first cause is a melancholy, gloomy, timid, and anxious character." This eighteenth-century spiritual master must have dealt with some tough cases. He reminds me of present-day psychiatrists commiserating with their colleagues over coffee when he describes the frustration of dealing with treatment-resistant OCDers:

> They hold obstinately to their own opinions and after having consulted a multitude of advisers, end at length by doing what they themselves think to be best.
>
> Their care is one of the most arduous tasks that can fall to the lot of a physician of souls. For even as these poor creatures are ever tormenting themselves with the self-same scruples, they fail not to torment their confessors with never-ending repetitions. It is arduous, because this malady is one from which few recover completely . . . if they go not mad themselves, they will at least make their confessors go mad.

Sound Advice from Saints Who Suffered OCD

SAINT IGNATIUS OF Loyola, Saint Therese of Lisieux, and John Bunyan are all celebrated for their unique spirituality. As discussed in Chapter 3, these three luminaries also suffered OCD early in their lives. Of special interest is the fact that Ignatius, Therese, and Bunyan incorporated into their writings what amounts to behaviorally sound advice for OCD: exposure to obsessions and prevention of compulsions.

The approach of Saint Ignatius (1491-1556), founder of the Jesuits, is strongly introspective and analytical. Ignatius emphasizes the cardinal importance of identifying the nature of the thought that one is experiencing. Some types of thoughts come from Satan, the traditional purveyor of all bad thoughts. One specific type is that which we now call obsessions. Once it is recognized that Satan is at work, and that obsessions are the problem, Ignatius recommends preserving peace in the mind by ignoring these particular thoughts. In a letter to a friend suffering apparent obsessions, Ignatius writes:

> It is necessary therefore to ascertain the nature of the condition we experience. . . . If the enemy discovers a conscience that is overly tender, he endeavors to torment, suggesting sin where there is none,

anything to be able to disturb and afflict us. . . . If it is [this kind of] temptation that besets us, we must bear up against it without any vexation, and await the consolation of the Lord with patience. . . . Pay no attention whatsoever to the bad, impure, and sensual thoughts.

This excellent advice is consistent with modern behavioral therapy: once it is recognized that an obsession is the problem, try to bear it with patience and avoid fighting it.

John Bunyan, whose Puritan spirituality influenced Protestantism, including modern-day Evangelicalism, to a degree that cannot be overestimated, wrote two pamphlets, *The Doctrine of the Law and Grace Unfolded* and *Some Gospel Truths Opened,* only a short time after recovering from his lengthy OCD crisis. In them he says:

Know it for a truth that the greater you see your sins to be, the more cause you have to believe. . . . You must come to Christ with the fire of hell in your conscience; come with your heart hard, dead, cold, full of wickedness and madness; come as a blood-red sinner. Throw yourself down at the foot of Christ and say, "Lord Jesus hear a sinner, a sinner that deserves to be damned." Resolve never to give over crying until you find that he has washed your conscience with his blood.

The important point here is that Bunyan encourages maximum exposure to obsessions. In fact, putting a remarkable spin on tormenting thoughts, Bunyan suggests that having sinful obsessions is actually good for you, because "the greater you see your sins to be, the more cause you have to believe." Bunyan's advice is to keep coming to God with the full weight of your obsessions until you feel peaceful, or, in behavioral terms, to keep exposing yourself maximally to obsessions until habituation takes place.

Bunyan also emphasizes response prevention. Having learned from painful personal experience that efforts to reform, performances of certain rituals, and reassurances gained from reading scripture were of no help for his OCD, he cautions against the use of compulsions.

Have care of putting off your trouble of spirit in the wrong way: by promising to reform yourself and lead a new life, by your performances or duties, [by being] content with any knowledge that you can attain to by yourself. They that are saved are saved by Grace through faith; not for anything they can do themselves.

Therese of Lisieux, called by a recent pope the greatest of modern-day saints, developed a spirituality centered on abandonment and trust. Like Bunyan, she discovered through personal experience that obsessions do not respond to acts of will. What worked was surrender to God. In *Story of a Soul* Therese writes: "Even though I have on my conscience all the sins that can be committed, I go, my heart broken with sorrow, and throw myself into Jesus' arms. . . . What pleases God is the blind hope that I have in His mercy."

Therese's cousin, Marie Guerin, suffered sexual obsessions. In a letter to Therese, Marie admits her shameful thoughts and requests counsel. Therese responds affectionately with advice that is behaviorally sound.

I understand everything, everything, everything, everything! You haven't committed the shadow of any evil; I know these kinds of temptations so well that I can assure you of this without any fear. . . . We must despise all these temptations and pay no attention whatsoever to them. . . . Don't listen to the devil. Mock him.

MEDICINE FINALLY EMBRACES BEHAVIOR THERAPY

DESPITE THE FACT that exposure and response prevention had been used for many centuries to deal with obsessions and compulsions, these techniques were not adopted specifically as medical treatments until the turn of the twentieth century, when French psychiatrist Pierre Janet (1859–1947) wrote his monumental, two-volume work on OCD: *Obsessions and Psychasthenia*. Janet may have appreciated the techniques used by spiritual directors, since he cites the case of a soldier who was cured of OCD when he entered a monastery, and he also remarks on several obsessive-compulsive women who remained well only as long as they lived in convents. In any case, he spells out clearly many of the principles of behavior therapy. Here, for instance, he explains how the psychiatrist should direct the OCD sufferer to expose himself to fearful obsessions:

> The therapist will specify the action as precisely as possible. He will analyze it into its elements if it should be necessary to give the patient's mind an immediate and proximate aim. By continually repeating the order to perform the action, that is, exposure, he will help the patient greatly by words of encouragement at every sign of success, however insignificant, for encouragement will make the patient realize these little successes and will stimulate him with the hopes aroused by glimpses of greater successes in the future.

PSYCHOANALYSIS

UNFORTUNATELY FOR THE development of behavior therapy, Janet's contributions were soon overshadowed by those of Austrian psychiatrist Sigmund Freud, who explained his ideas on the cause and cure of OCD in a famous 1909 case study known as "Rat Man." This case involved "a youngish man of university education" who was virtually incapacitated by multiple obsessions and compulsions, including blasphemous religious thoughts, repugnant sexual ideas, and gut-wretchingly terrifying images of rats eating him and his father. After relating the details of the case, Freud gives his theory:

> All through the patient's life, he was unmistakably victim to a conflict between love and hatred. . . . In the unconscious the hatred, safe from the danger of being destroyed by the operations of consciousness, was able to persist and even to grow. . . . We may regard the repression of his infantile hatred of his father as the event which brought his whole subsequent career under the dominion of the obsessional neurosis.

To cure such unconscious conflicts, Freud invented psychoanalysis, a technique in which the patient lies on a couch and says everything that comes into his mind. The hidden information in the unconscious gradually becomes known, often in the form of symbols, which must be interpreted by the physician. In the case of "Rat Man," Freud assures us that psychoanalysis, lasting for about a year, resulted in "the complete restoration of the patient's personality and to the removal of his inhibitions."

Psychoanalysis soon became the treatment of choice for OCD among psychiatrists in America and Central Europe and remained so for the next sixty years. Case reports were frequently cited as proof of its efficacy, but no controlled studies were done until the 1960s. Research since then has conclusively demonstrated that psychoanalysis does not work as a specific treatment for OCD. Well-known psychiatric researchers Donald Goodwin and Samuel Guze, authors of the authoritative text *Psychiatric Diagnosis,* reviewed the treatment of OCD with psychoanalysis and related therapies and concluded that there was no evidence at all to support their value.

In comparing psychoanalysis and behavior therapy as treatments for OCD, it is important to note that the two are not only very different but opposite in crucial points of emphasis. Behavior therapy emphasizes action, psychoanalysis introspection; behavior therapy says you have the ability to control your behavior, psychoanalysis says much of it is out of your control; behavior therapy holds that obsessions are random thoughts without special meaning, psychoanalysis that obsessions conceal important aspects of yourself.

Psychoanalysis may well have much to offer certain patients, particularly those with traumatic childhoods who suffer from such disorders as multiple personality, amnesia, and dissociation. In the case of OCD, however, psychoanalysis and other "uncovering" therapies are not only ineffective, they can actually be harmful. A 1995 report from the University of Cincinnati, for instance, cited cases where OCD was exacerbated by therapy aimed at uncovering childhood abuse. My own experience, too, is that in the treatment of OCD, therapies that search for unconscious meanings do more harm than good.

MODERN BEHAVIOR THERAPY

NOT UNTIL THE 1960s, when psychoanalysis began to fall from favor as a treatment for OCD, was anything on behavior therapy published that went beyond the writings of Pierre Janet. Then British researcher Victor Meyer, building on the earlier work of Joseph Wolpe and others who had successfully used behavior therapy to treat simple phobias, reported on the successful treatment of fifteen hospitalized OCD patients. Meyer used a program of classic exposure and response prevention: Patients were systematically exposed to situations that elicited their obsessional fears, such as public restrooms, and then prevented from performing responsive rituals, such as showering. The results were striking: Ten of the fifteen patients improved markedly.

Since then, over seventy published studies have demonstrated that behavior therapy is an effective treatment for OCD. English researchers Isaac Marks and Stanley Rachman, along with America's Edna Foa, have led the way in developing new behavior therapy techniques, such as using cassette loop tapes to facilitate exposure to obsessions and involving family members to aid in response prevention. Improvement in behavior therapy techniques has allowed greater numbers of patients to receive more benefit in a shorter length of time. In a widely reported 1994 study, three quarters of patients using behavior therapy two hours a day for a two-week period showed a drop in symptom scores of 30 percent or more.

MEDICATIONS

THE USE OF medication for OCD also dates back many centuries, although the number of OCD cases described by physicians and treated with medication is far fewer than the number described by clergymen and treated with behavior therapy. The ancient Greeks, founders of scientific medicine, were the first to put forth completely naturalistic explanations for all diseases, including mental disorders. The father of medicine, Hippocrates (460–377 B.C.), wrote:

> And men ought to know that from nothing else but thence [from the brain] come joys, delights, laughter, and sports, and sorrows, griefs, despondency, and lamentations. . . . And by the same organ we become mad and delirious, and fears and terrors assail us, some by night, and some by day, and dreams and untimely wanderings, and cares that are not suitable, and ignorance of present circumstances, desuetude, and unskillfulness. All these things we endure from the brain, when it is not healthy, but is more hot, more cold, more moist, or more dry than natural.

Hippocrates founded the "humoral theory" of disease. The body had four humors, black bile, yellow bile, blood, and phlegm, each of which differed from the others in being either hot or cold, and either moist or dry. All diseases were due to excesses of one or more of the four humors, and all diseases could be cured by draining off the humors that were in excess. Purgatives could empty the body of black bile by inducing bowel movements; emetics could empty it of yellow bile by inducing vomiting; salivants and blood letting could likewise drain the body of phlegm and blood.

Later Greeks divided all mental illnesses into depression, mania, and delirium. OCD—at least in its severe form—was viewed as a type of depression, or melancholia, which means, literally, an excess of black bile. An account is given by Plutarch (A.D. 46–120) of a probable OCD sufferer with religious obsessions and compulsions to roll on the ground:

> Nowhere can he find an escape from his imaginary terrors. Every little evil is magnified by the scaring specters of his anxiety. . . . Ever and anon he confesses about this and that sin. He has eaten or drunk something wrong; he has gone some way or other which the Divine Being did not approve of. . . . His reason always slumbers; his fears are always awake.

This OCDer would have been treated with the commonly prescribed drug for melancholia, the strong cathartic referred to as "black hellebore," to induce bowel movements and restore the balance of black bile.

One of the most astonishing aspects of the entire history of medicine is the length of time that the Grecian humoral theory of disease held sway. Physicians continued to try to balance the body's humors with laxatives, emetics, salivants, and blood letting until the 1700s. A case of clear-cut obsessive-compulsive disorder found in Hunter and Macalpine's *Three Hundred Years of Psychiatry* demonstrates that in the best academic centers of the eighteenth century not much had changed in the medical treatment of OCD over the course of two thousand years.

TREATMENT OF HARM OBSESSIONS IN 1716

JOHN WOODWARD (1665–1728) was a professor of medicine in London who kept detailed case histories on his patients, many of whom had psychiatric disorders. He was consulted on November 6, 1716, by Mrs. Holmes, a twenty-six-year-old woman, pregnant with child, for an illness that had started some five months before. Dr. Woodward explains that his patient had one day observed, pleasantly enough, a large porpoise playing in the Thames River. Strangely, however, thoughts of the porpoise had thereafter kept intruding on her mind, soon becoming quite unpleasant and bothersome. Subsequently other unpleasant thoughts had begun to torment Mrs. Holmes, including ideas of harm coming to her unborn baby: "The thoughts obtruded themselves upon her, much to her surprise, and without any reason that she could conceive. They molested and teased her . . . and persecuted her almost incessantly day and night. She never awakened but these thoughts first came into her mind, and they continued till she went to sleep again."

As the months went by, Mrs. Holmes's obsessions became worse and worse. Dr. Woodward tells us that "she had thoughts of the Devil tempting and vehemently urging her to fling her child into the fire, beat its brains out, and the like; to which she had the utmost horror and aversion; being naturally a mild, good natured, and very virtuous woman." The doctor notes that she developed what we would now call mental compulsions: "She frequently endeavored to cast the thought out, and to introduce another that might be more pleasing to her; in which she sometimes succeeded; but the new thought, however pleasant at first, became, in a little time, as troublesome and disturbing as that of the other." Eventually, he informs us, she became confined to her bed. "She was neither capable of business, nor any regular thought; she durst never be by her self, or alone, for fear of some ill accident."

Dr. Woodward understood the basic nature of obsessions and was severely critical of a previous physician who had advised Mrs. Holmes to overcome her bad thought by trying to think more cheerful ones:

> People in these cases are subject to the fury of a morbid principle, and wholly under the government of it. It is the nature and property of that principle to disturb the thoughts, pervert the reasoning power, and present melancholy and vexatious ideas and images of things. So that to advise them to think rightly, or to be cheerful, is just the same as to advise a man under a severe fit of the gout to be easy and to be in no pain.

Yet, despite a good deal of insight into the psychology of obsessions, Dr. Woodward, when finally consulted, merely prescribed strong purgatives and enemas, which, he tells us, "worked plentifully, giving at least a dozen stools." He repeated this therapy a number of times, after which the intrusive thoughts disappeared and, Dr. Woodward assures us, Mrs. Holmes became "cheerful, easy, and well." (What cured the patient? Not the laxatives and enemas, but perhaps Dr. Woodward's optimism that a cure was available, as well as his reassurance that she was not to blame for her dreadful thoughts. Also important was the successful completion of what had been for Mrs. Holmes a medically difficult and therefore very stressful pregnancy.)

During the eighteenth and nineteenth centuries, great advances were made in the newly established fields of neurology and psychiatry, particularly in understanding the causes of disease. Mental problems were no longer attributed to imbalances in the body's four humors but to imbalances in the brain and nervous system. Now, for the first time, it was possible to have a "nervous disorder." Yet, while other branches of medicine were witnessing sweeping advances in medication treatments, in that regard psychiatry was progressing at a snail's pace.

TREATMENT OF CONTAMINATION OBSESSIONS IN 1879

WILLIAM HAMMOND (1828–1900), who was surgeon-general of the U.S. Army and president of the American Neurological Association, is famous for coining the term "athetosis" to describe a common form of involuntary movement. This man of many talents also authored a psychiatric text, *A Treatise on Insanity in Its Medical Relations,* and was something of a specialist in OCD. Citing fourteen cases that he had personally treated, he described the obsessive fear of contamination and named it "mysophobia."

A typical case cited by Dr. Hammond is that of "a young lady, aged eighteen, tall and slender," who presented to him on January 23, 1879. She had been entirely well until a year and a half before, when she had discovered lice in her hair. Thereafter, despite repeated washings with soap, carbolic acid, and many other detergents and disinfectants, she could not shake a fear of lice infestation. She spent over an hour a day minutely examining and cleansing her combs and brushes. When she went out into the street, on passing any person, she carefully gathered her skirts together, and she would not for any reason allow a child to approach her. Gradually the fear of lice infestation broadened to encompass other areas of her life:

> Little by little the idea became rooted that she could not escape sources of contamination. She washed her hands, as her mother informed me she had ascertained by actual count, over two hundred times a day. Her fear of contamination extended to the soap with which she felt compelled to wash her hands, and she was then obliged to wash them again in pure water in order to remove all traces of the soap. Then as the towel with which she wiped them dry had been washed with soap, she rinsed her hands in water, and allowed them to dry without the aid of a towel.

In removing her clothes at night, she carefully avoided touching them with her hands, because then she would not have sufficient opportunity for washing. She therefore had someone else to loosen the fastenings, and then she allowed her garments to drop on the floor. A great source of anxiety with her was the fact that her clothes were washed in the laundry with the clothing of other people; but she saw no practicable way of escape from this circumstance.

When not washing her hands or examining her combs and brushes, she spent nearly all the rest of the day in carefully inspecting every article of furniture and dusting it many times. Thus, her whole life was one continued round of trouble, anxiety, and fear.

Dr. Hammond emphasizes that his mysophobia patients have full insight into the foolishness of their beliefs, a key diagnostic criterion for OCD. "I had no difficulty in getting her to admit the absurdity of her ideas. She stated that whenever she reflected upon the subject, she was convinced of their erroneous character, but that, nevertheless, she could not avoid acting as she did. For as soon as she was exposed to any possible source of contamination, the ideas returned in full force."

Dr. Hammond treated all cases of mysophobia with bromides. These simple salts, including potassium bromide, calcium bromide, and sodium bromide, were widely used at the turn of the twentieth century for sedation, having been introduced into medicine 1853 as the very first drugs specific for that action. Dr. Hammond notes of bromides: "There are few cases of morbid impulses and morbid fears, in the early part of their course, which resist their systematic and intelligent employment . . . the patient once more sleeps well, and the mind gradually gets rid of its aberrations and resumes its normal condition." He also often prescribed ergot preparations, strong drugs obtained from a wheat fungus that have a long history in medicine and a multitude of actions. Both bromides and ergot drugs, however, cause at best only a moderate antianxiety action and often are severely toxic. In addition, they have no direct antiobsessional effects at all. Along with these medications, and probably more helpfully, Dr. Hammond recommended keeping mentally and physically active.

Like many other physicians of his time, Dr. Hammond attributed mental disorders to local abnormalities in various parts of the brain. Mysophobia was due to edema, an excess of fluid, in certain brain areas. The medications he prescribed worked, he thought, by diminishing the caliber of the blood vessels in the brain, thus lessening the flow of blood and correcting the excess of fluid.

Another common theory in the late 1800s was that of Henry Maudsley (1835–1918), the most widely known English psychiatrist of the nineteenth century. Maudsley attributed OCD, which he viewed as a type of depression, to lowered "mental energy." In his 1895 *Pathology of the Mind,* the outstanding psychiatric textbook of that period, he hypothesizes that obsessions and compulsions are caused by "a drain of nerve force" due to either "innate nerve-weakness" or excessive life stresses:

> The fundamental fault is probably loose-knit cerebral centers, the inhibitory ties being weak, and consequently, separate thought-tracts taking on separate actions. Once an irregular action is established, it is a torment to the individual no matter what the particular tract and its conscious idea or impulse be. Thus he is in despair because he has the urgent impulse to do some ridiculous thing; or cannot help repeating an act foolishly over and over again; or he is constrained to think of doing an indecent act and is in a fright lest he should some day do it; or he is urged by a morbid spirit of curiosity to continually ask himself the reason of this and the reason again of that reason and so backwards the reasons of reasons without end.

Maudsley recommended treatment with "nerve tonics" such as opium and morphine prescribed three times a day. Low doses of arsenic were sometimes judged helpful as well, especially in combination with a narcotic. Maudsley also stressed the importance of living an active, disciplined, and self-controlled life and of exercising regularly.

Of course, it has turned out that no sorts of "edema" or "lowered mental energy" can be demonstrated in the brains of those who suffer OCD or other mental disorders. The medication treatments of the nineteenth century proved disappointing. Thus Freud, who had himself trained as a neurologist and had experimented with the use of cocaine as a therapeutic agent, became disenchanted with the state of psychiatry and proposed his revolutionary theories.

The textbook I used in medical school, Freedman and Kaplan's *Comprehensive Textbook of Psychiatry,* taught Freud's theories and suggested treating OCD with psychoanalysis. Regarding the use of medications, the authoritative text stated: "There are no drugs that have a specific action on the obsessive-compulsive symptoms, although the use of sedative and tranquilizers as an adjunct to psychotherapy may be helpful in cases where anxiety is excessive." I remember dutifully attempting to interpret my OCD patients' dreams in order to get to the roots of their unconscious conflicts, while avoiding prescribing anything.

It is notable that even while advocating his psychological theories, Freud wrote in 1920: "Biology is truly a land of unlimited possibilities. We may expect it to give us the most surprising information, and we cannot guess what answers it will return in a few dozen years to the questions we have put to it. They may be of a kind which will blow away the whole of our artificial structure of hypothesis." Regarding treatment, he predicted in 1938: "The future may teach us to exercise a direct influence, by means of particular chemical substances."

These prophesies were borne out shortly after I started training. Freud's prediction of "a few dozen years" wasn't off by much. In 1967, a Spanish psychiatrist, Lopez-Ibor, reported a drug that was specifically effective for OCD, clomipramine (Anafranil). Many case reports of its successful use followed, and in the 1980s more than fifteen double-blind and placebo controlled studies demonstrated beyond a doubt that it was a uniquely effective treatment for OCD.

Clomipramine was developed by chemists who added a chlorine atom to the molecular structure of the standard antidepressant imipramine in the hopes of finding a better antidepressant. Instead, fortuitously, the new agent was observed by psychiatrists to be helpful for OCD. Imipramine itself had been developed through experimental changes to the molecule of a certain antihistamine, done in the hope of building a better antihistamine. The compound was accidentally observed to work in the treatment of depression. All of the early breakthroughs in medication treatments for mental disorders were due to such serendipity.

In the 1970s, however, a remarkable advance in pharmacological research technique ushered in a whole new era in the development of drugs for psychiatric disorders. Solomon Snyder and colleagues at Johns Hopkins University developed a practical method of screening drugs for their effects on specific chemicals in the brain. The key discovery was finding a way to keep brain tissue chemically alive after an animal had been sacrificed. Using this technique, a rat could then be given a drug, sacrificed, and its brain tissue examined to see what effects that drug was having on various brain chemicals. Serendipity was no longer necessary. "Designer drugs" with specific effects on certain neurochemicals could now be developed.

Prozac, Luvox, Zoloft, and Paxil were all designer drugs, identified by their specific effects on serotonin. All have been proven very effective anti-OCD agents. Prozac was the first to be introduced in the United States, and its effectiveness in the treatment of OCD has been shown in more than a dozen double-blind studies, the largest a thirteen-week investigation of 355 OCD patients at eight different treatment centers. In this study, patients received either placebo, Prozac at a dose of 20 milligrams per day, Prozac at 40 milligrams per day, or Prozac at 80 milligrams per day. Mean drops in Y-BOCS scores (see Appendix A) were, respectively, 0.9, 4.6, 5.5, and 6.5. Similar multi-center studies involving hundreds of patients have now also proven clearly the efficacy of Luvox, Zoloft, and Paxil in treatment of OCD. All of the effective anti-OCD medications have approximately the same efficacy. So far, no study has convincingly shown one medication to work better than another.

RECENT ADVANCES

RESEARCH IN PSYCHIATRY and related fields is increasing exponentially. Every three to four years, the number of books written and studies published doubles. In the treatment of OCD, hot topics include how behavior therapy and medications can work best together and why a sizable minority of patients respond to neither treatment. One area of current clinical research that is especially interesting, and that may shed light on these very questions, suggests that there are essential similarities in the way behavior modification and medications work.

It has been clear since the early 1980s that approximately the same number of patients, 60–80 percent, are significantly helped by both behavior therapy and the serotonergic medications. (Although some studies do give a significant edge to behavior therapy, these usually do not include the relatively large number of patients, up to 30 percent, who drop out of behavior therapy. When dropouts are factored in, the two treatments again seem approximately equal.) Furthermore, the degree of improvement is similar with the two treatments. Even when they work, neither behavior therapy nor medication can cure OCD. They both produce similar drops in symptom scores, an average of 20–30 percent.

Another similarity is the length of time it takes the two treatments to work. Antiobsessional medications, it has been repeatedly observed, take more than two months to reach their full effect, a delay that has puzzled researchers, since the direct action of these medications on serotonin at the nerve synapses takes place within hours. Researchers have long concluded that secondary changes in the brain are responsible for the SRIs' therapeutic effects. A similar delay in therapeutic action is observed with behavior therapy. Obsessions and compulsions are not markedly decreased until after a person has employed behavioral techniques for a minimum of twenty to thirty exposure sessions, which usually takes a month or more.

Another similarity between behavior therapy and medication that has recently been reported—and this finding has even received attention in the lay press—points to a fundamental likeness in the biochemical effects of the two treatments in the brain. Lewis Baxter, Jeff Schwartz and colleagues at UCLA studied this phenomenon using PET scanning, the imaging technique that provides a moving picture of the brain at work. The surprising observation was that behavior therapy and medication, when effective, produced identical changes in the brains of OCD patients: specifically, decreased activity in a small part of the brain known as the orbital frontal area.

Baxter's research has forced a reanalysis of many basic assumptions about the differences between biological and psychological therapies. When I presented these findings to a group of general practitioners recently, a doctor put it this way: "But that can't be true, can it? Behavior therapy is by definition a psychological therapy, and it shouldn't produce physical changes in the brain." So many of us thought until recently, but this new evidence points otherwise. Behavior therapy and medication, two treatments that for millennia have seemed to have no common ground, do, in fact, share some sort of a final, common, biochemical pathway.

The best theory advanced so far to explain this finding is that of Harvard psychiatrist Steve Hyman, who speculates on a common biochemical action for behavior therapy and serotonergic medications in a recent book, *The Molecular Foundations of Psychiatry.* Hyman suggests that both forms of therapy cause the same effect at the same place in the brain: changes in the concentrations of neurotransmitters, particularly serotonin, at the brain cell junctures. In the case of medications, a large amount of evidence, some of which was reviewed in Chapter 9, demonstrates that they directly affect serotonin levels at the brain synapses. As for behavior therapy, Hyman speculates that all psychotherapies, indeed, all life events, also affect us by causing synaptic changes:

> Life experiences are perceived by an individual through sensory neurons—for example, sights by the retina and spoken words by the auditory system. This information is first analyzed in primary sensory areas of the cerebral cortex, then a wave of successive brain regions are recruited. . . . Perception, interpretation, response, and modulation are mediated via synaptic connections among a large number of individual neurons . . . leading to prolonged, and sometimes relatively stable, alterations in brain function, including memories.

The changes induced at synapses are, Hyman speculates, only the initial effects of medications and behavior therapy. "Secondary messengers" subsequently carry the chemical changes to the most basic of all cell structures, the genes. It is by altering the information that is transcribed from the genes that these two therapies are able to alter many different and far-reaching aspects of brain functioning, including those generally considered to be "psychological," such as memories, attitudes, and motivation.

The natural course of medicine in the twentieth century is this: A great discovery is made, it is implemented for a decade or two, then it is taken for granted. The first antibacterial drugs were introduced in the 1930s, and over the next decade the death rate from meningitis, pneumonia, and a number of other common infectious diseases dropped by more than 80 percent. As the discoverer of the sulfonamides, Gerhard Domagk, later noted, "We now accept as a matter of course the thousandfold miracle cures."

In historical perspective, psychiatry is in the midst of a leap forward that started about the time I was in medical school. In the case of OCD, spectacular treatments have been developed that are now in the early stages of implementation. As of now, many OCDers still do not know about them. My hope is this book will help behavior therapy and medication become accepted as a matter of course very soon.

APPENDIX A

THE YALE-BROWN
OBSESSIVE-COMPULSIVE SCALE

THE "Y-BOCS," THE most widely used of all OCD scales, is a ten-item questionnaire designed to quickly measure OCD's severity. Although excellent for following progress in treatment, it should not be relied upon to diagnose OCD, as it does not completely assess some important aspects of the disorder, such as degree of avoidance.

The Y-BOCS consists of five questions about obsessions and five very similar inquiries regarding compulsions. The items are well researched and reliable, although numbers 4 and 9 are a bit controversial. Each item is given a rating of 0 to 4, the total score for the test being the sum of the ratings for all ten. Usually, a score of 0–7 is within the normal range; 8–15 indicates mild OCD; 16–23 moderate OCD; 24–31 severe OCD; and 32–40 extreme OCD. Most people who present for treatment of OCD have scores in the 20–30 range. Studies suggest that 2 percent of the population will score 18 or above.

Instructions
READ AND ANSWER the following questions. Don't spend too much time trying to decide—just check the answer that seems to fit best.

1. How much of your time is occupied by obsessive thoughts? How frequently do the obsessive thoughts occur?

   0 = None.

   1 = Less than 1 hour per day, or occasional intrusions (occur not more than 8 times a day).

   2 = 1 to 3 hours per day, or frequent intrusions (occur more than 8 times a day, but most hours of the day are free of obsessions).

   3 = More than 3 and up to 8 hours per day, or very frequent intrusions.

   4 = More than 8 hours per day, or near-constant intrusions.

2. How much do your obsessive thoughts interfere with your work, school, social, or other important role functioning? Is there anything you don't do because of them?

   0 = None.

   1 = Slight interference with social or other activities, but overall performance not impaired.

   2 = Definite interference with social or occupational performance, but still manageable.

   3 = Causes substantial impairment in social or occupational performance.

   4 = Incapacitating.

3. How much distress do your obsessions cause you?

   0 = None.

   1 = Not too disturbing.

   2 = Disturbing but still manageable.

   3 = Very disturbing.

   4 = Near-constant and disabling distress.

4. How much of an effort do you make to resist the obsessive thoughts? How often do you try to turn your attention away from these thoughts as they enter your mind?

   0 = Try to resist all the time (or the symptoms are so minimal that there is no need to actively resist them).

   1 = Try to resist most of the time.

   2 = Make some effort to resist.

    3 = Yield to all obsessions without attempting to control them, but I do so with some reluctance.

    4 = Completely and willingly give in to all obsessions.

5. How much control do you have over your obsessive thoughts? How successful are you in stopping or diverting your obsessive thinking? (Note: Do not include here obsessions stopped by doing compulsions.)

    0 = Complete control.

    1 = Usually able to stop or divert obsessions with some effort and concentration.

    2 = Sometimes able to stop or divert obsessions.

    3 = Rarely successful in stopping obsessions, can only divert attention with difficulty.

    4 = Obsessions are completely involuntary, rarely able even momentarily to alter obsessive thinking.

6. How much time do you spend performing compulsive behaviors? How much longer than most people does it take to complete routine activities because of your rituals? How frequently do you perform rituals?

    0 = None.

    1 = Less than 1 hour per day, or occasional performance of compulsive behaviors (no more than 8 times a day).

    2 = From 1 to 3 hours per day, or frequent performance of compulsive behaviors (more than 8 times a day, but most hours are free of compulsions).

    3 = More than 3 and up to 8 hours per day, or very frequent performance of compulsive behaviors.

    4 = More than 8 hours per day, or near constant performance of compulsive behaviors.

7. How much do your compulsive behaviors interfere with your work, school, social, or other important role functioning? Is there anything that you don't do because of the compulsions?

    0 = None.

    1 = Slight interference with social or other activities, but overall performance not impaired.

    2 = Definite interference with social or occupational performance, but still manageable.

3 = Causes substantial impairment in social or occupational performance.

4 = Incapacitating.

8. How would you feel if prevented from performing your compulsion(s)? How anxious would you become?

    0 = None.

    1 = Only slightly anxious if compulsions prevented.

    2 = Anxiety would mount but remain manageable if compulsions prevented.

    3 = Prominent and very disturbing increase in anxiety if compulsions interrupted.

    4 = Incapacitating anxiety from any intervention aimed at modifying activity.

9. How much of an effort do you make to resist the compulsions?

    0 = Always try to resist (or the symptoms are so minimal that there is no need to actively resist them).

    1 = Try to resist most of the time.

    2 = Make some effort to resist.

    3 = Yield to almost all compulsions without attempting to control them, but with some reluctance.

    4 = Completely and willingly yield to all compulsions.

10. How strong is the drive to perform the compulsive behavior? How much control do you have over the compulsions?

    0 = Complete control.

    1 = Pressure to perform the behavior, but usually able to exercise voluntary control over it.

    2 = Strong pressure to perform behavior, can control it only with difficulty.

    3 = Very strong drive to perform behavior, must be carried to completion, can only delay with difficulty.

    4 = Drive to perform behavior experienced as completely involuntary and overpowering, rarely able to even momentarily delay activity.

APPENDIX B

THE DSM-IV DIAGNOSTIC CRITERIA
FOR OCD

PUBLISHED BY THE American Psychiatric Association, *The Diagnostic and Statistical Manual of Mental Disorders* is the standard guide for diagnosing mental disorders in the United States. Now published in fourteen languages, it is certainly the most authoritative and widely used manual of its type. Its diagnostic criteria are closely aligned to those of the official coding system for all medical disorders throughout the world, the International Classification of Diseases.

The DSM is an evolving document. Currently, it is in its fourth edition. New disorders are added when it becomes clear that they represent independent syndromes; old disorders are deleted if they are better included as parts others. When additional facts are learned about a particular disorder, its diagnostic criteria are modified to become more precise.

In the case of OCD, the most important recent change in diagnostic criteria has been the recognition of the importance of mental compulsions. Prior to the DSM-IV, compulsions were defined simply as behavioral, or observable, acts; now it is recognized that mental acts, or "thought compulsions," are also very common. The next major change in the DSM, some experts think, may be requiring that both obsessions and compulsions be present in order to make the diagnosis.

The DSM-IV, in introducing the topic of OCD, starts off with a helpful overview of the disorder:

> Obsessions are persistent ideas, thoughts, impulses or images that are experienced as intrusive and inappropriate and that cause marked

anxiety or distress. The intrusive and inappropriate quality of the obsessions has been referred to as "ego-dystonic." This refers to the individual's sense that the content of the obsession is alien, not within his or her own control, and not the kind of thought that he or she would expect to have. However, the individual is able to recognize that the obsessions are the product of his or her own mind and are not imposed from without.

Compulsions are repetitive behaviors (e.g., hand washing, ordering, checking) or mental acts (e.g., praying, counting, repeating words silently) the goal of which is to prevent or reduce anxiety or distress, not to provide pleasure or gratification. In most cases, the person feels driven to perform the compulsion to reduce the distress that accompanies an obsession or to prevent some dreaded event or situation.

The essential features of obsessive-compulsive disorder are recurrent obsessions or compulsions (Criterion A) that are severe enough to be time consuming (i.e., they take more than 1 hour per day) or cause marked distress or significant impairment (Criterion C). At some point during the course of the disorder, the person has recognized that the obsessions or compulsions are excessive or unreasonable (Criterion B). If another Axis 1 disorder is present, the content of the obsessions or compulsions is not restricted to it (Criterion D). The disturbance is not due to the direct physiological effects of a substance (e.g., a drug of abuse, a medication) or a general medical condition (Criterion E).

The DSM-IV then presents the official diagnostic criteria for OCD.
Obsessive-compulsive disorder is diagnosed when criteria A, B, C, D, and E are present:
A. Either obsessions or compulsions: Obsessions as defined by (1), (2), (3), and (4)
> (1) recurrent and persistent thoughts, impulses, or images that are experienced, at some time during the disturbance, as intrusive and inappropriate and that cause marked anxiety or distress
> (2) the thoughts, impulses, or images are not simply excessive worries about real-life problems
> (3) the person attempts to ignore or suppress such thoughts, impulses, or images, or to neutralize them with some other thought or action

(4) the person recognizes that the obsessional thoughts, impulses, or images are a product of his or her own mind (not imposed from without as in thought insertion)

Compulsions as defined by (1) and (2)

(1) repetitive behaviors (e.g., hand washing, ordering, checking) or mental acts (e.g., praying, counting, repeating words silently) that the person feels driven to perform in response to an obsession, or according to rules that must be applied rigidly

(2) the behaviors or mental acts are aimed at preventing or reducing distress or preventing some dreaded event or situation; however, these behaviors or mental acts either are not connected in a realistic way with what they are designed to neutralize or prevent or are clearly excessive

B. At some point during the course of the disorder, the person has recognized that the obsessions or compulsions are excessive or unreasonable. Note: This does not apply to children.

C. The obsessions or compulsions cause marked distress, are time consuming (take more than 1 hour a day), or significantly interfere with the person's normal routine, occupational (or academic) functioning, or usual social activities or relationships.

D. If another Axis 1 disorder is present, the content of the obsessions or compulsions is not restricted to it (e.g., preoccupation with food in the presence of Eating Disorder; hair pulling in the presence Trichotillomania; concern with appearance in the presence of Body Dysmorphic Disorder; preoccupation with drugs in the presence of a Substance Use Disorder; preoccupation with having a serious illness in the presence of Hypochondriasis; preoccupation with sexual urges or fantasies in the presence of a Paraphilia; or guilty ruminations in the presence of Major Depressive Disorder).

E. The disturbance is not due to the direct physiological effects of a substance (e.g., a drug of abuse, a medication) or a general medical condition.

APPENDIX C

SUGGESTED READINGS

American Psychiatric Association. *Diagnostic and Statistical Manual of Mental Disorders.* 4th ed. Washington, D.C.: American Psychiatric Association, 1994.
(Widely used and authoritative manual for the diagnosis of psychiatric disorders. It is clearly written and simple enough for the average person to comprehend.)

Baer, Lee. *Getting Control: Overcoming Your Obsessions and Compulsions.* Boston: Little, Brown, 1991.
(One of the best self-help books. The most complete account of behavior modification techniques for OCD.)

Foa, Edna, and Wilson, Reid. *Stop Obsessing!* New York: Bantam Books, 1991.
(Another excellent self-help book. I usually recommend this one to patients suffering from mental compulsions.)

Freud, Sigmund. "Notes upon a Case of Obsessional Neurosis." In Sigmund Freud, *Collected Papers,* trans. James Strachey. Vol. 3. London: Hogarth Press, 1950.
(Freud's famous OCD case study, "Rat Man." Absolutely enthralling, but Freud's psychoanalytic interpretations are, of course, out of date.)

Goodwin, Donald, and Guze, Samuel. *Psychiatric Diagnosis.* 5th ed. New York: Oxford University Press, 1996.
(The clearest up-to-date explanation of how psychiatric disorders, including OCD, are diagnosed.)

Hollander, Erik. *Obsessive-Compulsive-Related Disorders*. Washington, D.C.: American Psychiatric Press, 1993.
(Best book on OCD spectrum disorders.)

Hunter, Richard, and Macalpine, Ida. *Three Hundred Years of Psychiatry*. Hartsdale, N.Y.: Carlisle, 1982.
(A fascinating compilation of psychiatric cases in centuries past. Of great historical interest.)

Hyman, Steven, and Nestler, Eric. *The Molecular Foundations of Psychiatry*. Washington, D.C.: American Psychiatric Press, 1993.
(The best overview of recent advances in the biochemistry of psychiatric disorders.

Jenike, Michael, Baer, Lee, and Minichiello, William. *Obsessive-Compulsive Disorders: Theory and Management*. 2d ed. Chicago: Year Book, 1990.
(Best textbook on OCD. New edition coming out soon.)

Kramer, Peter. *Listening to Prozac*. New York: Viking Press, 1993.
(More than just a thought-provoking book on Prozac possibilities; an interesting commentary on the entire field of biological psychiatry.)

Lewis, Aubrey. "Problems of Obsessional Neurosis." *Proceedings of the Royal Society of Medicine* 29 (1935): 325–336.
(A classic article in which Lewis, the greatest English psychiatrist of the twentieth century, discusses OCD with great foresight.)

March, John. *Anxiety Disorder in Children and Adolescents*. New York: Guilford Press, 1995.
(Up-to-date and informative. Various experts discuss topics such as neurobiology, social development, and behavioral inhibition.)

Pato, Michele, and Zohar, Joseph. *Current Treatments of Obsessive-Compulsive Disorder*. Washington, D.C.: American Psychiatric Press, 1991.
(Especially good on group and family approaches to OCD. Medications chapters now out of date.)

Peschel, Enid, and Peschel, Richard. *Neurobiological Disorders in Children and Adolescents*. San Francisco: Jossey-Bass, 1992.
(Excellent book emphasizing the implications of OCD being a neurobiologic disorder, including insurance coverage and helping OCDers in school.)

Rachman, Stanley, and De Silva, Padmal. *Obsessive-Compulsive Disorder: The Facts*. New York: Oxford University Press, 1992.
(Simply written, good summary of what is known about the disorder.)

Rachman, Stanley, and Hodgson, Ray. *Obsessions and Compulsions*. New York: Prentice Hall, 1980.
(One of the best books ever written on OCD. Unfortunately, now somewhat dated.)

Rapoport, Judith. *The Boy Who Couldn't Stop Washing.* New York: Dutton, 1989.

(The best-seller and a great overview on OCD. Although it is getting a little out of date, I still recommend it to patients because of the power of its case histories.)

Schwartz, Jeffrey. *Brainlock.* New York: Regan Books, 1996.

(An excellent self-help book; my patients like it.)

Steketee, Gail. *Treatment of Obsessive Compulsive Disorder.* New York: Guilford Press, 1993.

(This is by far the best treatment manual for therapists who want to learn behavior therapy for OCD.)

Steketee, Gail, and White, Kerrin. *When Once Is not Enough.* Oakland, Calif.: New Harbinger, 1990.

(Another excellent self-help book, particularly for classic washing and checking rituals.)

Wegner, Daniel. *White Bears and Other Unwanted Thoughts.* New York: Penguin Books, 1989.

(Very readable and thought-provoking. Should be read by anyone interested in learning more about the psychological cause of obsessions.)

APPENDIX D

WHERE TO FIND HELP

HOW TO FIND A THERAPIST

THE USUAL METHODS of finding qualified therapists, such as asking someone for a recommendation, do not necessarily work for OCD. The fact is that many psychiatrists, psychologists, and social workers with excellent reputations have not kept up with the rapid advances in the understanding and treatment of this disorder. But there are two strategies for finding a good therapist that are almost foolproof.

The first is to call a teaching center, preferably a medical school's department of psychiatry or a university's department of psychology. Ask if they have a specialist in OCD, or, better yet, an OCD clinic. If they do, you can be reasonably assured of getting good treatment there.

If no teaching center is nearby, then the best bet is to call the OC Foundation, our national, nonprofit, nonpolitical, OCD advocacy group. The foundation has a top-notch scientific advisory board, and it keeps an up-to-date listing of OCD specialists and clinics throughout the world.

OC Foundation, Inc.
P.O. Box 70
Milford, Connecticut 06460
Telephone: (203) 878-5669

FINDING INFORMATION ON OCD

TWO OCD CENTERS carry books, articles, videos, and pamphlets on the disorder. The OC Foundation publishes a regular newsletter, sponsors numerous conferences, and has a large publication list. Every OCDer should join this national foundation and take advantage of its educational opportunities.

Another very helpful Obsessive-Compulsive resource is the Information Center, which has just about every book or article ever published on OCD. The librarians are extremely helpful.

Obsessive-Compulsive Information Center
2711 Allen Blvd.
Middletown, Wisconsin 53562
Telephone: (608) 827-2390
Fax: (608) 827-2399

FINDING HELP ON THE INTERNET

MORE THAN A dozen good OCD resource pages are to be found on the Internet. Two large sites have listings of other OCD web pages:

http://www.pages.prodigy.com/alwillen/ocf.html
(home page of the Obsessive-Compulsive Foundation)

http://www.fairlite.com/ocd/
(a well-run bulletin board for OCD sufferers)

OCD SUPPORT GROUPS

THERE ARE MORE than two hundred active OCD groups in the United States and Canada. They are led by either OCDers or professional therapists. Most of these groups are primarily for support and discussion; some of them, particularly those that are professionally led, have a behavior therapy focus; and a few groups are part of Obsessive-Compulsive Anonymous, self-help for OCD that is based on the twelve-step model.

I believe that any of these groups can be extremely helpful. As noted in

Chapter 6, OCDers tend to hide their disorder and to think that no one else in the world suffers from it. Group therapy is not infrequently the most important treatment that a person can find.

The OC Foundation maintains a master list of OCD support groups. At the time of this writing, early 1998, the following OCD groups were in operation.

ALABAMA

Birmingham

Contact: Phil Shell (205) 322-1797 or Ralph Dobbs (205) 786-8288 or 888-841-8335, then enter 0747; after tone, enter your phone number with area code

Open to: Individuals with OCD

Frequency: 1st and 3rd Thursday, 7–9 P.M.

Location: Brookwood Medical Center, Gallery Complex, Room 545

Self-help group

Updated April 1997

Huntsville

Contact: Jane Sucic (205) 881-2295

Open to: Individuals diagnosed with OCD by a physician and in treatment

Frequency: 2nd and 4th Monday, 6 P.M.

Location: Mayfair Church of Christ

Professionally assisted group

Updated February 1996

ARIZONA

Tempe

Contact: Shelly (602) 497-8054

Open to: Individuals with OCD and family members, and friends

Frequency: 4th Monday, 7–8:30 P.M.

Location: Bay Spring United Methodist Church

Updated November 1997

Scottsdale

Contact: Steve (602) 935-7725

Open to: Individuals with OCD, spectrum disorders, and family members

Frequency: 2nd and 4th Thursday, 7–9 P.M.

Location: Samaritan Behavioral Hlth. Ctr. (board room),
7575 E. Earll Dr.

Self-help group

Updated January 1996

Tucson

Contact: Susan Silva-Salgado (520) 622-5582

Frequency: 4th Wednesday, 7:30 P.M.

Open to: Individuals with OCD and family members

Location: Amisa Conference Room, 1st floor, 738 N. 5th Ave.

Self-help group

Updated January 1996

Contact: Randall J. Garland, Ph.D. (520) 322-9334

Open to: Individuals with OCD and adolescents. Request that individuals be professionally diagnosed previously or evaluated by Dr. Garland before entering group.

Frequency: Wednesday, once a month, 7–8:30 P.M.

Location: 5447 E. 5th St., Suite 210-A

Fee: $10 per group

Professionally assisted group

Updated May 1997

Contact: Randall J. Garland, Ph.D. (520) 322-9334

Open to: Individuals with trichotillomania *only*. Request that individuals be professionally diagnosed previously or evaluated by Dr. Garland before entering group.

Location: 5447 E. 5th St., Suite 210-A

Frequency: Once monthly, typically on Mondays, 6:30 P.M.

Fee: $10

Professionally assisted group

Updated May 1997

ARKANSAS

Little Rock

Contact: Jackie Weser (w) (800) 237-3675, 8:30-4:30; (h) (501) 397-5202

Open to: Individuals with OCD and trichotillomania

Frequency: 3rd Tuesday, 7:00 P.M.

Location: Hendricks Hall, Room 150

Self-help group

Updated November 1997

CALIFORNIA

El Sobrante

Contact: Irv Bork (510) 222-3535

Open to: Individuals with OCD, family members and friends

Frequency: Thursday, 7 P.M.

Location: Call for information

Updated September 1996

Fullerton

Contact: Bob Hohenstein, Ph.D. (714) 528-9335

Open to: Individuals with OCD, family members

Frequency: Weekly Wednesday, 7:00-8 P.M.

Format: Cognitive behavioral approach

Location: 3350 E. Borch, Suite 206

Fee: $20 per session

Updated July 1996

Contact: Fred Ilfeld, M.D. (916) 488-7795

Open to: Individuals with OCD

Frequency: Wednesday, once a month, 4:30 P.M.

Location: 4300 Auburn Blvd. #205

Format: Support/Behavioral Therapy

Updated March 1996

Garden Grove

Contact: John Henry Foundation (714) 539-9597

Open to: Individuals with OCD, anxiety, and depression

Frequency: Thursday 6-7:30 P.M.

Location: 12812 Garden Grove Blvd., Suite J

Updated March 1996

Glendale
Contact: Dr. Boone (310) 375-4855
Open to: Individuals with OCD
Frequency: Monday, 12 noon–12:50 P.M.
Location: 116 N. Maryland Ave. #200
Updated September 1997

Long Beach
Contact: John (310) 867-2907
Open to: Individuals with OCD
Frequency: Every Saturday, 4:30 P.M.
Type: 12-step
Location: Geneva Presbyterian Church, 2625 E. 3rd St. (NW corner 3rd and Molino)
Updated March 1996

Loomis
Contact: Dan Lloyd (916) 427-3935
Open to: Individuals with OCD only
Frequency: 1st and 3rd Monday, 7–9 P.M.
Location: 5645 Rocklin Road
Format: Self-help
Updated October 1997

Los Angeles
Contact: Courtney Jacobs, Ph.D. (310) 358-5984
Open to: Individuals with OCD
Frequency: Monday, 8:00-9:30 P.M.
Location: 1100 Glendon Ave., Suite 1601
Fee: $37.50 per month
Updated March 1997

Contact: Tom Corboy, M.A. (310) 335-5443, (310) 374-6407
Open to: Individuals with OCD
Frequency: Tuesday, 7:00–8:30 P.M.
Location: Coast Counseling Center
Updated September 1994

Contact: Edward Glaser (213) 465-1216
Open to: Individuals with OCD, Trichotillomania. Family members welcome.
Frequency: Tuesday, 7:00-9 P.M.
Type: 12-step

Location: Dialog Copy Shop, 8766 Holloway Drive North Hollywood
(basement)
Updated March 1996

Contact: Dr. Schwartz (310) 392-4044, or Dr. Gorbis 213-651-1199
Open to: Individuals with OCD
Frequency: 1st Thursday, 4:30-6:30 P.M.
Type: Cognitive/Behavioral
Location: UCLA
Fee: Requires prior evaluation
Updated May 1997

Contact: Karron Maidment (310) 794-7305
Open to: Family members and other loved ones of people with OCD
Frequency: last Thursday, 4:30-6:00 P.M.
Type: Support/Educational
Location: UCLA
Updated May 1997

Contact: Karron Maidment (310) 794-7305
Open to: Individuals with OCD
Frequency: Friday, 3-4:30 P.M.
Type: Research/Treatment
Location: UCLA Neuropsychology Research
Updated May 1997

NW Los Angeles County
Contact: David Mellinger, MSW, LCSW, BCD (818) 758-1200
Open to: Individuals who are members of Kaiser Permanente
Format: Cognitive beh. therapy group
Updated September 1997

Orange
Contact: Katie Monarch, M.S.W. (717) 771-8243 x8243
Open to: Individuals with OCD
Frequency: Every other Wednesday, 6-7 P.M.
Location: St. Joseph Hospital Comm. Couns.
Fee: $5.00 donation
Updated November 1996

Palo Alto
Contact: Scott Granet, L.C.S.W. (415) 858-2875
Open to: Individuals with OCD, Spectrum disorders
Frequency: Monday, 5-6:30 P.M.
Fee: $30 per session
Updated July 1996

Petaluma
Contact: June Taylor (707) 769-7869
Open to: Adults with OCD
Frequency: $1^{1}/_{2}$ hour weekly meetings
Type: Parents group
Fee: $25 per session
Location: 7 Fourth Street, Suite 8
Updated March 1996

Pleasanton
Contact: Don (510) 828-5184, Naomi Gaunt (510) 455-5748
Open to: Individuals with OCD, family members
Frequency: Wednesday, 7 P.M.
Location: 4725 First Street, Suite 200
Updated March 1997

Redlands
Contact: Colleen Woodhouse (909) 796-3412
Open to: Individuals with OCD, family members
Frequency: 2nd and 4th Monday 7-9 P.M.
Location: Loma Linda University Behavioral Medical Center
Updated March 1996

Sacramento
Contact: Rachele Junkert (916) 966-5917
Open to: Individuals with OCD, family members
Frequency: 2nd and 4th Monday, 7 P.M.
Location: 7700 Folsom Blvd.
Updated May 1997

San Diego
Contact: Ana Maria Andia, M.D. (619) 476-2260
Open to: Individuals with OCD, family members
Frequency: Wednesday, 4:30-6:00 P.M.
Type: Psycho educational
Location: Call for information
Updated March 1997

Contact: Guy (619) 427-7635
Frequency: 1st Wednesday, 6:30-8 P.M.
Location: 3427 Fourth Ave., Room 214 UCSD Gifford Clinic (enter through walnut entrance and go to top stairs)
Type: 12-step
Updated March 1996

Contact: Jayne (619) 295-6129
Open to: Individuals with OCD
Frequency: Thursday, 5:30-6:45 P.M.
Type: 12-step; please contact leader before attending
Location: 3851 Rosecrans Street Harbor Room
Updated May 1997

Contact: Jim Hatton, Ph.D. M.F.C.C. (619) 457-8428, Bonnie (619) 475-8527
Open to: Trichotillomania only
Frequency: 2nd Monday, 7-8:30 P.M.
Location: Mesa Vista Hospital, 7850 Vista Hill Ave.
Updated March 1997

Contact: Jorge (619) 479-4417
Open to: Individuals with OCD, family members
Frequency: 1st and 3rd Friday of each month, 7:00-9 P.M.
Location: Bayview Hospital, 330 Moss Street
Updated March 1997

Contact: Jim Hatton, Ph.D. M.F.C.C. (619) 457-8428, Bonnie (619) 475-8527
Open to: Individuals with OCD, family members
Frequency: 2nd & 4th Friday
Location: Charter Hospital, 11878 Ave. of Industry
Updated March 1997

San Francisco

Contact: (415) 591-7688; Peninsula Network of Mental Health Clients
Open to: Individuals with OCD
Frequency: Call for information
Location: Call for information
Updated March 1996

Contact: David (415) 206-1656
Open to: Individuals with OCD, family members
Frequency: 1st Thurs. and 3rd Monday, 7:00-9:00 P.M.
Location: UCSF
Updated March 1996

Santa Cruz

Contact: Christina Dubowski 408-457-1004
Open to: Individuals with trichotillomania only
Frequency: Weekly, quarterly newsletter
Type: 12-step
Location: Trichotillomania Learning Center
Updated March 1997

Contact: Audrey (408) 438-1043, Rhonda (408) 684-0568
Open to: Individuals with OCD, family members
Frequency: Thursday, 7:30 P.M.
Updated March 1996

Santa Monica

Contact: David Fogelson, M.D. (310) 828-5015
Open to: Individuals with OCD, family members
Frequency: call for information; professional referral required
Location: 2730 Wilshire Blvd. #325
Fee: $50
Updated March 1996

Torrance

Contact: Dr. Rodney Boone (310) 375-4855
Open to: Individuals with OCD
prior to group, individuals must meet with Dr. Boone
Frequency: Saturday 10–11:30 A.M.
Location: 24445 Hawthorne Blvd. #105
Fee: Updated September 1997

Contact: Dr. Boone (310) 375-4855
Open to: Individuals with trichotillomania
Frequency: Wednesday 6:30–7:50 P.M.
Location: 24445 Hawthorne Blvd. #105
Fee: Updated September 1997

Contact: James S. Pratty, M.D. (310) 217-8877
Open to: Individuals with OCD
Frequency: Call for information
Location: Azimuth Mental Health Associates, 21081 Western Ave.,
    Suite 250
Updated March 1996

Ventura
Contact: Richard Reinhart, Ph.D. (805) 652-6747
Open to: Individuals with OCD, family and friends
Frequency: 1st and 3rd Thursday, 7:30-9:00 P.M.
Location: 300 Hillmont Avenue
Updated March 1997

West Hills
Contact: Carla Huffman, M.A. M.F.C.C. (818) 710-9433
Open to: Young adults with OCD
Frequency: Tuesday evenings, adults; Saturday, children
Fee: $25 per session
Updated January 1996

Westminster
Contact: Mary (714) 893-3137
Open to: Individuals with OCD, Trichotillomania
Frequency: Every other Wednesday, 7-9 P.M.
Location: 8854 Grandville Circle
Updated November 1997

COLORADO

Boulder

Contact: Judy Goldstein (303) 938-1360
Open to: Individuals with OCD
Location: Boulder Mental Health Center
Frequency: 1st Monday, 7–9 P.M.; informational meeting 3rd Wednesday, 7–9 P.M.
No fee
Mental health professional may attend.
Updated January 1997

Colorado Springs

Contact: Edna Huston (719) 599-7694
Interested in starting a support group.
Self-help group
Updated January 1996

Fort Collins

Contact: Gene Haimson (970) 498-8363 for further information about
support groups
Open to: Individuals with OCD
Self-help group
Updated February 1996

Northglenn

Contact: Ed Sears (303) 452-2376
Open to: Individuals with OCD, and family members, and individuals
with Trichotillomania
Frequency: 1st Saturday, 11 A.M.
Location: 622 Melody Circle
Self-help group
Updated January 1996

CONNECTICUT

Danbury

Contact: Maria Urban (203) 778-2924
Open to: Individuals with OCD and their support people
Frequency: Tuesday, 2 P.M.
Location: Exodus, 64 West St.
Self-help group
Updated October 1997

Contact: Bruce Mansbridge, Ph.D. (203) 790-7001

Frequency: Informational meeting, 1st Monday, 7–8:30 P.M.

Open to: Individuals with OCD, OC spectrum patients, family, and friends

Location: First Congregational Church of Danbury

No fee

Professionally assisted group

Enfield

Contact: Joe Rinaldi (860) 745-5363

Open to: Individuals with OCD, family & friends

Frequency: Twice a month, first Tuesday, 7–9:00 P.M.

Location: (1st meeting) Johnson Wellness Center, Grounds of Johnson Memorial Hosp.-Stafford Springs, CT. (2nd meeting location) Hartford Courant Bldg., Phoenix Ave., 6–8 P.M.

Farmington

Contact: Nancy Fidler, M.S.W. (860) 679-6700 (answer machine)

Frequency: Every other week

Open to: Individuals with OCD

Fee

Cognitive therapy group

Updated October 1997

Messie Anonymous

Contact: Tonya (860) 267-2812

Open to: Individuals who have a desire to be clutter-free and acquire an organized lifestyle.

Location: Meetings in Greenwich, Westport, Unionville, and E. Hampton

Updated July 1997

Middletown

Contact: Ginger Blume (860) 346-6020

Open to: Individuals with OCD

Frequency: Monday, 4–5:30 P.M.

Fee: $50, or $60 with insurance

Therapy group, six-week

Updated October 1997

Milford

Contact: Susan Duffy or Sheryl Esposito (203) 877-0563

Open to: Individuals with OCD, family, and friends

Frequency: Every other Thursday, 7:30 P.M. May be canceled due to inclement weather or rescheduled due to special meetings. Please call to confirm dates and times.

Location: OCF Headquarters, 9 Depot Street. From New Haven: Route 95 South, take Exit 39A (second 39 exit), take right off exit, take left fork onto Cherry St., go through four lights, at fourth light bear left down the hill into Milford Center, at next light turn right (the Milford Green is directly in front of you), after the Milford Bank turn right onto Depot St. Look for three-story brick building directly behind Milford Bank. From New York: Route 95 North, take Exit 39B (first 39 exit), go through light, turn onto Cherry St., and follow directions as above.

Self-help group

Updated October 1997

Contact: Jim Broatch 878-5669

A teenager is interested in starting and co-leading a support group for teenagers with OCD. An adult volunteer is also needed to help lead this group. For more information, please call.

Orange

Contact: Emotions Anonymous 795-3351 (call any time before 9 P.M.)

Open to: Individuals willing to become well emotionally; call before attending group

Frequency: Friday, 7:30–9:30 P.M.

Location: Church of the Good Shepherd Episcopal, basement, 680 Race Brook Rd.

12-step approach, self-help group

Updated October 1997

West Hartford

Contact: Emily Bailey (800) 842-1501 ext. 13 or (800) 529-1970

Frequency: Thursday 7–9 P.M.

Location: West Ministry Church

Open to: Individuals with OCD

Updated July 1997

Contact: Terry Parkerson (860) 247-2606 (day) (860) 528-2050 (evenings)
Open to: Individuals with OCD, family members
Format: Based on Dr. Jeffrey Schwartz's book
Location: Unity Church, 730 Farmington Ave., W. Hartford, CT 06119
Frequency: Saturday, 11–12 noon
Updated October 1997

DELAWARE

Dover
Contact: Joseph Redden (302) 731-4339
Open to: Individuals with OCD, family, and friends. Please call coordinator for further information.
Frequency: 1st and 3rd Monday, 7–9 P.M.
Location: People's Church of Dover
No fee. Optional $1–2 donation
Self-help group
Updated January 1996

Newark
Contact: Joseph Redden (302) 731-4339
Open to: Individuals with OCD
Frequency: 2nd and 4th Wednesday, 7:30–9 P.M.
Location: St. Nicholas Church (corner of Chestnut Hill Rd. and Old Newark Rd.)
Self-help group
Updated January 1996

Wilmington
Contact: Kathy Parrish, M.A. (610) 891-9024 X125
Open to: Adolescents with OCD, 12–18 years
Frequency: Every other Thursday, 6:30–7:30 P.M.
Location: Center for Cognitive and Behavioral Therapy, 3411 Silverside Rd., Hagley Bldg., Suite 102
Fee: $10
Updated August 1997

FLORIDA

Cocoa Beach

Contact: Faith Brigham (407) 631-1312
Open to: Individuals with OCD, family members
Frequency: Tuesday, 8 P.M.
Location: Teacher's Lounge, St. Mary's Catholic School, Rock Ledge
12-step approach, self-help group
Updated February 1996

Del Rey Beach

Contact: Michelle (305) 341-6830
Open to: Individuals with OCD. Please call Michelle before attending.
Frequency: Every other Thursday, 7 P.M.
Professionally assisted group
Updated January 1996

Fort Lauderdale

Contact: Support Group Information (954) 434-5333
Open to: Individuals with OCD, family members
Frequency: 1st and 3rd Wednesday, 7:30 P.M.
Location: Florida Medical Center South, 6701 Sunrise Blvd.
No fee
Self-help group
Updated February 1996

Gainesville

Contact: Janis McClure (904) 726-0918
Open to: Individuals with OCD and support people
Frequency: 1st and 3rd Monday, 7 P.M.
Location: Mandarin Middle School, Room 51, 5100 Hood Rd.
Self-help group
Updated October 1997

Contact: Janis McClure (904) 726-0918
Open to: Individuals with OCD; family members
Location: University of Florida campus
Frequency: Every other Saturday, 11 A.M.–1 P.M.
Self-help group
Updated October 1997

Hollywood

Contact: Bruce M. Hyman, Ph.D. (954) 557-4495

Open to: Adolescents with OCD. Must meet with Dr. Hyman prior to admission to group.

Frequency: Tuesday afternoon

Location: 4350 Sheridan St., Suite 200

Fee

Professionally assisted group

Updated October 1997

Contact: Bruce M. Hyman, Ph.D. (954) 557-4495

Open to: Adults with OCD. Must meet with Dr. Hyman prior to admission to group.

Frequency: Tuesday evenings

Location: 4350 Sheridan St., Suite 200

Fee

Professionally assisted group

Updated February 1997

Lakeland

Contact: Sylvia Hart (941) 688-7865

Open to: Individuals with OCD, family members

Frequency: Friday, 7 P.M.

Location: Jeanine Brown Drop-in Center, 2968 Lakeland Highlands Rd.

Self-help group

Updated February 1996

Largo

Contact: Barbara Rhode, M.S. (813) 586-0636

Location: 10225 Ulmerton Rd., Suite 8B

Fee: $30

Self-help group

Updated May 1997

Contact: Angela J. Gibson, L.C.S.W. (813) 586-0636

Open to: Individuals with OCD and family members

Frequency: Saturday, 11 A.M.–12:30 P.M.

Location: 10225 Ulmerton Rd., Suite 8B

Fee: $20

Professionally assisted group

Updated May 1997

Miami

Contact: Arlene Miller, L.C.S.W. (305) 279-1715 or Ellen Rock, LCSW (305) 279-1715

Open to: Individuals with OCD and family members. Please contact Ellen prior to attending.

Frequency: 1st and 3rd Monday, 7–8:30 P.M.

Location: Baptist Hospital of Miami, 8900 N. Kendall Dr.

Self-help group

Updated February 1996

GEORGIA

Atlanta

Contact: Charles Melville, Ph.D. (404) 266-8881

Open to: Individuals with OCD and family members

Frequency: 2nd Thursday, 6:30–8 P.M.

Professionally assisted group

Updated April 1997

Contact: Karen Strickland, R.N.C., Anxiety Disorders Institute of Atlanta, (770) 395-6845

Open to: Individuals with anxiety disorders

Group name: CINAP (PANIC spelled backward)

Frequency: Tuesday, 6–7 P.M.

12-step approach, self-help group

Updated February 1996

Contact: Delanna Protas (770) 952-1441

Open to: Individuals with OCD, family, and friends

Frequency: 2nd and 4th Saturday, 10 A.M.

Location: Sandy Springs Christian Church, 301 Johnson Ferry Rd., NW

No fee

Self-help group

Updated May 1996

Contact: Lisa Terry, L.P.C., (770) 396-2929 X28

Open to: Teens with mental health disorders

Frequency: Tuesday, 6:30–7:30 P.M.

Professionally assisted group

Updated March 1996

HAWAII

Honolulu

    Contact: Ginny (808) 261-6987

    Open to: Professionally diagnosed individuals with OCD and family members

    Frequency: 2nd Saturday, 11 A.M.–1 P.M.

    Location: 4470 Aliikoa St.

    Self-help group

    Updated May 1997

IDAHO

Boise

    Contact: Charles Bunch, M.C., N.C.C. (208) 344-5254; ckestrel@aol.com

    Frequency: Every 2nd Tuesday, 7:30 P.M.

    Location: 303 Allumbaugh St., Library

    No fee for first hour meeting; diagnostic letter of referral required after second visit.

    Support group

    Updated April 1997

    Contact: Charles Bunch, M.C., N.C.C. (208) 344-5254; ckestrel@aol.com

    Frequency: 4th Wednesday, 6:30 P.M.

    Fee covers lecture, process of treatment work, recreation; some insurance covered.

    Team treatment

    Updated April 1997

Hayden Lake

    Contact: Karen Grove (208) 772-4156

    Open to: Individuals with OCD, trichotillomania, anxiety

    Frequency: Thursday, 7–8:30 P.M.

    Location: 251 W. Miles Ave.

    Guest speakers periodically

    Self-help group

    Updated May 1997

ILLINOIS

Chicago

Contact: Pam Kohlbeck, M.S. (847) 604-2502
Open to: Individuals with OCD and significant others
Frequency: 3rd Tuesday, 6–7:30 P.M.
Fee: $5
Professionally assisted group
Updated February 1997

Contact: Angela di Manno (773) 973-8243
Open to: Individuals with OCD, family, and friends
Location: Loyola University campus
Frequency: 1st and 3rd Tuesday, 7–8:30 P.M.
Mutual-help support group
Updated February 1997

Contact: Susan Richman (773) 880-2035
Open to: Individuals with OCD, family, and friends
Frequency: 2nd and 4th Thursday, 7:30–9 P.M.
Fee: $5
Mutual-help support group
Updated February 1997

Contact: Sharon Vlasak, R.N., M.S. (773) 413-0997 or Dr. A. J. Allen,
    M.D., Ph.D. (773) 413-1710
Open to: Older children and adolescents with OCD and their parents
Frequency: 1st Saturday, 10 A.M.–noon
Location: UIC Institute
Fee: $10 per family
A series of informational programs given by University of Illinois,
Chicago Pediatric OCD and TIC Disorders Clinic Staff. The first
hour will be an interactive didactic program on some aspect of OCD.
During the second hour, older children and adolescents will meet in
one group and parents in another group to discuss what was learned
and provide each other with mutual support. A series of six topics
will be repeated every six months.
Updated February 1997

Chicago—North Chicago
 Contact: John Calamari (847) 578-3305
 Open to: Individuals with OCD, family, and friends
 Frequency: 1st and 3rd Wednesday, 7–8:30 P.M.
 Fee: $10 (can be waived)
 Instruction on cognitive behavior principles, including ERP
 Professionally assisted group
 Updated February 1997
Chicago—Northwest suburbs
 Contact: Kristen (630) 980-1328 (best time to call: late afternoon or
  evening)
 Open to: Children and adolescents with OCD
 Frequency: 2nd and 4th Monday, 7:30–8:30 P.M.
 Mutual-help support group
 Updated February 1997
Crystal Lake
 Contact: Tim Re (800) 765-9999
 Open to: Individuals with OCD
 Frequency: 2nd and 4th Monday, 7–8:30 P.M.
 Location: Horizons, 970 S. McHenry Ave.
 Leader has therapy group in Elgin.
 Updated February 1997
Downers Grove
 Contact: Dennis Nakanishi, M.A. (708) 939-4441
 Open to: Individuals with OCD
 Frequency: Monday, 6–7 P.M.
 Fee: $25 per group
 Goal-oriented ERP group
Evanston
 Contact: James Dod, Ph.D., Evanston Hospital (847) 570-2720 or
  (708) 570-1585 (voice mail)
 Open to: Individuals with OCD
 Fee: Sliding scale for Evanston residents; others, $30 per group session
 Professionally assisted group

Contact: James Dod, Ph.D., Evanston Hospital (847) 570-2720 or (708) 570-1585 (voice mail)

Open to: Home-based exposure treatment (leaving office and going to houses)

Fee: Sliding scale for Evanston residents; others, $30 per group session

Professionally assisted group

Glenview

Contact: Karol K. (847) 965-1225

Open to: Individuals with OCD

Frequency: Friday, 7:30 P.M.

Location: Glenview Community Church, 1000 Elm St.

12-step approach, Obsessive-Compulsive Anonymous

Updated May 1997

Homewood

Contact: Mark Bornstein, Psy.D. (708) 461-2333 (pager)

Open to: Individuals with OCD, family, and friends

Frequency: 2nd and 4th Monday, 7:30–8:30 P.M.

Fee: $5 per group

Professionally assisted group

Updated February 1997

Lisle

Contact: Margaret Wehrenberg, Psy.D. (708) 852-3870

Open to: Individuals with OCD

Frequency: Wednesday, 7:30–9 P.M.

Location: 5007 Lincoln Ave., Suite 215

Fee: $25 per group

Professionally assisted group

Updated February 1997

Naperville

Contact: Jane Bodine, M.A. (630) 416-3146

Open to: Individuals with OCD, family, spectrum disorder; must contact leader prior to attending group

Frequency: 2nd and 4th Wednesday, 6:30–7:45 P.M.

Location: 10 W. Jefferson

Fee: $25

Professionally assisted group

Updated May 1997

Contact: Jane Bodine, M.A. (630) 416-3146
Open to: Young adults
Frequency: Wednesday, 3:30 P.M.
Location: 10 W. Jefferson
Fee: $25
Professionally assisted group
Updated May 1997

Contact: Jane Bodine, M.A. (630) 416-3146
Open to: Trichotillomania group, support people, children and adolescents
Frequency: 1st and 3rd Wednesday
Location: 10 W. Jefferson
Fee: $15
Professionally assisted group
Updated May 1997

Contact: Jane Bodine, M.A. (630) 416-3146
Open to: Individuals in current treatment
Frequency: 3–4 times a year
Location: 10 W. Jefferson
Fee: $25
Goal-oriented ERP group; ten-week therapy group
Updated May 1997

New Town Alamo Center
Contact: Patrick (312) 929-7275 or (312) 271-6822
Open to: Individuals with OCD
Frequency: Saturday (contact group leader for time)
Updated February 1997

Northbrook
Contact: Pam Kohlbeck, M.S. (847) 604-2502
Open to: Parents of children with OCD
Frequency: 4th Monday, 7:30 P.M.
Location: Glencoe Public Library
Professionally assisted group
Updated February 1997

Northfield
Contact: Karen Cassiday, Ph.D. (847) 577-8809
Open to: Individuals with OCD, family, and friends
Frequency: 1st and 3rd Monday, 7:30–9 P.M.
Location: Anxiety and Agoraphobia Treatment Center
Fee: $5 per group

Contact: Penny Silverman (847) 432-0446
Interested in starting a group for body dysmorphic disorder
Springfield
Contact: Janice Phelan (217) 523-2740
Open to: Individuals with OCD, family members
Frequency: Last Monday of the month, 5:30–7 P.M.
Location: Christ Episcopal Church, Jackson St.
Updated October 1997

INDIANA

Fort Wayne
Contact: Robert Collie, Ph.D. (219) 485-6687
Open to: Individuals with OCD and family members
Location: Good Shepherd United Methodist Church, Room 37
Frequency: Monday, 7–8:30 P.M.
Professionally assisted group
Updated July 1997
Indianapolis
Contact: Kerri Bova (317) 888-6753, Vikki Sutton (317) 963-3210,
Homer (317) 576-0625, or Phil Clendenen (317) 297-0625
Open to: Individuals with OCD, family, and friends
Frequency: 1st, 2nd, and 3rd Monday, 6:30 P.M.
Location: 7440 N. Shadeland Ave., Room 202
Mutual-help support group
Professionally assisted group
Updated April 1997

Contact: Kerri Bova (317) 888-6753, Vikki Sutton (317) 963-3210,
    Homer (317) 576-0625, or Phil Clendenen (317) 297-0625
Open to: Individuals with trichotillomania
Frequency: 2nd Monday
Location: 7440 N. Shadeland Ave., Room 202
Mutual-help support group
Professionally assisted group
Updated April 1997

Contact: Kerri Bova (317) 888-6753, Vikki Sutton (317) 963-3210,
    Homer (317) 576-0625, or Phil Clendenen (317) 297-0625
Open to: Individuals with general anxiety
Frequency: 4th Monday, 6:30–8 P.M.
Location: 7440 N. Shadeland Ave., Room 202
Professionally assisted group
Updated April 1997

Contact: Dr. Hilgendorf (317) 578-4213
Open to: Individuals with OCD
Frequency: Monday, 7:30–8 P.M.
Location: 7440 N. Shadeland Ave., Room 202
Professionally assisted group
Updated April 1997

South Bend
Contact: Nancy Sechrest (219) 299-1483
Open to: Individuals with OCD
Frequency: Thursday, 7 P.M.
Updated April 1997

IOWA

Iowa City
Contact: Nancee Blum (319) 353-6180
Open to: Individuals with OCD
Frequency: 2nd and 4th Thursday, 7–8:30 P.M.
Location: 1942 JPP, University of Iowa
No fee
Professionally assisted group
Updated May 1997

Contact: Nancee Blum (319) 353-6180
Open to: Family members of individuals with OCD
Frequency: 2nd Thursday, 7–8:30 P.M.
Location: 1942 JPP, University of Iowa
No fee
Professionally assisted group
Updated May 1997

KANSAS

Lenexa

Contact: Jane Condra (816) 763-8174
Open to: Individuals with OCD and family members
Frequency: Thursday, 7–9:30 P.M.
Location: CPC College Meadows Hospital, 14425 College Blvd., con-
ference room
Self-help group
Updated May 1997

Wichita

Contact: Rob Zettle, M.D. (316) 978-3081
Open to: Individuals with OCD
Frequency: 1st and 3rd Monday, 7 P.M.
Location: Charter Hospital of Wichita, Room 23
Mutual-help support group
Updated April 1997

KENTUCKY

Lexington

Contact: Deborah A. Krause, Ph.D. (606) 271-2881
Open to: Individuals with OCD and significant others
Frequency: 1st Thursday, 7 P.M.
Professionally assisted group
Updated May 1997

Louisville

Contact: Dr. Jeff Romer, C.M.F.T. (502) 899-5991
Open to: Individuals with OCD, spectrum disorders. Contact group
leader prior to attending group.
Frequency: Tuesday, 7–8:30 P.M.
Location: Lutheran Child and Family Counseling
Professionally assisted group
Updated January 1996

LOUISIANA

New Orleans

Contact: Pattie Lemonn (504) 588-5405

Open to: Individuals with OCD, family, and support people.

Contact group leader prior to attending group.

Frequency: 2nd Tuesday, 6–8 P.M.

Self-help group

Updated January 1996

MAINE

Bangor

Contact: Charles Casey (207) 794-3501 or (207) 794-3161

Open to: Individuals with OCD and family members. Contact Charles prior to attending.

Frequency: Date to be determined each meeting, 7–9 P.M.

Location: Bangor Counseling Center

Self-help group

Updated May 1997

Berwick

Contact: Sandy Skammels (603) 692-9851

Interested in starting a support group again. Contact if interested.

Updated January 1996

Clinton

Contact: Tina Couturier (207) 873-0145

Open to: Individuals with trichotillomania, family, and friends

Frequency: 3rd Friday, 7–9 P.M.

Location: Brown Memorial United Methodist Church

Self-help group

Updated January 1996

MARYLAND

Annapolis

Contact: Peg Duvall (410) 544-5918 or Charlotte Lindsley, M.S.W. (410) 263-3987

Open to: Individuals with OCD, and support people

Frequency: 1st Wednesday, 7:30–9 P.M.

Updated October 1997

Arnold

    Contact: Peg Duvall (410) 544-5918 or Charlotte Lindsley, M.S.W.
    (410) 263-3987

    Open to: Individuals with OCD and family members

    Frequency: First Wednesday, 7–9 P.M.

    Location: Please contact group leader for location.

    Updated October 1997

Kensington

    Contact: Lorett Gaiser (301) 929-0156

    Available twenty-four hours a day to talk with individuals with OCD
    or trichotillomania and guide to meetings.

    Updated January 1996

Rockville

    Contact: Roslyn Lehman, L.C.S.W.-C. (301) 469-0108; fax (301) 762-
    5711

    Open to: Support for family members

    Frequency: 1st Thursday, 2–4 P.M.

    Location: 20 Courthouse Square, Suite 217

    Self-help group

    Updated April 1997

Wheaton

    Contact: David (301) 495-7806

    Open to: Individuals with OCD. Contact David prior to attending.

    Frequency: 1st and 3rd Tuesday, 7:30–9:30 P.M.

    Location: 2424 Reedie Dr.

    Self-help group

    Updated January 1996

MASSACHUSETTS

Belmont

    Contact: Diane Baney, R.N., M.B. (617) 855-3279

    Location: OCD Institute, McLean Hospital

    Partial hospital and intensive residential care for individuals seventeen
    and older who suffer from severe or treatment-resistant OCD.

Boston

OCF Greater Boston Affiliate

Debbie McDowell, president (781) 376-3784

Greater Boston affiliate sponsors four self-help groups: Professionally assisted group for individuals with OCD, family, and friends; Trichotillomania group; Spectrum disorders; Child and adolescents group

For further information, please call helpline: (617) 376-3784.

Contact: (617) 376-3653

Open to: Individuals with OCD

Frequency: Wednesday, 7:30 P.M.

Location: United Presbyterian Church, 32 Harvard St., basement

12-step approach, Obsessive-Compulsive Anonymous

Self-help group

Updated January 1996

Contact: Christina (617) 231-9053

Open to: Individuals with OCD and family members

Frequency: Wednesday, 7–8 P.M.

Location: Shaughnessy-Kaplan Rehabilitation Hospital

12-step approach, Obsessive-Compulsive Anonymous

Updated November 1995

Brookline

Contact: Roberta Brucker, L.I.C.S.W. (617) 499-7979

Open to: Individuals with OCD. Must contact leader prior to attending.

Frequency: Weekly for 1½ hours

Fee

Professionally assisted group

Updated January 1996

Contact: Roberta Brucker, L.I.C.S.W. (617) 499-7979

Open to: Family members of individuals with OCD. Must contact leader prior to attending.

Frequency: Weekly for 1½ hours

Fee

Professionally assisted group

Updated January 1996

Cambridge
    Contact: HPA, P.O. Box 614, Cambridge, Massachusetts 02140
    Open to: Individuals with trichotillomania only
    Frequency: Wednesday, 7:15–8:45 P.M.
    Location: Cambridge Hospital, Macht Bldg., Room 148, 1493 Cambridge St.
    12-step approach, self-help group
    Updated May 1997

Chicopee
    Contact: Leslie or Mary (413) 567-5633
    Open to: Individuals with OCD, family and friends
    Frequency: 1st and 3rd Tuesday of the month, 7 P.M.
    Location: Charles River Hospital, West 350 Memorial Dr.
    Updated July 1997

Great Barrington
    Contact: Brent (413) 229-2994
    Brent is interested in starting a mutual-help support group.

Ludlow
    Contact: Patricia Ricci (413) 583-6750
    Open to: Family members
    Frequency: Wednesday evening short-term support group
    Fee
    Professionally assisted group
    Updated January 1996

North Cambridge
    Contact: Joris Jones or David Ligon, 458-0925 (beeper) or (617) 864-9902. He will return your call.
    Open to: Individuals with OCD, family, and friends
    Frequency: 3rd Wednesday, 7–9 P.M.
    Location: Rear Mefitz Gerald School, 70 Rindge Ave.
    Self-help group
    Updated January 1996

Stoughton
    Contact: Phil (508) 583-3205
    Open to: Individuals with OCD in treatment
    Frequency: Monday, 7–9 P.M.
    Location: Goddard Center, Conference Room A. Call (617) 297-8200 for directions.
    Self-help group
    Updated May 1997

Worcester

Contact: Ann (508) 799-6784

Open to: Individuals with OCD and family members

Frequency: Every other Tuesday, 7:30–8:30 P.M.

Location: Hahnemann Hospital, 281 Lincoln St., 4th floor, Classroom 2. Use rear entrance.

12-step approach, Obsessive-Compulsive Anonymous

Self-help group

Updated January 1996

Contact: William Ferrarone (508) 792-8785

Open to: Individuals with OCD. Must contact group leader for evaluation and diagnosis.

Frequency: Friday, 3–4:30 P.M. Follow-up group meets monthly.

Location: Psychiatric Patient Services Medical Center, 15 Belmont, Lincoln Pavillion

Updated January 1996

MICHIGAN

Ann Arbor

Contact: Mary Jo (313) 761-9167

Frequency: 4th Wednesday, 6–8 P.M.

Location: Washtenaw County Mental Hospital, 2140 Ellsworth

Updated August 1997

Battle Creek

Contact: Gerda (616) 965-4529

Frequency: 3rd Tuesday, 7–9 P.M.

Location: St. Peter's Lutheran Church, 1079 Riverside

Updated August 1997

Dearborn

Contact: Wally Green (313) 563-5200

Open to: Individuals with OCD

Frequency: 1st and 3rd Thursday, 7–9 P.M.

Location: First United Methodist Church, Garrison and Mason St.

Mutual-help support group

Updated August 1997

Escanaba
>   Contact: Val (906) 474-9369
>   Open to: Public
>   Frequency: 3rd Monday, 7–9 P.M.
>   Location: Delta Community Mental Health Building, 2820 College Avenue
>   Mutual-help support group
>   Updated August 1997

Farmington Hills
>   Contact: Bobbie (313) 522-8907, or write THEO (Trichotillomania Helping Each Other), P.O. Box 871083, Canton, MI 48187
>   Open to: Individuals with trichotillomania *only*
>   Frequency: 1st and 3rd Sunday, 1–4 P.M.
>   Location: Botsford Hospital, 28050 Grand River
>   Self-help group
>   Updated August 1997

>   Contact: Greg (313) 438-3293
>   Open to: Adolescents and their supporters
>   Frequency: 3rd Wednesday, 7–9 P.M.
>   Location: Davis Counseling Center Park on the Green Center, 37923 West 12 Mile Rd. Building A (between Haggerty and Halstead)
>   Updated August 1997

Flint
>   Contact: David (810) 694-4845
>   Open to: Individuals with OCD and family members
>   Frequency: 2nd Wednesday, 7–9 P.M.
>   Location: Perry Center, 11920 S. Saginaw St., Grand Blanc
>   Updated August 1997

Grand Blanc
>   Contact: Ellen Craine (810) 695-0055
>   Open to: Parents of children and adolescents with OCD
>   Frequency: Tuesday, once a month, 6–7:30 P.M.
>   Location: 8341 Office Park Dr.
>   Fee: Most insurance accepted
>   Professionally assisted group
>   Updated August 1997

Lake Orion
Contact: Susan (248) 628-8029
Open to: Individuals with OCD
Frequency: Every Saturday 10 A.M.
Location: The Keep Coming Back Club, 33 Broadway St.
Updated October 1997
Lansing
Contact: Jon (517) 485-6653
Open to: Individuals with OCD and family members
Frequency: 1st and 3rd Thursday, 7–9 P.M.
Location: Delta Presbyterian Church, 6100 W. Michigan Ave.
Self-help group
Updated August 1997

Contact: Sandi (517) 484-8205 or (517) 351-7362
Open to: Individuals with trichotillomania
Frequency: 2nd Sunday, 2–4 P.M.
Location: 3340 Hospital Road, Dining Room B
Mutual-help support group
Updated August 1997
Monroe
Contact: Doug (313) 390-6484
Frequency: 1st and 3rd Tuesday 6–8 P.M.
Location: Monroe Community Mental Health, 1001 Raisonville Rd.
Updated September 1997
Plymouth
Contact: Lois Turpel (313) 522-3022
Open to: Individuals with OCD and family members
Frequency: 2nd and 4th Thursday, 7 P.M.
Location: First Baptist Church, 45000 N. Territorial Rd.
Self-help group
Updated August 1997
Royal Oak
Contact: Bob Cato (248) 542-5909
Open to: Individuals with OCD and family members
Frequency: 1st and 3rd Tuesday, 7–9 P.M.
Location: St. John Episcopal Church, 115 S. Woodward
Self-help group
Updated August 1997

Saginaw
    Contact: Barb Bacon (517) 777-6042
    Open to Individuals with OCD and family members
    Frequency: Tuesday, 7:30–8:30 P.M.
    Location: Healthsource, Dining Room B, 3340 Hospital Road

West Bloomfield
    Contact: Ellen Craine, J.D., C.S.W., A.C.S.W. (810) 539-3850
    Open to: Children and adolescents with OCD
    Frequency: Monday and Wednesday, 4–5:30 P.M.
    Fee: $40 per session
    Education/support, professionally facilitated
    Professionally assisted group
    Updated April 1997

    Contact: Ellen Craine, J.D., C.S.W., A.C.S.W. (810) 539-3850
    Open to: Parents and family members with a child or adolescent with
      OCD
    Frequency: Monday and Thursday, 6–7:30 PM
    Fee: $40 per session
    Education/support, professionally facilitated
    Professionally assisted group
    Updated April 1997

MINNESOTA

Chanhassen
    Contact: Sharon Lohmann (612) 646-5615
    Open to: Parents and children with OCD
    Frequency: 3rd Saturday, 1 p.m.
    Updated July 1997

Hopkins
    Contact: Justus Burggraf (612) 724-0931
    Open to: Individuals with OCD, family, and friends
    Frequency: Monday, 7–8:30 P.M.
    Location: Eisenhower Community Center
    Fee: donation
    Self-help group
    Updated May 1997

Minneapolis/St. Paul

Contact: Sharon Lohmann, president, OC Foundation Affiliate (612) 646-5615 or (612) 646-5616
Open to: Individuals with OCD, family, and friends
Frequency: 2nd and 4th Saturday, 11 A.M.–1 P.M.
Location: Please contact leader for meeting place.
Self-help group
Updated July 1997

Contact: Gail Meyer, R.N., M.S.N., C.S. (612) 649-1105 or (612) 649-0050, ext. 3
Open to: Individuals with OCD. Must be Pioneer Clinic patients.
Location: Pioneer Clinic, 2550 University Ave., W.
Professionally assisted group
Updated May 1997

Contact: Gail Meyer, R.N., M.S.N., C.S. (612) 649-1105 or (612) 649-0050, ext. 3
Open to: Individuals with trichotillomania
Frequency: Monthly, or ten-session treatment group; or 1-week intensive treatment group program (April, June, and August)

St. Louis Park

Contact: Sharon Lohmann (612) 646-5615 or (612) 825-0963
Open to: Children with OCD and parents
Frequency: 1st, 3rd, and 5th Saturday afternoon
No fee
Self-help group
Updated July 1997

MISSOURI

Kansas City

Contact: Jane Condra (913) 469-1100
Open to: Individuals with OCD and families
Frequency: Thursday, 7 P.M.
Location: College Meadows Hospital, CPC-Pink Unit, Room A
Self-help group
Updated January 1996

St. Louis

Contact: Edna or Bernie (314) 842-7228
Open to: Individuals with OCD, family members, and friends
Frequency: 3rd Saturday, 10 A.M.; professional speaker
Location: St. John's Mercy Medical Center, 615 S. New Ballas Rd.
Self-help group, OCD support group
Updated April 1997

Contact: George M. (314) 394-2662
Open to: Individuals with OCD
Frequency: Saturday, 10 A.M. (except the 3rd Saturday, when St. John's
    OCD support group meets)
Location: Missouri Baptist Hospital, Nursing School Bldg., Room 108
Obsessive-Compulsive Anonymous
Updated January 1996

Contact: Elliot Nelson, M.D. (314) 362-2465
Frequency: 2nd and 3rd Wednesday, 7–8:15 P.M.
Location: Barnes Hospital, 15th floor
Professionally assisted group
Updated January 1996

MONTANA

Bozeman

Contact: Sharon Mohr (406)587-5718 or Bozeman Help Center (406)
    586-3333
Open to: Individuals with OCD and support people, and spectrum dis-
    orders
Frequency: Thursday, 7 P.M. Please call coordinator. Time and place are
    subject to change.
Self-help group
Updated May 1997

NEBRASKA

Hastings

Contact: Nabil Faltas, M.D. (402) 463-7711
Open to: Individuals with OCD. An initial screening interview is nec-
    essary.
Fee
Updated May 1996

Lincoln

Contact: Pat Diesler (402) 483-3480

Open to: Individuals with OCD and family members, and individuals with trichotillomania

Frequency: 1st Wednesday, 7–8 P.M.

Location: Bryan Memorial Hospital, 1600 S. 48th St.

Self-help group

Updated February 1996

Omaha

Contact: Creighton-Nebraska Dept. of Psychiatry

Open to: Parent of a child with OCD and a child group

Frequency: 1st and 3rd Monday, 4:15–5:15 P.M.

Location: Child and Adolescent Division, 3528 Dodge, Omaha, NE 68131

Updated October 1997

Omaha

Contact: Dan Hegarty (402) 496-0242 or (402) 390-6093

Open to: Individuals with OCD, family members, and support people

Frequency: 3rd Thursday, 7–9 P.M.

Location: Pathways Center, Building 7701, Suite 319

Self-help group

Updated February 1996

NEVADA

Contact: Jeff (702) 642-8775

Open to: Individuals with all types of OCD

Frequency: Monthly

Location: Varies

No fee

The Tourette O.C.D. Society of Southern Nevada, Inc.

Self-help group

Updated January 1996

Las Vegas

Contact: Nancy Quinones (702) 252-4596 or ADD Clinic (702) 796-1919

Open to: Adults and parents of children with OCD, trichotillomania, and/or Tourette's syndrome

Frequency: 2nd Wednesday

Professionally assisted group

Updated April 1997

NEW HAMPSHIRE

Portsmouth

Contact: Kim (603) 778-2906
Open to: Individuals with OCD
Frequency: 2nd and 4th Sunday, 7–8:30 P.M.
Location: Pavillion Hospital, P.H.P. Room, 343 Borthwick Ave.
Mutual-help support group
Updated September 1996

Contact: Tom Luby (603) 683-7991
Open to: Individuals with OCD and support people
Frequency: Sunday, 7–8:30 P.M.
Also has a group in Lebanon, NH
Updated October 1997

NEW JERSEY

Cliffside Park

Contact: James Pinto (201) 941-8143
Open to: Individuals with OCD
Frequency: Thursday, 6–7 P.M.
Location: The Oasis, 619-A Palisade Ave.
Updated May 1997

Dover

Contact: Michelle Shine (201) 347-7508 or Helene (201) 335-6185
Frequency: Wednesday, 7:30 P.M.
Open to: Individuals with OCD and family members
Self-help group
Updated January 1996

Lakewood

Contact: Nancy Spader (908) 295-8883
Open to: Individuals with OCD and families with OCD member
Frequency: 2nd Tuesday, 7 P.M.
Location: Axelrad Bldg., Route 9
Self-help group
Updated January 1996

Montclair

Contact: New Jersey Self-Help Clearinghouse (800) 367-6274 or (201)
625-7101
Self-help group

Contact: Nancy Maller (201) 472-8215
Open to: Individuals with OCD and family members
Frequency: 1st and 3rd Thursday, 8–10 P.M.
Location: Mountainside Hospital, 300 Bay Ave., Room 6191
Self-help group
Updated January 1996

Newton

Contact: OCD Support Group (201) 619-1207
Open to: Individuals with OCD, family, and friends
Frequency: 1st and 3rd Thursday, 8–9 P.M.
Location: Newton Memorial Hospital, Center for Mental Health, Conference Room 239, 175 High St.
Self-help group

Oradell

Contact: Nina Simon, A.C.S.W. (201) 265-4793
Open to: OCD family group, behavioral cognitive group
Frequency: To be established
Fee: Sliding scale ($25 per patient/per family)
Location: 377 Loretta Dr.
Professionally assisted group
Updated May 1997

Parsippany

Contact: Helene (201) 335-6185
Open to: Individuals with OCD
Frequency: Wednesday, 7:30–9:30 P.M.
Self-help group
Updated April 1995

Pennington

Contact: Linda Flower, ACSW (609) 737-0233
Open to: Individuals with trichotillomania
Frequency: Monthly therapy group
Fee: $35 for 1 ½ hours
Contact Linda for further information.
Professionally assisted group
Updated January 1996

Piscataway

    Contact: Dr. Michael Petronko (908) 445-5384

    Open to: Individuals with OCD

    Frequency: 1st and 3rd Wednesday, 7–8:30 P.M.

    Location: Rutgers University, 807 Hoes Lane

    Fee: $1 donation per session

    Professionally assisted group

    Updated January 1996

Princeton

    Contact: Dr. Allen (609) 921-3555, ext. 21 or (908) 905-3777

    Open to: Individuals with OCD, family, and friends

    Frequency: 2nd and 4th Thursday, 7 P.M.

    Location: 256 Bunn Dr., Suite 6

    Self-help group

    Updated January 1996

Randolph

    Contact: Christopher Lynch, Ph.D. (201) 366-9444

    Open to: Individuals with OCD

    Frequency: Tuesday, 7–8 P.M.

    Fee

    Updated March 1996

    Contact: Karen (908) 269-9044 or (908) 315-1912 (pager)

    Open to: Individuals with OCD, family, and friends

    Frequency: Friday, 7:30–9 P.M.

    Location: Community Medical Center, Auditorium C

    Mutual-help support group

    Updated April 1997

Somerdale

    Contact: Ruth (609) 627-2971

    Available for phone help.

    Updated January 1996

Somerville

    Contact: Joseph A. Donnellan, M.D. (609) 683-4547

    Open to: Individuals with OCD and family members

    Frequency: 3rd Thursday, 7:30–9 P.M.

    Location: Somerset Medical Center, Fuld Auditorium

    No fee

    Also has a therapy group. Please call for information.

    Professionally assisted group

    Updated January 1996

Sussex County

Contact: Wade/Joan (201) 619-1207
Open to: Individuals with OCD and family members
Frequency: 1st and 3rd Thursday, 8–9 P.M.
Location: Newton Memorial Hospital, 2nd floor, Conference Room 239
Self-help group
Updated January 1996

NEW YORK

Brooklyn

Contact: Ron (718) 624-5716
Open to: Individuals with OCD, family members
Frequency: Thursday 7–8:30 PM
Location: Father Demphsey Center Format: 12-step OCA group
Updated October 1996

Contact: Susan (718) 332-2225 (pager)
Open to: Individuals with OCD, family, and friends
Frequency: 1st Tues. 7:30 P.M.
Location: Coney Island Hospital
Updated August 1996

Buffalo

Contact: Jerry Horowitz (716) 881-2186
Open to: Individuals with OCD, family, and friends
Frequency: 1st & 3rd Tues., 7–9 P.M.
Location: Bry-Lin Hospital
Updated February 1996

Contact: Patti (716) 885-1106
Open to: Individuals with OCD
Frequency: 1st and 3rd Fri. 7:30 P.M.
Location: 1272 Delaware Avenue
Updated February 1996

Contact: Susan Arnold Gunn (716) 859-2703
Open to: Individuals with OCD
Frequency: Tues. 7 P.M.
Location: Buffalo General Hospital Auditorium
Format: Professionally assisted
Updated April 1997

Commack

   Contact: Warren (516) 681-7861
   Frequency: Every Monday, 7–8:45 P.M.
   Location: 155 Indian Head Road (enter through rear building entrance)
   Open to: Individuals with OCD and family members
   Updated January 1996

Farmingdale

   Contact: Linda (516) 249-8175, (516) 741-4901
   Open to: Individuals with OCD
   Frequency: Monday, 8 P.M.
   Location: Brunswick Medical Center, Brunswick Hall
   Format: 12-step
   Updated January 1996

Glen Oaks

   Contact: Emily Klass, Ph.D. (718) 470-3500
   Open to: Parents of Children with OCD (must call group coordinator first)
   Location: Call for information
   Updated January 1992

Great Neck

   Contact: Institute for Bio-Behavioral Therapy and Research
       (516) 487-7116
   Open to: Individuals with OCD
   Location: 935 Northern Blvd, Suite 102
   Updated February 1996

Huntington

   Contact: Fred Penzel, Ph.D. (516) 351-1729
   Open to: Individuals with OCD
   Frequency: Monthly, 2nd Friday, 7:30-9 P.M.
   Location: 755 New York Ave., Suite 2000
   Format: Professionally assisted
   Updated January 1996

   Contact: Christine Cannella, Ph.D. (516) 351-1729, (516) 424-5408
   Open to: Family members
   Frequency: Monthly, 2ndThursday, 7:30–9 P.M.
   Location: Western Suffolk Psychiatric Services

Contact: Robert Araujo (516) 351-1828
Open to: Families of those with OCD, children of parent with OCD
Frequency: Tuesday, 6:45-8:15 P.M.
Location: 755 New York Avenue
Format: Professionally assisted

Contact: Fred Penzel (516) 661-2718
Open to: Individuals with OCS who have been in treatment
Frequency: Every other Tuesday, 7 P.M.
Location: 755 New York Avenue, Suite 200
Format: Post-recovery self-help
Updated February 1996

Manhasset
Contact: Roy (516) 741-4901 (Obsessive Compulsive Anonymous)
Location: Manhasset Congregational Church, 1845 Northern Blvd.
Format: OCA/12-Step

Manhattan
Contact: Howard (212) 229-1043
Frequency: 1st Monday, 6:15 P.M.
Location: Payne Whitney, Room 129
Type: Support/12-step
Updated February 1996

Contact: Howard (212) 229-1043
Frequency: 2nd Wednesday, 7 P.M.
Location: 423 E. 77th St.
Type: Support/12-step
Updated February 1996

Contact: Shelby Howatt, C.S.W., Naomi Sarna, C.S.W. (212) 865-1331
Frequency: Wednesday and Thursday, 6:30-8 P.M.
Open to: Women with trichotillomania only
Format: Professionally assisted group therapy
Fee: $25 per session
Updated January 1996

Contact: Naomie Sarna, C.S.W. (212) 802-9496
Open to: Individuals with trichotillomania
Frequency: Monthly, 1-4:00 P.M.
Location: Washington Square United Methodist Church, 135 West 4th Street
Updated January 1996

Contact: Dr. Phillipson (212) 686-8778
Open to: Individuals with OCD
Frequency: Tuesday, 6:45 P.M., Friday 6:15 P.M.
Type: Behavioral therapy
Location: Institute for Behavior Clinic
Updated January 1996

Contact: Shelly Goldberg, C.A.C. (718) 852-2390 (interested in starting a group for those who self-injure)

Contact: Elizabeth Brondolo, Ph.D. (212) 942-8532
Open to: Those diagnosed with OCD; must meet with Dr. Brondolo prior to attending group
Frequency: Every other Monday, 6–7:00 P.M.
Fee: $40
Format: Behavioral therapy group
Location: Call for information
Updated February 1996

Contact: Stacie (212) 696-8692
Open to: Hoarders, and individuals with OCD and family members
Frequency: Every other Monday 6–7:00 P.M.
Fee: $40
Format: Behavioral therapy group
Updated February 1996

Contact: Norman Levy (212) 684-FAMI
Open to: Individuals with OCD
Frequency: 3rd Tuesday, 6:00 P.M.
Updated February 1996

Contact: Joa Silvestre, C.S.W. (212) 960-5627, Mark Hollander Ph.D.
(718) 935-7681
Open to: Individuals with OCD
Frequency: Wednesday evening for 20 sessions
Fee: Call for information
Updated September 1997

Contact: Marlene Cooper, Ph.D. (212) 877-8017
Open to: Family members of individuals with OCD
Frequency: Call for information
Fee: Monthly
Location: Call for information
Updated January 1997

Contact: Charity Paul (212) 242-7893
Open to: Individuals with OCD spectrum related disorders
Frequency: Monday and Thursday 7:00-9 P.M.
Location: 74 Perry St.
Fee: Sliding scale
Updated August 1997

Contact: The Center for Holistic Therapy (212) 961-1378
Open to: Individuals with OCD
Frequency: Monthly
Location: Call for information
Updated February 1996

Contact: Dr. Josephson, PhD (212) 288-2777 (interested in starting a
group)
Updated January 1996

Peekskill

Contact: Robin Goldsand (914) 739-4029
Open to: Individuals with OCD
Frequency: Every other Tuesday, 7–9 P.M.
Location: 401 Claremont Ave.
Fee: $20
Format: Cognitive therapy group
Updated October 1997

Pomona

    Contact: Self-Help Clearinghouse (914) 639-9431

    Open to: Individuals with OCD

    Frequency: Monday, 7:30 P.M.

    Location: Pomona Health Center F, Room 112

    Format: Self-help

    Updated January 1996

Poughkeepsie

    Contact: Krista (914) 473-2500; e-mail Chris Vertullo a Marist.Edu.

    Open to: Individuals with OCD, family and friends

    Frequency: 2nd and 4th Tuesday, 7–9 P.M.

    Location: Vassar Hospital, cafeteria

    Updated September 1997

Queens:

    Contact: Albert (718) 441-7718

    Open to: Individuals with OCD

    Frequency: Tuesday, 8 P.M.

    Location: Saint John's University

    Format: 12-step

    Updated February 1996

    Contact: Albert (718) 441-7718

    Open to: Individuals with OCD

    Frequency: Saturday, 1-2:30 P.M.

    Location: Resurrection Ascension Church

    Format: 12-step

    Updated February 1996

Schenectady

    Contact: Barbara O'Connor, (518) 372-6198

    Open to: Individuals with OCD, and family members with permission

    Frequency: First Friday

    Location: Ellis Hospital, Conference Room #A6

    Updated April 1997

Staten Island

    Contact: Jeanie or Theresa (718) 351-1717

    Open to: Individuals with OCD, family members

    Frequency: 2nd Monday, 7:30 P.M.

    Location: 308 Seaview Avenue

    Format: Self-help

    Updated January 1996

Syracuse

    Contact: Joanne Kuneman or Carol Bass (315) 451-6340

    Open to: Individuals with OCD, family members

    Frequency: Tuesday, 7:30-9:30 P.M.

    Location: Lyncourt Wesleyan Church

Utica

    Contact: Kathy (315) 735-2370 or (315) 831-8070

    Open to: Individuals with OCD

    Frequency: Tuesday, 6:00–8:30 P.M.

    Location: Mohawk Valley Community College, Rm. 218, College Center

    Updated September 1997

    Contact: Susan Connell or Scott (315) 768-8947; (315) 768-7031

    Open to: Individuals with OCD, family members

    Frequency: Monday, 6:30–8 P.M.

    Location: St. Elizabeth Hospital School of Nursing, 2215 Genesee St.

    Updated September 1997

Vestal

    Contact: Tim Peters (607) 785-4621

    Open to: Individuals with OCD and family members

    Frequency: Thursday, 7:30 P.M.

    Location: Vestal Library

    Format: Self-help

    Updated August 1995

Westchester

    Contact: Meryl (914) 478-4212

    Open to: Parents of Children and Adolescents with OCD

    Frequency: Call for information

    Location: Call for information

    Updated January 1997

White Plains

    Contact: Lisa or Sharon (800) 345-0199

    Open to: Individuals with OCD, family and friends

    Frequency: Tuesday, 6:30–8 P.M.

    Location: 5 Waller Street, Ste. 302

    Fee: $75, or sliding scale

    Format: Professionally assisted

    Updated January 1996

Contact: Dr. Alvin Yapalater (800) 345-0199
Open to: Individuals with OCD and family members
Frequency: Tuesday, 6:30–8 P.M.
Fee: Sliding scale
Location: Call for information
Updated August 1995

NEW MEXICO
Albuquerque
Contact: Kathleen McLellan (505) 299-0266
Frequency: 3rd Thursday, 7:30–9 P.M.
Open to: Individuals with OCD and family members
Location: Charter Heights Psychiatric Hospital, 5901 Zuni, S.E.
Professionally assisted group
Updated May 1997

NORTH CAROLINA
Burlington—Central Piedmont
Contact: Lisa (910) 227-3893 before noon
Open to: Individuals with OCD and family members
Frequency: 2nd and 4th Wednesday, 7 P.M.
Location: First United Methodist Church of Elon College, 1630 West-
brook Ave.
Self-help group
Updated May 1997
Charlotte
Contact: Cecil King (704) 367-0005
Open to: Individuals with OCD
Frequency: Wednesday, 7 P.M.
Location: 1903 Charlotte Dr.
Frequency: Call for more information
Self-help group
Updated May 1997

Greensboro

Contact: Robert Milan (910) 378-1200
Open to: Individuals with OCD
Frequency: Every other Thursday or every Friday
Location: 200 E. Bessemer Ave.
Fee: Sliding scale
Support, education, cognitive-behavior therapy
Professionally assisted group
Updated May 1997

Contact: Robert Milan (910) 378-1200
Open to: Individuals with trichotillomania only
Frequency: Every other Wednesday
Location: 200 E. Bessemer Ave.
Fee: Sliding scale
Support, education, cognitive-behavior therapy
Professionally assisted group
Updated May 1997

Wilmington

Contact: Nancy Formy-Duval (910) 791-5859
Open to: Individuals with OCD or OCD spectrum disorder
Frequency: 1st and 3rd Thursday, 7 P.M.
Location: First Baptist Activity Center, 1939 Independence Blvd.
No fee
Updated July 1997

Winston-Salem

Contact: Mary Beck (910) 722-7760 (w)
Open to: Individuals with OCD, family, and support people
Frequency: Tuesday, 7:30–9 P.M.
Location: New Philadelphia Moravian Church, Country Club Rd.
Self-help group
Updated February 1996

OHIO

Cincinnati

Contact: Tami (513) 662-3830
Open to: Individuals with OCD and support members
Frequency: Monday, 7 P.M.
Location: Holy Name Church, 2448 Auburn Ave., basement
Self-help group
Updated May 1997

Contact: Susan R. Eppley, EdP (513) 861-9797
Open to: Individuals with OCD and significant others
Location: 2330 Victory Parkway
Fee: $45
Behavior and cognitive therapy
Professionally assisted group
Updated January 1996

Cleveland

Contact: Dennis Klinkiewicz (216) 883-4801, Andrea (216) 656-3653,
 or Tim (216) 747-3944
Open to: Individuals with OCD
Frequency: Monday, 7 P.M.
Location: Independence, Ohio, public library
12-step approach, self-help group
Updated January 1996

Contact: Mary Ann Miley (216) 442-1739
Open to: Individuals with OCD, family, and friends
Frequency: 2nd and 4th Thursday, 7 P.M.
Location: Merida Hillcrest Hospital
Self-help group
Updated May 1996

Contact: The Benhaven Program, Gene Benedetto (216) 526-0468
Open to: Individuals with OCD, anxiety disorders
Frequency: Tuesday, 7 P.M.
Location: Brecksville Commons Bldg. 4, 8221 Brecksville Rd.
No fee
Professionally assisted group
Updated May 1997

Columbus

Contact: Larry R. (614) 444-8806 or OCA Hotline (614) 470-0935

Open to: Individuals with OCD, family, and friends

Frequency: Wednesday, 8:00 P.M.

Location: 95 W. Fifth Ave.

Obsessive-Compulsive Anonymous

Updated February 1996

Cuyahoga County

Contact: Bob (216) 252-1065

Bob is forming a self-help group for friends and family of individuals with OCD.

Self-help group

Updated January 1996

Dayton

Contact: Susan Kaspi, Ph.D. (513) 220-2554 (Tuesday, Wednesday, Thursday)

Open to: Individuals with OCD, family, and friends

Frequency: 1st and 3rd Monday, 7–9 P.M.

Location: Miami Valley Hospital

No fee

Professionally assisted group

Updated January 1996

Marion

Contact: Amy Baldauf (614) 387-1577

Interested in starting a support group.

Updated January 1996

Newark

Contact: Joyce Williams (614) 366-2885

Open to: Individuals with OCD and support people

Frequency: Wednesday, 6:30–8 P.M.

Location: Mental Health Association Messimer Dr.

Combined OCD and eating disorder

No fee

Updated September 1996

Parma

   Contact: Mrs. Zorko (216) 582-1310 (leave message); 591-8684 (pager)

   Open to: Individuals with OCD and family members

   Frequency: Tuesday, 7–8:30 P.M.

   Location: Parma Hospital, 7007 Powers Blvd., Orientation Classroom
   For directions, call the hospital 888-1800

   Self-help group

   Updated February 1996

Toledo

   Contact: Nancy (419) 882-1602, Sally (419) 475-6963, or Lola (419) 352-6476

   Open to: Individuals with OCD, family, and friends

   Frequency: 2nd and 4th Wednesday, 7–9 P.M.

   Location: Harbor Behavioral Healthcare, 4334 Secor Rd.

   Self-help group

   Updated May 1997

OKLAHOMA

Edmond

   Contact: Joe Hale, L.P.C., Christian Growth Resources (405) 478-8101

   Open to: Individuals with OCD.

   Frequency: Tuesday, 7:30–9 P.M.

   Location: 2801 E. Memorial Road #101

   Updated August 1997

Lawton

   Contact: Stacy Winzelman (405) 357-1457

   Open to: Individuals with OCD

   Mutual-help support group

   Updated January 1997

OREGON

Portland

   Contact: Dr. James Hancey, M.D. (503) 494-6173

   Open to: Individuals with OCD, trichotillomania, family members

   Individual must meet with Dr. Hancy prior to attending group. Some
   meetings include family members.

   Frequency: 1st and 3rd Thursday, 7–8:30 P.M.

   Location: Oregon Health Science University

   Professionally assisted group

   Updated February 1996

PENNSYLVANIA

Allentown

Contact: Marilyn Barkan (610) 821-8929
Open to: Individuals with OCD and family members
Frequency: 1st and 3rd Tuesday, 6:30–7:30 P.M.
Location: St. James Evangelical Church, 11th and Tilghman St.
No fee
12-step approach, Obsessive-Compulsive Anonymous
Updated October 1997

Clearfield

Contact: Ian Osborn, M.D. (814) 765-5337
Open to: Individuals with OCD of Clearfield-Jefferson Community
    Mental Health Center with doctor's diagnosis of OCD
Frequency: 1st and 3rd Monday, 2:30–4 P.M.
Location: Clearfield-Jefferson Community Mental Health Center
No fee
Professionally assisted group
Updated May 1997

Erie

Contact: Kimberly Morrow (814) 838-9155
Open to: Children and adults with OCD; Union Station group for
    adults with OCD
Frequency: 1st and 3rd Thursday, 6:30–7:30 P.M.
Location: 183 W. 14th St.
Professionally assisted group
Updated May 1997

Johnstown

Contact: Ed (814) 536-3038
Open to: Individuals with OCD and family members
Frequency: 2nd Wednesday, 7–9 P.M.
Location: Cornemaugh Memorial Hospital, Education Bldg., Room
    117
Professionally assisted group
Updated October 1997

Lancaster

Contact: Christina Slick (717) 397-7461
Open to: Individuals with OCD and family members
Frequency: 2nd and 4th Wednesday, 7 P.M.
Location: MHA of Lancaster County, 630 Janet Ave., Community Service Bldg., Blair Room
Self-help group, professionally assisted group
Updated May 1997

Malvern

Contact: Connie Krasucki, RN (610) 644-9749
Open to: Individuals with OCD
Frequency: Every other Wednesday, 7–8:30 P.M.
Updated October 1997

Monroe County

Contact: Carol L. Denny (717) 424-8725
Open to: Individuals with OCD
Frequency: 2nd Tuesday
Location: Laurel Manor Nursing Home, living room
Self-help group
Updated October 1996

New Castle

Contact: Beverly Morosky (412) 652-6019 or Roger Smith (412) 658-3578
Would like to start a support group. Please contact if interested.
Updated February 1996

Philadelphia

Contact: Dr. Harvey Doppelt (610) 446-8555
Open to: Family members of individuals with OCD
Fee: $10
Professionally assisted group
Updated May 1995

Wilkes-Barre

Contact: Ruth (717) 675-5867
Open to: Individuals with OCD
Frequency: 3rd Wednesday, 7 P.M.
Location: Human Services Building, 111
Self-help group, Obsessive-Compulsive Anonymous
Updated October 1997

Contact: Paula Ward (412) 531-8631

Open to: Parents with children or teens suffering from OCD; separate group for parents, childrens, and teens

Location: St. Clair Hospital

No fee

Contact Paula for further information.

Updated February 1996

Contact: Joan Kaylor, M.S.Ed. (412) 942-5448

Open to: Individuals with OCD and family members. Call group leader.

Frequency: Friday, 2–3 P.M., no fee; Tuesday, 7–9 P.M., sliding scale

Location: Bethel Park

Updated May 1997

Rosemont

Contact: Jon Grayson, Ph.D. (610) 667-6490

Open to: Individuals with OCD

Frequency: Every other Wednesday, 8 P.M.

Location: Rosemont Counseling Associates, 1062 Lancaster Ave., Suite 9

Self-help group, professionally assisted group

Updated January 1996

Contact: Sally Allen, Ph.D. (610) 525-1510

Open to: Individuals with trichotillomania

Frequency: Every other Wednesday, 6:45–8 P.M.; family members of individuals with trichotillomania, every other Wednesday, 8–9:30 P.M.

Location: Rosemont Counseling Center, Suite 9

No fee

Self-help group, professionally assisted group

Updated 1996

Contact: Diane Lee (610) 525-1510

Open to: Children and adolescents with OCD

Frequency: Every other Thursday, 7–8 P.M.

Location: Rosemont Counseling Center, Suite 9

No fee

Updated January 1996

Contact: Kathy Parrish (610) 891-9024, ext. 125
Open to: Adolescents 12–19 years
Frequency: Every other Wednesday, 7:00 P.M.
Location: Rosemont Counseling Associates
No fee
Updated July 1997

Scranton

Contact: Beverly Day (717) 562-4044
Open to: Individuals with OCD and support people
Frequency: 1st Saturday, 2 P.M.
Location: 846 Jefferson Ave., Mental Health Association
Self-help group
Updated January 1996

University Park

Contact: Ian Osborn, M.D. (CAPS Center) (814) 863-0395
Open to: Individuals diagnosed with OCD
Frequency: Wednesday, 3:30 P.M.
Location: Ritenour Health Center, Pennsylvania State University
No fee
Self-help group, professionally assisted group
Updated May 1997

West Reading

Contact: Berks County Mental Health Association (610) 376-3905 or
Rusty (610) 372-3080
Open to: Individuals with OCD, family, and friends of individuals with
OCD
Frequency: Wednesday, 7:30–9 P.M.
Location: First Church of the Brethren, 2200 Bern Rd. (across from
Hechinger's)
Self-help group
Updated January 1996

Williamsport Area

Contact: Andrew Hollopeter 324-2067
Open to: Individuals with OCD
Frequency: 4th Monday
Location: Divine Providence Hospital
Self-help group
Updated October 1996

York

Contact: Julie (717) 845-6417 or Mental Health Association (717) 843-6973

Open to: Individuals with OCD, family, and friends

Frequency: 4th Monday, 7:30–9 P.M.

Location: Luther Memorial Evangelical Lutheran Church, 1907 Hollywood (next to York Suburban High School)

No fee

Mutual-help support group

Updated May 1997

RHODE ISLAND

OC Foundation Rhode Island Affiliate

Contact: Catherine Snell, president (401) 635-8888

Open to: Individuals with OCD

Frequency: 1st Tuesday, 7 P.M.

Location: Ray Conference Center, Butler Hospital

Fee: $2 per person

Self-help group

Updated October 1996

SOUTH CAROLINA

Columbia

Contact: Kay York, M.S.W. (803) 252-0914 or (803) 799-2406

Open to: Individuals with OCD, family members, and friends

Frequency: 3rd Tuesday, 6:45 P.M.

Location: Family Connections Office

Professionally assisted group

Updated January 1996

Greenville

Contact: Albert C. Bennett, M.A. (864) 232-6216

Open to: Individuals with OCD and family members

Frequency: 4th Thursday, 6:30–8 P.M.

Fee: $10 per individual, $15 per family

Professionally assisted group

Updated May 1997

Hartsville

    Contact: Jane Crowley (803) 332-2823, Nick Menendez (803) 383-3780, Lynn Jordan (803) 332-1386, or Judy Johnson (803) 332-3005

    Open to: Individuals with OCD and family members

    Frequency: 2nd Monday, 7–9 P.M.

    Location: 302 Dunlap Dr., St. Luke Methodist Church

    Self-help group

    Updated May 1997

SOUTH DAKOTA

Rapid City

    Contact: Ron Schuller (605) 341-1261

    Interested in starting a support group.

TENNESSEE

Knoxville

    Contact: Kelly (615) 693-8389

    Open to: Individuals with OCD and family members

    Frequency: 1st Tuesday, 7:30 P.M.

    Location: St. Mary's Hospital, classroom 7

    Self-help group

    Updated January 1996

Memphis

    Contact: Hadley Hury, executive director (901) 323-0633

    Open to: Individuals with OCD, family, and friends

    Frequency: Every other Saturday, 10–11:30 A.M.

    Location: Mental Health Association of the Mid-South, 2400 Poplar Ave., Suite 410

    Professionally assisted group

    Updated January 1996

TEXAS

Arlington

    Contact: Kathleen Norris, M.A. (817) 461-5454

    Open to: Individuals with OCD

    Frequency: Monday, 5:45 P.M.

    Location: 1521 N. Cooper St., Suite 480

    No fee

    Professionally assisted group

    Updated February 1996

Contact: Andrew Howard (512) 305-4548
Open to: Individuals with OCD and family members
Frequency: Tuesday, 7–9 P.M.
Location: Call leader for location.
Self-help group
Updated February 1996

Clear Lake City

Contact: Claire Vaughn (713) 472-7114
Interested in starting a support group for individuals with OCD and families members. Call for information.
Updated January 1996

Dallas

Contact: OCD Association–DFW (214) 278-0318 or e-mail <slitskin@nkn.net>

Fort Worth

Contact: Bette Bolles (817) 336-1112
Interested in starting up a support group again for individuals with OCD and family members.
Updated February 1996

Houston

OC Foundation of Texas, Inc.
Contact: Donna Friedrich, president (713) 482-2147
Open to: Individuals with OCD and family members, and friends *only*
Frequency: 2nd and 4th Thursday, 7:30–9:30 P.M.
Location: Memorial Southwest Hospital, 7600 Beechnut, Level C (2nd Thursday, Room E; 4th Thursday, Room C)
Self-help group
Updated January 1996

San Antonio

Contact: Rick (210) 816-2019
No meetings are scheduled. Phone support only.
Updated September 1996

Contact: Penny Cooperider (210) 614-9595 or Jean McRae (210) 614-9597

Open to: Individuals with OCD who have been evaluated by Dr. Nathan

Frequency: Tuesday, 4–5:30 P.M.

Location: 2829 Babcock Rd., Suite 640

Fee: $65

Professionally assisted group

Updated January 1996

Contact: Jean (512) 305-4548

Open to: Individuals with OCD, family and friends

Frequency: Tuesday, 7–9 P.M.

Location: call for information

Updated January 1997

UTAH

Salt Lake City

Contact: Suze Harrington, LCSW, (801) 474-2100

Open to: Individuals with OCD

Frequency: Monday, Wednesday, or Friday

Location: 1414 East 2100 South

Fee: $25

Updated: July 1997

VERMONT

Burlington

Contact: Williams J. McCann

Open to: Individuals with OCD

Frequency: call for information

Location: call for information

Professionally assisted group

Updated: May 1994

VIRGINIA

Abington

Contact: Bill Hayes, M.ED. (540) 889-3145, (540) 628-1676
Open to: Individuals with OCD
Frequency: 1st Tuesday at 7 P.M.
Location: Abington Bible Church, 2400 Elementary Road
Professionally assisted group
Updated: January 1996

Arlington

Contact: Marie Ogur (703) 978-6425
Open to: Family members of individuals with OCD
Frequency: 1st Wednesday, 7:30 P.M.
Location: St. Andrews Episcopal Church, 4000 Lorcom Lane
Self-help group
Updated: February 1998

Contact: Betty Beach (703) 533-8434
Open to: Individuals with OCD
Frequency: Mondays, 8–10 P.M.
Location: St. Andrews Episcopal Church, 4000 Lorcom Lane
Self-help group
Updated: February 1996

Lynchburg

Contact: Shelba Lindstrom (804) 237-4176
Open to: Individuals with OCD, family friends, concerned individuals
Frequency: 2nd Thursday, 7 P.M.
Location: Virginia Baptist Hospital, chaplin's conference room
12-step group
Updated: July 1997

Richmond

Contact: Laura Cribbs (804) 282-1323
Open to: Individuals with OCD and family members
Frequency: 1st and 3rd Tuesday, 7:15–9:30 P.M.
Location: Skipworth United Methodist Church, 2211 Skipworth Road
Self-help group
Updated: February 1996

Contact: Ronna Saunders, L.C.S.W. (804) 270-4111, (804) 270-4111
Open to: Individuals with OCD
Frequency: 1st and 3rd Tuesday, 7:15–8:45 P.M.
Location: Center for Behavioral Change, 3212 Skipworth Road, Suite
    104
Updated: May 1997

Roanoke

Contact: Ted Petrocci, LPC (540) 344-3211, (540) 345-6468
Open to: Individuals with OCD
Frequency: Last Thursday, 6–7:30 P.M.
Location: 16 Walnut Avenue
Professionally assisted group
Fee: None
Updated: February 1996

WASHINGTON

Bellevue

Contact: Yvonne Younger (206) 641-7647
Open to: Individuals with OCD
Frequency: call for information
Location: call for information
Updated: February 1996

Seattle

Contact: Phil (206) 322-3621
Open to: Individuals with OCD, family members
Frequency: Saturdays, 10 A.M.–12 P.M.
Location: Swedish Hospital, Level B, Conference Room B
Self-help group
Fee: Free
Updated: May 1997

Contact: Gerald Rosen, Ph.D. (206) 343-9474
Open to: Individuals with OCD
Frequency: Tuesday, call for time
Location: call for information
Professionally assisted group
Fee: $40 per session

Contact: Yvonne Younger, (206) 641-7647
Open to: Individuals with trichotillomania
Frequency: Thursdays, 6–8 P.M.
Location: call for information
Self-help group
Fee: no fee
Updated: January 1996

WASHINGTON, D.C.

Contact: Diane Rubin (202) 973-2127, call before attending
Open to: Individuals with OCD
Frequency: 1st Tuesday 7 P.M.
Location: George Washington Ambulatory Care Center
Self-help group
Updated: January 1996

WISCONSIN

Eau Claire

Contact: Marilyn Goodman, MS (715) 834-2751
Open to: Individuals with OCD, family members, and friends
Frequency: 7:15 P.M. 1998 dates:1/29, 2/26, 3/25, 4/29, 5/20
Location: Sacred Heart Hospital, ground floor, Conference Room 4
Professionally assisted group

Green Bay

Contact: Annette Grunseth (920) 433-7554
Open to: Individuals with OCD
Frequency: call for information
Location: call for information

Madison

Contact: Jay Freuhling, M.L.S. (608) 263-6171
Open to: Children or teens with OCD
Frequency: 1st Monday, 6–8 P.M.
Location: call for information
Self-help group
Updated May 1997

Contact: Jay Freuhling, M.L.S. (608) 263-6171
Open to: Teens with OCD and Parents of Children with OCD
Frequency: call for information
Location: call for information
Professionally assisted group
Updated October 1997

Contact: Lisa (608) 288-0783
Open to: Individuals with Trichotillomania
Frequency: Last Monday, 5 P.M.
Location: 600 Highland Avenue
Self-help group
Fee: $15
Updated January 1996

Contact: Lisa (608) 288-0783
Open to: Individuals with Trichotillomania
Frequency: 2nd Monday, Noon
Location: 600 Highland Avenue
Self-help group
Fee: $15
Updated January 1996

Contact: Colette Girard (608) 263-6081
Open to: Individuals with OCD, family and friends
Frequency: 3rd Tuesday, 12 P.M.–5 P.M.
Location: WISPIC 6001 Tokay Blvd.
Professionally assisted group
Fee: $15
Updated January 1996

Platteville
Contact: Josh (608) 348-4768
Open to: Individuals with OCD
Frequency: call for information
Location: 35 East Main Street
Professionally assisted, Self-help
Updated November 1997

Wauwatosa

Contact: Bill Ford (414) 454-6669, (414) 454-6500
Open to: All persons
Frequency: call for information
Location: Milwaukee Psychiatric Hospital, 1220 Dewey Avenue
Professionally assisted, self-help
Updated January 1997

CANADA

BRITISH COLUMBIA

Coquitlam

Contact: Truman Spring (604) 936-0491
Open to: Parents of children with OCD
Professionally assisted group
Updated November 1997

Vancouver

Contact: Leslie Solyom, MD (604) 872-7880
Open to: Individuals with OCD (need to be doctor's patient to partici-
pate)
Frequency: Tuesday, 4–6 P.M.
Fee: Non-Canadian, $40; Canadians are covered by Medical Services
Plan
Psychoeducational cognitive behavior therapy
Professionally assisted group
Updated January 1996

MANITOBA

Winnipeg

Contact: Calvin (204) 947-4514 (voice mail); OCAD/The Obsessive-
Compulsive and Anxiety Disorders [OCD] and Akin Matters Asso-
ciation
Open to: Individuals with OCD, anxiety disorder
Frequency: Wednesday, 6–7:30 P.M.
Location: Health Action Center 425 Elgin Ave., 2nd floor
Self-help group
Updated January 1996

Contact: OC Information and Support Center, c/o Manitoba Clearing
   House (204) 772-6979 or (204) 786-0860 (fax)
Frequency: Every Tuesday, 7–9 P.M.
Location: 825 Sherbrook St.
Self-help group
Updated January 1996

NOVA SCOTIA

Sydney

Contact: Fred Chezenko (902) 733-3018
Open to: Individuals with OCD and family members
Frequency: Once a month, 7–9 P.M.
Location: McConnel Library
Self-help group
Updated May 1997

ONTARIO

London

Contact: Jim Wallis (519) 644-2368
Open to: Individuals with OCD and family members
Frequency: 1st Tuesday, 7–9 P.M.
Location: 648 Huron St.
Updated May 1997

Markham

Contact: Obsessive-Compulsive Disorder Network (OCCDN)
   (905) 294-0494, or write P.O. Box 151, Markham, Ontario L3P
   3J7, Canada
Open to: Individuals with OCD
Self-help group
Updated October 1997

New Market

Contact: Marianne Small (905) 836-4777
Open to: Individuals with OCD and significant others
Frequency: 1st and 3rd Monday, 7:30 P.M.
Self-help group
Updated October 1997

Ottawa

Contact: Rolland Boisvenu (613) 722-3607

Frequency: Every other Wednesday, 7:30–10 P.M.

Location: Hintonburg Community Center, Champlain Room, Wellington St.

Self-help group

Updated March 1996

Pickering

Contact: Free from Fear, or The Anxiety Disorders Network (905) 831-3877, or write to 1848 Liverpool Rd., Suite 199, Pickering, Ontario, L1V 6M3, Canada, for information about support groups in your area.

Self-help group

Updated October 1997

Toronto

Contact: Jan Stewart (416) 364-0222

Open to: Parents of children with OCD

Location: Hospital for Sick Children

Updated October 1997

Unionville

Contact: Diane (905) 472-0494; oocdm@interhop.net

Open to: Individuals with OCD

Frequency: 1st and 3rd Thursday, 7:30 P.M.

Location: St. Justine Lamarter Church, 3898 Highway 7

Self-help group

Updated October 1997

Waterloo

Contact: Astride (519) 746-9644

Open to: Individuals with OCD and family members

Frequency: 2nd and 4th Thursday, 7 P.M.

Location: Adult Recreation Centre, 185 King St. South

Updated October 1997

Windsor

Contact: Family YMCA, PATH Program (519) 258-9622 ext. 57 or 58

Open to: Individuals with OCD, family, and friends

Frequency: 2nd and 4th Thursday, 7–9 P.M.

Location: 511 Pelissier

Self-help group

Updated August 1997

QUEBEC

Montréal

Contact: Stephanie Aylwin, Ami Quebec (514) 486-1448
Open to: Individuals with OCD, family and friends
Frequency: Two groups per month. Periodically, psychoeducational
programs are offered.
Updated October 1997

North Bay

Contact: Larry (705) 497-9460
Open to: Individuals with OCD
Frequency: Thursday, 7 P.M.
Location: 163 First Avenue East
Updated October 1997

Contact: Jan Stewart (416) 364-0222
Open to: Parents of children with OCD
Location: Hospital of Sick Children
Updated October 1997

ACKNOWLEDGMENTS

I AM FIRST of all indebted to my OCD patients, every one of whom played a role in the writing of this book. My thanks goes out especially to those who graciously allowed me to share their experiences. A few of the case studies in this book, for extra confidentiality, combine symptoms of two or three patients. The great majority of case studies, however, accurately present the story of one person's battle with OCD with only minimal changes in personal identifying data.

This book could not have been written without the encouragement and suggestions of friends here at Penn State. Bernie Asbel and Wendell Harris got me started. Rob Gannon, Margaret Lyday, and Sherry Hogan provided helpful suggestions. David Pacchioli, editor at *Research Penn State,* generously provided invaluable and ongoing editorial assistance.

I am much obliged to Regina Ryan, who gave help that went well beyond that usually provided by a literary agent; and to Linda Healey, my editor at Pantheon Books, who managed a host of details from start to finish. I want to thank my colleagues who provided me with opportunities to work intensively with OCD patients, including Rex McClure, Dennis Clark, Paul Tabone, Jane Gorman, and Sandy Gaffney at the Clearfield-Jefferson Community Mental

Health Center; and Dennis Heitzmann and Sue Gibson at the CAPS center at Penn State. I am grateful to the Centre Community Hospital library for obtaining many obscure journal articles and books that were out of print.

I have also greatly appreciated the time that a number of experts in the field of OCD have given me. This list includes, but is not limited to, Jon Grayson, Michael Jenike, Lee Baer, John March, Gail Stektee, Edna Foa, Jeffrey Schwartz, and Alec Pollard. The OC Foundation has also been extremely helpful, especially Jim Broatch, Patricia Perkins-Doyle, and Susan Duffy.

Lastly, no one deserves more thanks than my wife Rosa and my three children, Frank, Paula, and Billy, who were always encouraging and who put up with my working on the book on Saturday and Sunday mornings.

INDEX

ABOUT THE AUTHOR

Ian Osborn, M.D., is a practicing psychiatrist in State College, Pennsylvania, and a specialist in the treatment of OCD. He lectures frequently to mental health professionals and the general public.